The
Big Book
of
Fascinating
Facts

---

i before e (except after c)

---

*Under the Covers and
between the Sheets*

---

*A Certain
"Je Ne Sais Quoi"*

PROJECT STAFF
i before e (except after c)
   U.S. Project Editor: Sandra Kear
   Copy Editor: Marilyn Knowlton
   Project Production Coordinator: Wayne Morrison

Under the Covers and between the Sheets
   Copy Editor: Ellen Bingham
   Project Designer: Elizabeth Tunnicliffe
   Indexer: Lina Burton

A Certain "Je Ne Sais Quoi"
   Consulting Editor: Candace Levy

READER'S DIGEST TRADE PUBLISHING
U.S. Project Editor: Kim Casey
Copy Editors: Barbara Booth, Marilyn Knowlton
Project Designer: Jennifer Tokarski
Senior Art Director: George McKeon
Executive Editor, Trade Publishing: Dolores York
Associate Publisher, Trade Publishing: Rosanne McManus
President and Publisher, Trade Publishing: Harold Clarke

We are committed to both the quality of our products and the service we provide to our customers.
We value your comments, so please feel free to contact us.

   The Reader's Digest Association, Inc.
   Adult Trade Publishing
   44 S. Broadway
   White Plains, NY 10601

For more Reader's Digest products and information, visit our website, www.rd.com
(in the United States)

Printed in China

1 3 5 7 9 10 8 6 4 2

❧ Contents ❧

I BEFORE E (EXCEPT AFTER C)
Old-School Ways to Remember Stuff

Introduction   6

1. The English Language   9
2. To Spell or Not to Spell   20
3. Think of a Number   39
4. Geographically Speaking   60
5. Animal, Vegetable, Mineral   70
6. Time and the Calendar   80
7. The Sky at Night and by Day   90
8. The World of Science   98
9. World History   106
10. Musical Interlude   122
11. Foreign Tongues   129
12. Religious Matters   135
13. The Human Body   143
14. Lifesaving Tips   153
15. The World of Work   161
16. Other Favorites   168

UNDER THE COVERS AND BETWEEN THE SHEETS
The Inside Story behind Classic Characters, Authors, Unforgettable Phrases, and Unexpected Endings

Introduction   178

1. Shot Out of the Canon   180
2. Guilty Pleasures   214
3. Young at Heart   246
4. Stranger Than Fiction   270
5. Off the Page   302

Index of Authors and Titles   331

A CERTAIN "JE NE SAIS QUOI"
The Origin of Foreign Words Used in English

Introduction   342

From "A cappella" to "Zeitgeist"   344

A Brief List of Sources   510

i before e
(except after c)

old-school ways
to remember stuff

JUDY PARKINSON

Introduction

"Thirty days hath September, April, June, and November…"

How many times, perhaps anxiously awaiting payday, have you repeated this saying to yourself? Or racked your brains for the name of the eleventh president of the United States in order to stump some impertinent know-it-all at a dinner party?

No doubt about it, memory's a funny business. But in a pre-Google, less hectic age, many useful, if not invaluable, facts were taught by mnemonics—simple memory aids, which once learned, fixed information in the brain forever. In fact, the concept of memory devices began in ancient Greece, before the written word. Rather than memorize information by rote, the Greeks developed a technique called the Method of Loci (pronounced LOW-sigh), or method of locations or places.

With this method a person creates an image that associates the necessary information with a location or place along a familiar and well-traveled route. To retrieve the items from memory, the person then mentally travels through that visualization, picking up the previously associated items.

As Cicero tells it in his work *De Oratore*, this method was invented by a Greek poet named Simonides of Ceos (c. 556-468 B.C.). After a recitation at a dinner party, Simonides was apparently called outside. While he was outside, the roof of the building he was in collapsed, killing all inside, many beyond recognition. Simonides was able to identify the victims by associating their names with their respective positions at the dinner table, and it is believed that through this tragedy, an ancient system of mnemonics was born.

Since then, hundreds of new mnemonic devices have been created that clearly give knowledge seekers an advantage. Studies have shown time and time again that people who use mnemonics remember at least twice as well as those who don't.

This book assembles many of those quirky and amusing ways that people have devised to remember tidbits of information in school—all of them still handy devices for solving today's problems. Packed with clever verses, entertaining acronyms, curious—and sometimes hilarious—sayings, *i before e (except after c)* includes all the mnemonics you could ever need (and some you probably don't).

This book is your one-stop shop for finding basic mnemonics. Soon you'll be recalling them to pass a test or include in a speech. They can help remind you when to turn your clocks back and forward, as well as important anniversaries and that special someone's birthday. Mnemonics could even save you from contacting poison ivy and may help you save a life. By the end of it, you'll definitely remember *i before e* as an amusing and handy collection of ingenious mind tricks devised to help us learn and understand the idiosyncrasies of this world and beyond.

1
The English Language

━━

The Alphabet

Children, of course, must first learn the alphabet before they successfully embark upon reading the complete works of Shakespeare. So it is that for many of us, learning our ABCs to the tune of "Twinkle, Twinkle, Little Star" (made famous by *Sesame Street's* Big Bird) becomes our first introduction to the world of mnemonics.

It was Charles Bradlee, a Boston music publisher, who first copyrighted that combination in 1835, calling it "the ABC, a German air with variations for flute with an easy accompaniment for the pianoforte."

> *a–b–c–d–e–f–g,*
> *h–i–j–k–l–m–n–o–p,*
> *q–r–s–t–u–v,*
> *w–x–y and z.*
> *Now I know my ABCs,*
> *next time won't you sing with me?*

For the rhyme to work with the Z, you have to use the U.S. pronunciation of zee rather than zed. If you didn't sing your ABCs to the tune of "Twinkle, Twinkle, Little Star," then you might have used the tune of "Baa, Baa, Black Sheep" instead, which has a similar rhythm and the same melody.

Because the letters l—m—n—o—p have to be sung twice as fast as the rest of the letters in the rhyme, some children have mistakenly assumed that "elemenopee" is

a word. *Sesame Street's* DVD, "The Alphabet Jungle Game" pokes fun at this type of error. In the video Telly thinks he's been stumped when Zoe introduces the next letter after K, called "Elemeno." After some worrisome bantering, Elmo enlightens his friends to the error, and an animated short on each letter follows, in classic *Sesame Street* style.

In the nineteenth century, a popular way to teach

children the ABCs was through a rhyme entitled, "The Tragical Death of A, Apple Pie, Who Was Cut in Pieces, and Eaten by Twenty-Six Gentlemen, With Whom All Little People Ought To Be Very Well Acquainted." The text dates back as far as the reign of Charles II (1660–1685).

A was an apple pie
B bit it,
C cut it,
D dealt it,
E eats it,
F fought for it,
G got it,
H had it,
I inspected it,
J jumped for it,
K kept it,
L longed for it,
M mourned for it,
N nodded at it,
O opened it,
P peeped in it,
Q quartered it,
R ran for it,
S stole it,
T took it,
U upset it,
V viewed it,
W wanted it,
X, Y and **Z** all wished for
and had a piece in hand.

The Five Vowels

The English alphabet has five soft vowels: **A E I O U**. This sequence of letters generally tends to roll off the tongue quite naturally, but for anyone who has trouble remembering the order of vowels, here are a couple of useful phrases:

Ann's **E**gg **I**s **O**n **U**s.

Anthony's **E**go **I**s **O**ver **U**sed.

The Parts of Speech

After learning the alphabet, the next step is to devise coherent sentences. The rhyme below categorizes each of the parts of speech, giving a clear example of each grammatical term. The rhyme dates back to 1855 and was written by educators David B. Tower and Benjamin F. Tweed:

A NOUN's the name of any thing;
As, *school or garden, hoop, or swing.*

ADJECTIVES tell the kind of noun;
As, *great, small pretty, white, or brown.*

Three of these words we often see
Called ARTICLES — *a, an,* and *the.*

Instead of nouns the PRONOUNS stand;

John's head, his face, my arm, your hand.

VERBS tell of something being done;
As, *read, write, spell, sing, jump,* or *run.*

How things are done the ADVERBS tell;
As, *slowly, quickly, ill,* or *well.*

They also tell us *where* and *when;*
As, *here,* and *there,* and *now,* and *then.*

A PREPOSITION stands *before*
A NOUN; *as, in,* or *through,* a door.

CONJUNCTIONS sentences unite;
As, kittens scratch *and* puppies bite.

The INTERJECTION shows surprise

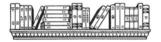

A different rhyme called "The Parts of Speech" is similarly concise as a reminder of the different components of the English language. The origin of these verses is unknown.

Every name is called a **noun,**
As *field* and *fountain, street* and *town.*

In place of noun the **pronoun** stands,
As *he* and *she* can clap their hands.

The **adjective** describes a thing,
As *magic* wand and *bridal* ring.

The **verb** means action, something done—
To *read,* to *write,* to *jump,* to *run.*

How things are done, the **adverbs** tell,
As *quickly, slowly, badly, well.*

The **preposition** shows relation,
As *in* the street, or *at* the station.

Conjunctions join, in many ways,
Sentences, words, *or* phrase *and* phrase.

The **interjection** cries out, "Hark!
I need an exclamation mark!"

Through poetry, we learn how each
Of these make up the **Parts of Speech.**

What's a Preposition?

To further remember the function of a preposition, insert any word into the following sentence:

The squirrel ran_____the tree.

For example, over, under, after, around, through, up, on, to, from, by, and so forth. Other prepositions include in, at, for, between, among, and of.

What's a Conjunction?

Conjunctions are words used to join two independent clauses. Most people are careless with punctuation, especially these days when shortcuts in e-mails and text messages have become commonplace. But this FAN

BOYS mnemonic helps if you want to remember the coordinating conjunctions, of which the most important are *and, or,* and *but.*

FAN BOYS

For, **A**nd, **N**or, **B**ut, **O**r, **Y**et, **S**o

The Rules of Punctuation

Cecil Hartley's poem from *Principles of Punctuation* or *The Art of Pointing* (1818) reveals the old-fashioned way that people were advised on how to interpret punctuation when reading sentences out loud.

> The stops point out, with truth, the time of pause
> A sentence doth require at ev'ry clause.
> At ev'ry comma, stop while *one* you count;
> At semicolon, *two* is the amount;
> A colon doth require the time of *three*;
> The period *four*, as learned men agree.

Though it's not a verse that most grammarians would encourage these days, it does give you an idea of the difference between each type of punctuation mark.

On Commas

A cat has claws at the ends of its paws.
A comma's a pause at the end of a clause.

On Colons

The English teacher and prominent lexicographer H. W. Fowler creates a useful visual image of the job done by the colon, which he says, "delivers the goods that have been invoiced in the preceding words."

On the Exclamation Point

The following anonymously authored seventeenth-century rhyme appeared in *Treatise of Stops, Points, or Pauses, and of Notes Which Are Used in Writing and Print* (1680):

This stop denotes our Suddain Admiration,
Of what we Read, or Write, or giv Relation,
And is always cal'd an Exclamation.

Writing Stories

And when you put all these elements together to write your first novel, don't forget the main elements of storytelling:

Viewpoint
Mood
Plot
Characters
Theme
Setting

If the VMPCTS acronym doesn't roll easily off the tongue, this phrase should help to keep it firmly in mind:

Very **M**any **P**upils **C**ome **T**o **S**chool

Learning Lines

How do actors memorize scripts? Learning lines by repetition is the most obvious way, but many actors also refer to the beat of the script that is, the rhythm of the words, which actors literally tune into. Some plays are easier to learn than others. Shakespeare's texts are highly memorable because they are rich and full of puns (often extremely bawdy ones), rhymes, and alliterations.

Whereat, with blade, with bloody blameful blade,
He bravely breach'd his boiling bloody breast.

Another mnemonic secret of the English poetic tradition is the rhythm of the iambic pentameter. An iamb is a beat with one soft syllable and one strong syllable, and a series of five iambs forms the heartbeat of classic poetry: its familiarity makes it easy to remember, especially in the works of Shakespeare.

From *Hamlet*

To be / or not / to be / that is / the question.

From the Sonnets

Shall I / compare / thee to / a sum/mer's day?
Thou art / more love/ly and / more tem/perate:
Rough winds / do shake / the dar/ling buds / of May,
And sum/mer's lease / hath all / too short / a date.

Setting a text to a well-known tune and rhythm is a useful method of memorizing the words. Why not try singing Homer's *Odyssey*, Coleridge's "The Rime of the Ancient Mariner," or one of Shakespeare's sonnets to the tune of your favorite nursery rhyme or song? You can remember the words using a combination of rhymes, rhythms, and repetition.

> *English usage is sometimes more than mere taste, judgment, and education—sometimes it's sheer luck, like getting across the street.*
>
> — E. B. White

2
To Spell or Not to Spell

Although there are some people who can spell *supercalifragilisticexpialidocious* without blinking an eye, others draw blanks at the simplest word. Everyone has a different level of ability when it comes to spelling. For those who fall into the latter category, perhaps they weren't taught the right sort of spelling mnemonics…

I before E (except after C)

Teachers often drum this phrase into children's heads in grammar school, and it does apply in the sentence: "Receive a Piece of Pie." But all rules invariably have exceptions, just to make life difficult:

> *i* before *e*, except after *c*
> or when sounded like *a*
> as in *neighbor* and *weigh*.

A similar version ends with the line: "as in *weigh, neigh,* or *sleigh.*" Numerous exceptions to the rule include the words *neither, height, leisure,* and *weird.*

A rhyme with an extended rule used more commonly in British schools clarifies things a little further:

> When the sound is *ee*
> It's *i* before *e* except after *c*.

However, even the extended rule has a number of exceptions: words such as *caffeine, protein*, and *seize* are *e* before *i* despite having a long *ee* sound. Also, the plurals of −*cy* words end with −*cies*, which is another exception to this *i* before *e* rule, as are many −*cie* words, such as *science* and *conscience*.

Therefore, another addendum has been applied to the original saying:

> *i* before *e*, except after *c*
> Or when sounding like *a*
> As in *neighbor* and *weigh*.
> Drop this rule when -*c* sounds as -*sh*.

Words such as *ancient, efficient*, and *species* become covered by this additional rule.

The Complexities of English Spelling

The English language is full of convolutions and contradictions, which can make the spelling and pronunciations of certain words difficult to predict. The following poem, which appeared in the *NEA Journal*, a publication of the National Education Association, in 1966/67, by educator Vivian Buchan, expresses the idiosyncrasies and frustrations with so-called spelling rules.

Phony Phonetics

One reason why I cannot spell,

Although I learned the rules quite well

Is that some words like *coup* and *through*

Sound just like *threw* and *flue* and *Who*;

When *oo* is never spelled the same,

The *duice* becomes a guessing game;

And then I ponder over *though*,

Is it spelled *so*, or *throw*, or *beau*,

And *bough* is never *bow*, it's *bow*,

I mean the *bow* that sounds like *plow*,

And not the *bow* that sounds like *row*—

The *row* that is pronounced like *roe*.

I wonder, too, why *rough* and tough,

That sound the same as *gruff* and *muff*,

Are spelled like *bough* and *though*, for they

Are both pronounced a different way.

And why can't I spell *trough* and *cough*

The same as I do *scoff* and *golf*?

Why isn't *drought* spelled just like *route,*
or *doubt* or *pout* or *sauerkraut?*
When words all sound so much the same
To change the spelling seems a shame.
There is no sense—see sound like cents—
in making such a difference
Between the sight and sound of words;
Each spelling rule that undergirds
The way a word should look will fail
And often prove to no avail
Because exceptions will negate
The truth of what the rule may state;
So though I try, I still despair
And moan and mutter "It's not fair
That I'm held up to ridicule
And made to look like such a fool
When it's the spelling that's at fault.
Let's call this nonsense to a halt."

Commonly Misspelled Words

It has almost become cliché among educators and orthographers (who study spelling) to misspell the word *misspell* in order to prove a point. It does, however, demonstrate how easily words can run astray. You need only do an Internet search of the misspelled word *equiptment* to see how poor spelling has become commonplace.

Their/They're/There

Instructors and editors often find errors with this group of words, because the words all sound the same. They're all pronounced the same but spelled differently. The possessive is *their*, and the contraction of "they are" is *they're*. Everywhere else, it is *there*. Think directions for *there*: it's either *here* or *there*. The word *here* can be found in *there*. Think of ownership for *their*: children are *heirs* before they inherit *their* fortune. If there is an *"I"* in it, then it is the one that refers to people.

Principal/Principle

Remember the following spelling principle: the school *principal* is a *prince* and a *pal* (despite what you may think of him or her). The *principal's principle* dictates: a *principle* is a rule!

Lay and Lie

As a rule, irregular verbs pose problems for people who like neat, cut-and-dried methods to live and learn by. One forms the past and past participle of regular verbs by adding *-d* or *-ed* to the stem of the infinitive *(touch, touched)*, but this process does not apply to irregular verbs such as *lie*. So just remember the phrase:

You'll lay an egg if you don't lie down.

Affect or Effect?

The RAVEN mnemonic is useful when working out whether to use *affect* or *effect* in a sentence:

Remember: **A**ffect, **V**erb, **E**ffect, **N**oun

The woman was *affected* by the *effect* of the film.

A Useful Selection of Spelling Aids

Many of the words in the following list appear to have no logical spelling rule whatsoever, but reciting the clever mnemonic phrase that accompanies the word may help keep you out of the dunce's chair.

Accelerator
A Cruel **C**reature—imagine words and pictures to remind you to write two Cs.

Acceptable
Remember to accept any table offered, and you will spell this word correctly.

Accessible
—able or —ible?
Say out loud, "**I** am always accessible."

Accidentally
Two Cs and an ally. Make up a story:
Two cats accidentally scratched your friend and ally.

Accommodation
Again two Cs and two Ms,
And don't forget that second O after the second M.
Comfortable **C**hairs, **O**r **M**odern **M**ats, **O**r…

Address
Directly **D**elivered letters are **S**afe and **S**ound.

Aeroplane
All **E**ngines **R**unning **O**kay.

Almond
ALmonds are ov**AL**s.

Amateur
Amateurs need not be mature.

Argument
A **R**ude **G**irl **U**ndresses—**M**y **E**yes **N**eed **T**aping.

(Another way to check your spelling is to find short words within.
Think of chewing GUM when you chew over an arGUMent.)

Arithmetic
A **R**at **I**n **T**he **H**ouse **M**ay **E**at **T**he **I**ce **C**ream.

A **R**ed **I**ndian **T**hought **H**e **M**ight **E**at **T**urkey
In **C**hurch.

Assassination

This word is comprised of four short words:

Ass Ass I Nation.

Asthma

The cause of Asthm**A**:

Sensitivity **T**o **H**ousehold **M**ites.

Autumn

There's an N at the end of autumn.

Think of N standing for November, because it's the end of autumn and the beginning of winter.

Bare or Bear

Imagine scenarios relating to the two words.

It's bath time with a bar of soap on your bare skin.

A bear is scary and fills you with fear.

Beautiful

Big **E**lephants **A**re **U**sually **BEAU**tiful.

Because

Big **E**lephants **C**an **A**lways **U**nderstand **S**mall **E**lephants.

Big **E**lephants **C**an't **A**lways **U**se **S**mall **E**xits.

Believe

This word obeys the *i* before *e* rule, and there's also a perfect word association within.

Do you beLIEve a LIE?

Biscuit

Some believe this word is derived from two French words—*bis cuit* meaning twice cooked. The easy way to remember how to spell it is with this phrase:

BIScuits are Crumbled Up Into Tiny pieces.

Broccoli

We know it's healthy, but it's tricky to spell.

Remember that broccoli would never Cause COLIc.

Calendar

Just remember that this word has an *e* between two *a*s. The last vowel is *a*.

Capital or Capitol

The capitAl city of Greece is Athens.

PAris is the capital of FrAnce.

Most capitOl buildings have dOmes.

There's a capitOl in WashingtOn.

Chaos
Cyclones, **H**urricanes **A**nd **O**ther **S**torms create chaos.

Character
CHARlie's **ACT** is **ER**otic.

Committee
Remember: **M**any **M**eetings **T**ake **T**ime— **E**veryone's **E**xhausted!

Conscience
It's not pronounced how it's spelled.

It's **S**cience with **C**on at the beginning.

Consensus
The census does not require a consensus, since they are not related.

Correspondence
CORRect your **CORR**espon**DEN**ce in the **DEN**.

Definitely
Find the word **FINITE** within.

Deliberate
It was a de**LIBERATE** plan to **LIBERATE** the hostages.

Desert (as in the Sahara) or Dessert (as in apple pie)
Remember that the sweet one has two Sugar**S**.

Or that the double "s" in dessert stands for "sweet stuff."

Diarrhea
If you need to know how to spell this—here you go!

Dash **I**n **A** **R**eal **R**ush—**H**urriedly **E**vading **A**ccident.

Doubt
Sometimes it's only natural to **B**e in doubt.

Dumbbell
Even smart people forget one of the *b*s in this one.
(So be careful whom you call one when you write.)

Eccentric
The word literally means "off center," so imagine an
eccentric **C**razy **C**at, running around in circles.

Eczema
It's pronounced with an X, but there's no X factor
with this problem:

Even **C**lean **ZE**alots **MA**y get eczema.

Embarrass
Do you turn **R**eally **R**ed **A**nd **S**mile **S**hyly when
embarrassed?

Exaggerate
If he's br**AGG**ing, then he's surely exaggerating.

Fascinate
Are you fa**SCI**nated by **SCI**ence?

Fiery
The silent *e* on fire is so cowardly: it retreats inside the word rather than face the suffix -y.

Forty
FORget the *u* in four when you spell **FOR**ty.

Friend
FRIEs are for sharing with your **FRIE**nd.

Geography
General **E**isenhower's **O**ldest **G**irl **R**ode **A** **P**ony **H**ome **Y**esterday.

Grammar
There's no *e* in grammar.

Think about Grand**MA**, who teaches perfect grammar.

Grateful
You should be grateful to know that keeping "great" out of "grateful" is great.

Handkerchief

It's shortened to "hanky," but the long form has a **D**.

Think of holding a handkerchief in your **HAND**.

Heard or Herd

If you heard something, you used your **EAR**.

There are lots of animals in a herd, so there can't be a single one on its own in this word.

Indispensable

Only the most **ABLE** are indispens**ABLE**.

Interrupt

It's a fact that it's **R**eally **R**ude to interrupt.

Liaison

Dangerous and often misspelled.

To spot a liaison, use your two eyes (2 **I**s).

Lightning

Lighten the load of the word lightning by learning how to eliminate the e.

Memento

Commonly misspelled as "momento."

A souvenir from your holiday is a memento, and it represents happy **MEM**ories.

Millennium
A thousand years—**MILLE**—that's more than
Ninety-**N**ine years.

Miniature
It means tiny, and there are tiny words in the
middle—**I** and **A**.

Misspell
The subject of this section of the book.

Don't mi**SS** that extra s in **Mi**SSpell.

Necessary
Not **E**very **C**at **E**ats **S**ardines—**S**ome **A**re **R**eally
Yummy.

Or think of a shirt—it is necessary for a shirt to
have one **C**ollar and two **S**leeve**S**.

Or think of your necessary coffee each morning with
one **C**ream and two **S**ugar**S**.

Occasion
If it's a special one, you'd travel over two seas (**C**s).

Ocean
Only **C**at's **E**yes **A**re **N**arrow.

Parallel
There are three **L**s in parallel, but think of the middle ones acting as parallel lines next to each other.

Parliament
Think: **I AM** parliament.

People
People **E**at **O**ther **P**eople's **L**eftovers **E**agerly.

Pneumonia
People **N**ever **E**xpect **U**s to come down with **PNEU**monia.

Possession
Very sweet—four **S**ugar**S**.

Potassium
One **T**ea and two **S**ugar**S**.

Recommend
No need for confusion with this word.
It's simply commend with *re-* at the beginning.

Rhythm
Rhythm **H**elps **Y**ou **T**o **H**ear **M**usic.

Rhythm **H**elps **Y**our **T**wo **H**ips **M**ove.

Separate
The *e*s surround the *a*s.

Or think of your old Father or **PA** in his den as a se**PA**rate kind of person.

Stationery or Stationary
A or E? Every office intern gets the spelling of this word wrong at least once in his or her life. You only have to remember one, and by process of elimination, the other one must be right. Think of the initial *e* in envelope for stationery, or keep in mind the following sentences:

PEns are items of stationery.

CArs when parked are stationary.

Subtle
To **B**e subtle—**B**e silent.

Succeed
Succeed, **P**roceed, **E**xceed are the only three English words that end in **CEED**.

Take the initial letters of these words and think **SPEED**.

Together

Split it up into three separate words:

To get her.

Weather or Whether

WE look **AT HER** (the TV weather girl) to check the forecast and discover whether it will be sunny or rainy.

Wednesday

WE Do **N**ot **E**at **S**oup **D**ay.

Weird

Weird doesn't follow the *i* before *e* rule, because weird is just weird.

You're or Your

YOU'RE never going to get it right if you don't use **YOUR** head.

If something belongs to us, it is **OUR**s, just as something that belongs to you is **YOUR**s.

Eye halve a spelling checker
It came with my pea sea
It plainly marques for my revue
Miss steaks eye kin knot sea.

Eye strike a key and type a word
And weight four it to say
Weather eye am wrong oar write
It shows me strait a weigh.

As soon as a mist ache is maid
It nose bee fore two long
And eye can put the error rite
It's rare lea ever wrong.

Eye have run this poem threw it
Eye am shore your pleased two no
It's letter perfect awl the weigh
My checker tolled me sew.

—Margo Roark

www.spellingsociety.org/news/media/poems.php

3
Think of a Number

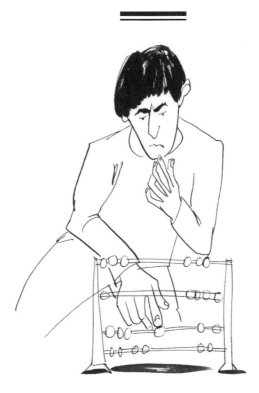

First Steps: Counting Rhymes

Learning to count is the first step to understanding arithmetic. Most children learn counting by reciting nursery rhymes, which contain the essential ingredients of mnemonics: imagery, rhyme, and fun. "One, Two, Buckle My Shoe" was devised many years ago as a fun way to teach children how to count to 20 using visual language and repetitive rhythm. Here are two slightly different versions of the famous verse:

One, Two, buckle my shoe,
Three, Four, knock at the door,
Five, Six, pick up sticks,
Seven, Eight, lay them straight,
Nine, Ten, a big fat hen,
Eleven, Twelve, dig and delve,
Thirteen, Fourteen, maids a-courting,
Fifteen, Sixteen, maids in the kitchen,
Seventeen, Eighteen, maids in waiting,
Nineteen, Twenty, my plate's empty.

One, Two, buckle my shoe,
Three, Four, knock at the door,
Five, Six, pick up sticks,
Seven, Eight, don't be late,
Nine, Ten, a good fat hen,
Eleven, Twelve, dig and delve
Thirteen, Fourteen, maids a-courting,
Fifteen, Sixteen, maids a-kissing,
Seventeen, Eighteen, maids a-waiting,
Nineteen, Twenty, I've had plenty.

"One, Two, Three, Four, Five," also known as "Once I Caught a Fish Alive," is another famous counting rhyme. Though its origins are unknown, its earliest date of publication has been traced back to 1888:

> One, two, three, four, five.
> Once I caught a fish alive.
> Six, seven, eight, nine, ten.
> Then I let it go again.
> Why did you let it go?
> Because it bit my finger so.
> Which finger did it bite?
> This little finger on my right.

This shorter counting rhyme was also popular with children:

> One, Two, Three, Four,
> Mary's at the cottage door.
> Five, Six, Seven, Eight,
> Eating cherries off a plate.

Writing Numbers

Mastering numbers out loud is one thing, but writing them down is something else entirely. However, the number-writing poem on the next page doubtless helped countless youngsters.

Around to the left to find my hero,
Back to the top, I've made a zero.

Downward stroke, my that's fun,
Now I've made the number 1.

Half a heart says, "I love you."
A line—now I made the number 2.

Around the tree, around the tree,
Now I've made the number 3.

Down and across and down once more
Now I've made the number 4.

The hat, the back, the belly—a 5.
Watch out! It might come alive.

Bend down low to pick up sticks,
Now I've made the number 6.

Across the sky, and down from heaven,
Now I've made the number 7.

Make an "S" and close the gate,
Now I've made the number 8.

An oval and a line,
Now I've made the number 9.

One (1) egg (0) laid my hen.
Now I've made the number 10.

Roman Numerals

Imagine doing sums using Roman numerals. They are still used today for indicating successive same-name successors to kings and queens, as well as for movie sequels, dates, Olympic Games, and the Super Bowl, but their usage is quite rare. I, V, and X are more commonly used, particularly on clock and watch faces, making it more familiar that they represent 1, 5, and 10 respectively. It's a good idea to remember that C stands for "century," i.e., 100 years:

I	V	X	L	C	D	M
1	5	10	50	100	500	1,000

The Romans did not have a notation for zero, which meant that early in the second millennium the system was gradually replaced by the Arabic numerals used today. Modern society rarely uses Roman numerals anymore; there's a danger that this system may become obsolete. This simple mnemonic helps keep the numbers in order:

I Value **X**ylophones **L**ike **C**ows **D**ig **M**ilk.

Remember the first three letters IVX, then recite the following to recall LCD and M:

Lucy **C**an't **D**rink **M**ilk.

The poem on the next page provides a rhythmic visual image for learning Roman numerals.

> X shall stand for playmates Ten,
> V for Five stout stalwart men,
> I for One as I'm alive,
> C for Hundred and D for Five,
> M for a Thousand soldiers true,
> And L for Fifty, I'll tell you.

As is this brief yet concise verse:

> M's mille—or 1,000 said,
> D's half—500 quickly read.
> C's just a 100—century
> And L is half again—50.
> So all that's left is X and V
> Or 10 and 5 and I is easy.

The Metric System

Metrication, or the decimal system, began in France in the 1790s. Although the United States has been slow to adopt metrics, it is gradually finding its way into the U.S. marketplace. Two-liter soft drinks are not uncommon; dental floss is often measured in meters; and prior to digitization, 35-mm film became a popular standard. Don't be terrified, get metrified. Here are some clever mnemonics to help you remember. Don't despair. If all else fails, use one of the many metric conversion calculators available on the Internet.

Kilometer	1,000 meters
Hectometer	100 meters
Decameter	10 meters
Meter (base)	1 meter
Decimeter	⅒ of a meter
Centimeter	⅟₁₀₀ of a meter
Millimeter	⅟₁₀₀₀ of a meter

The first letters stand for the metric prefixes and base unit: Kilo, Hecto, Deca, Meter (base), Deci, Centi, Milli. The following phrases help to remember the correct order:

King **H**enry **D**ied **M**ightily **D**rinking **C**hocolate **M**ilk

Keep **H**er **D**iamond **M**ine **D**own **C**reek, **M**ister

King **H**enry **D**ied—**M**other **D**idn't **C**are **M**uch

King **H**ector **D**ied **M**iserable **D**eath—**C**aught **M**easles

If the base unit is a gram rather than a meter we would have:

King **H**enry **D**ied—**G**ranny **D**idn't **C**are **M**uch

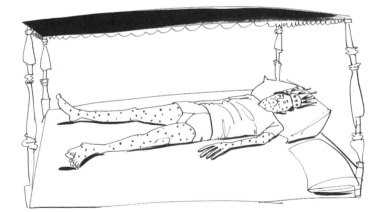

Times-Table Tricks

Ten Times-table

When multiplying a number by 10, add a zero to it. This is a simple mnemonic device— $3 \times 10 = 30$, just as $26{,}350 \times 10 = 263{,}500$. As the numbers get larger, add a zero and move the comma to the right by one place.

Nine Times-table

The study of arithmetic presents an infinite number of patterns to discover. One involves the nine times-table.

$9 \times 1 = 9$	$9 \times 6 = 54$
$9 \times 2 = 18$	$9 \times 7 = 63$
$9 \times 3 = 27$	$9 \times 8 = 72$
$9 \times 4 = 36$	$9 \times 9 = 81$
$9 \times 5 = 45$	$9 \times 10 = 90$

Notice that the product of 9×5 inverts at 9×6 to 54:

$$9 \times 5 = 45; 9 \times 6 = 54$$

Also, up to 9×10, the digits in the products of numbers multiplied by 9 always add up to 9:

$$9 \times 2 = 18 \ (1 + 8 = 9), 9 \times 3 = 27 \ (2 + 7 = 9).$$

Nine Times-table: By Hand

Many people learned this clever way to remember our nine times-table.

First, hold your two hands up with the palms facing you, and number each digit from 1 to 10, starting with the thumb on your left hand (1) through to the thumb on your right hand (10).

For 9×2, you need to bend digit number 2 (your left index finger) to signify *times 2*. This leaves your thumb (1) outstretched to the left of your bent index finger, and 8 digits outstretched to the right of it. Put 1 and 8 together to form the product of 9×2.

For 9×6, you need to bend digit number 6 (your right pinky) to represent *times 6*. This leaves all the digits on your left hand outstretched (5) and the remaining digits on your right hand outstretched (4). Put 5 and 4 together to make the product of 9×6.

The key involves looking at the number of fingers to the left side of the folded-down finger to find the number for the tens column of the answer, and looking to the right of the folded-down finger to find the number for the ones column.

More Times-table Tricks

Eight Times-table
8×8 fell on the floor, when I picked it up, it was 64!
8 and 9 are nice, but I like seven, too (72).

Seven Times-table
Three 7s had drinks and fun, and so they must be 21.
7 × 7 were in a mine, it must be 1849.

Six Times-table
6 and 7 went on a date and secured a table four two (42).

Five Times-table
Learn to count by fives, and remember that the products always end with a 5 or an 0.

Four Times-table
To 4 × 4 it would seem, long ago was sweet 16.

Three Times-table
Three cats have nine lives before heaven, until they turn 27.

Two Times-table
To multiply by two is great; it must end in 0, 2, 4, 6 or 8.

Long Division

When it comes to the technique for remembering which steps to follow when doing long division—**D**ivide, **M**ultiply, **S**ubtract, **B**ring down—use one of these memorable phrases:

Dad, **M**om, **S**ister, **B**rother.
Dead **M**onkeys **S**mell **B**ad.

The Order of Calculation

The order to work out a sum is: **M**ultiply and **D**ivide before you **A**dd and **S**ubtract. Any mathematical statement with an "equals" sign is an equation; that is, one side of the equation equals the other side. For example, $1 + 1 = 2$ is an equation, just as $2 \times 10 = 4 \times 5$ is an equation.

Some people find that the following phrase helps them remember the MDAS correct order:

My **D**ear **A**unt **S**ally

When things get more complicated and several functions become necessary to solve for the sum, the PEMDAS order tackles the problem:

Parentheses **E**xponents **M**ultiplication
Division **A**ddition **S**ubtraction

Certain phrases are useful for keeping the correct order in mind:

Please **E**xcuse **M**y **D**ear **A**unt **S**ally.

Please **E**xecute **M**y **D**og **A**nd **S**oon.

Put **E**very **M**an **D**own **A**nd **S**hout.

The **BIDMAS** acronym offers another alternative, but works in exactly the same way:

Brackets **I**ndices **D**ivision **M**ultiplication
Addition **S**ubtraction

BIDMAS allows you to calculate the sum written as:

$$(8 - 3) \times 4 + \frac{15}{5} - 3 = 20$$

The B for Brackets in BIDMAS means the same as the P for Parentheses in PEMDAS, as does the I for Indices and the E for Exponents. The order of Division and Multiplication is flexible, so the order can either be DM or MD.

Finding Averages

Here is an excellent way to remember the names of the four methods of finding averages, using the **Medium-Range Mean Model** method:

Median—the number exactly in the middle when a set of numbers is listed in order.

Range—the difference between the highest and lowest numbers in a set.

Mean—the sum of a set of numbers, divided by the number of numbers in the set.

Mode—the number (or numbers) that appears most frequently in a set.

Isosceles Triangles

To help distinguish between an isosceles triangle and all other types of triangles, this song sung to the tune of "Oh, Christmas Tree" proved invaluable:

> Oh, isosceles, oh, isosceles,
> Two angles have
> Equal degrees.
> Oh, isosceles, oh, isosceles,
> You look just like
> A Christmas tree.

Dividing by Fractions

A fraction is a numerical quantity that is not a whole number, for example ½ or $^{19}\!/_{20}$, which are quantities that form part of a whole.

The definition of a fraction is a numerator divided by a denominator, but which is which?

Think of "Notre Dame":

NUmerator **U**p, **D**enominator **D**own.

Therefore, in ½, 1 is the numerator, 2 is the denominator.

In $^{19}\!/_{20}$, 19 is the numerator, 20 is the denominator.

This rhyme will help every student who gets into a muddle when dividing by fractions:

> The number you're dividing by,
> Turn upside down and multiply.

e.g., 10 divided by ½ = 10 × ²⁄₁ = 20
or 15 divided by ⅕ = 15 × ⁵⁄₁ = 75

The Value of Pi

Pi is the Greek letter π. It is a mathematical constant and calculated as the ratio of the circumference of a circle to its diameter. Pi is the number 3.14159, although in reality, it has an infinite number of decimal places.

The traditional way to remind yourself of the decimals is to use phrases containing word-length mnemonics, where the number of letters in each word corresponds to a digit.

Pi to six decimal places is:

> How I wish I could calculate pi = 3.141592

And to 14 places:

> How I like a drink,
> alcoholic of course,
> after the heavy lectures involving
> quantum mechanics = 3.14159265358979

And here's a rhyme to 20 decimal places of pi:

> Now, I wish I could recollect pi.
> "Eureka," cried the great inventor.
> Christmas Pudding, Christmas Pie,
> Is the problem's very center.
> = 3.14159265358979323846

And to 31 decimal places:

> Sir, I bear a rhyme excelling
> In mystic force, and magic spelling
> Celestial sprites elucidate
> All my own striving can't relate
> Or locate they who can cogitate
> And so finally terminate. Finis.
> = 3.1415926535897932384626433832795

Unfortunately, this useful method of remembering pi only works up to 31 decimal places, because the thirty-second number after the decimal point is 0.

Omni, the celebrated science magazine of the late 1970s and early 1980s, devised this fun verse to help students calculate the circumference of a circle using pi:

> If you cross a circle with a line,
> Which hits the center and runs from spine to spine,
> And the line's length is d
> The circumference will be d times 3.14159.

The area of a circle is calculated as $\pi \times$ r squared (where r is the radius) $= \pi r^2$.

To help remember the formula, think:

> Apple Pie Are Square.

The circumference of a circle is calculated as $\pi \times$ d (where d is the diameter) $= \pi d$.

One memorable way to recall the formula is to think:

> Cherry Pie Delicious.

The following rhyme helps teach the difference between circumference and area:

> Fiddlededum, fiddlededee,
> A ring round the moon is π times d.
> If a hole in your sock you want repaired,
> You use the formula πr squared.

Square Roots

Just as subtraction is the opposite of addition and division is the opposite of multiplication, so square roots are the opposite of squaring; that is, multiplying a number by itself, so the square root of 4 is 2 (i.e., $2 \times 2 = 4$).

This example shows a perfect square root and is therefore quite simple. Things get more interesting when math instructors explore more complicated concepts, such as the square root of 2. Which number multiplied by itself makes 2? It's not a round number, and so, as with pi, the length of each word in the following rhyme represents each digit:

> For the square root of 2,
> I wish I knew
> 1.414—the root of two.
>
> For the square root of 3,
> O, charmed was he
> 1.732—to know the root of three.
>
> For the square root of 5,
> So we now strive
> 2.236—to know the root of five.
>
> For the square root of 6,
> We need more logistics
> 2.449—to know the root of six.

Pythagoras's Theorem

Pythagoras (c. 580–500 B.C.) was a Greek mathematician and philosopher from Samos, sometimes known as the "Father of Numbers." His famous theorem is a math standard that reveals how to calculate the lengths of the three sides of a right-angled triangle.

In essence, Pythagoras's theorem states that the

square of the hypotenuse is equal to the sum of the squares of the other two sides, or HYPOTENUSE squared = BASE squared + HEIGHT squared.

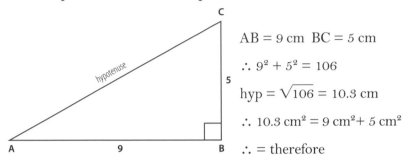

AB = 9 cm   BC = 5 cm

$\therefore 9^2 + 5^2 = 106$

hyp $= \sqrt{106} = 10.3$ cm

$\therefore 10.3 \text{ cm}^2 = 9 \text{ cm}^2 + 5 \text{ cm}^2$

$\therefore$ = therefore

To help math students remember the formula, a visual aid in the form of the "teepee story" was devised, which featured a memorable mnemonic punch line:

A Red Indian chief had three squaws in three teepees. When he came home late from hunting, he never knew which squaw was in which teepee, because it was always dark. One day he killed a hippopotamus, a bear and a buffalo. He put one hide from each animal into each teepee so that when he came home late he could feel inside the teepee and he would know which squaw was which. After a year, all three squaws had had children. The squaw on the bear hide had a baby boy, the squaw on the buffalo hide had a baby girl. But the squaw on the hippopotamus hide had a girl and a boy. And the moral of the story?

The squaw on the hippopotamus is equal to the sum of the squaws on the other two hides.

Trigonometry: Sine Cosine Tangent

By definition, triangles are all about threes—sides and angles. If you know two elements of a right-angled triangle—whether it be sides, angles, or one of each—you can then calculate the third.

In a right-angled triangle, if the value of a second angle is given:

the **S**ine of the angle = the ratio of the **O**pposite side to the **H**ypotenuse

the **C**osine of the angle = the ratio of the **A**djacent side to the **H**ypotenuse

the **T**angent of the angle = the ratio of the **O**pposite and the **A**djacent sides

For example, in this diagram:

$$\sin (A) = \frac{a}{c}$$

$$\cos (A) = \frac{b}{c}$$

$$\tan (A) = \frac{a}{b}$$

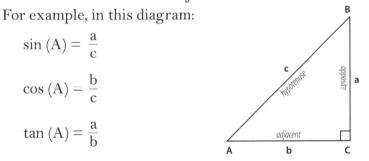

The initials spell **SOH–CAH–TOA,** which is easy to recall because it rhymes with Krakatoa, the volcanic island in Indonesia. If, however, the volcano comparison is less than effective, one of the examples on the next page might prove more memorable.

Smiles **O**f **H**appiness **C**ome
After **H**aving **T**ankards **O**f **A**le.

Some **O**ld **H**ag **C**aught
A **H**ippy **T**ripping **O**n **A**cid.

Some **O**ld **H**orse **C**aught **A**nother **H**orse
Taking **O**ats **A**way.

Graph Coordinates

From simple bar charts showing hours of sunshine against months of the year to advanced calculus graphs indicating rates of change, this is the rule for all graphs:

X along the corridor,
Y up and down the stairs.

The convention for labeling a pair of coordinates (x and y) is that x is the horizontal axis and y the vertical axis.

Converting Miles to Kilometers

Fibonacci numbers are named after the thirteenth-century mathematician Leonardo of Pisa, who was also called Leonardo Fibonacci. They are whole numbers in sequence: 0, 1, 2, 3, 5, 8, 13, 21, 34, 55, 89 . . . and so on to infinity. Each number in the series is the sum of the previous two numbers.

There are approximately 8 (8.05 km) kilometers in 5 miles, and since both 8 and 5 are Fibonacci numbers, you can convert kilometers to miles and miles to kilometers by looking at the consecutive numbers. Just remember, there will always be more kilometers (longer word) than miles (shorter word).

$$8 \text{ km} = 5 \text{ miles}$$
$$13 \text{ km} = 8 \text{ miles}$$
$$21 \text{ km} = 13 \text{ miles}$$
$$34 \text{ km} = 21 \text{ miles}$$
$$55 \text{ km} = 34 \text{ miles}$$
$$89 \text{ km} = 55 \text{ miles}$$

The hardest arithmetic to master is that which enables us to count our blessings.

—Eric Hoffer
Reflections on the Human Condition

4
Geographically Speaking

───

Learning Directions

The four main compass directions: north, south, east, and west form the introduction to many geography lessons. Remembering exactly where these points fall on a compass should be quite straightforward, but to avoid memory loss, a number of useful phrases have been devised.

Consider, for example, the acronym NEWS:

North at the top
East on the right
West on the left
South at the bottom

Alternatively, the first letter of each word in these sentences indicates the points of the compass in clockwise order:

Never **E**at **S**hredded **W**heat.

Never **E**at **S**limy **W**orms.

Never **E**nter **S**anta's **W**orkshop.

Never **E**at **S**oggy **W**affles.

Naughty **E**lephants **S**quirt **W**ater.

Latitude and Longitude

If you've ever had problems remembering the direction of latitude and longitude lines, here are a few mnemonic pointers to ensure you won't get lost.

The Latin word *latus* means "side"; hence, latitude lines go from side to side.

The phrase "Lat is fat" should help remind us that the central lines of latitude go around the "belt" of the equator.

*Long*itude lines seem *long*er, going from top to bottom or north to south.

The Tropics of Cancer and Capricorn

These are two imaginary lines running parallel to the equator (the longest line of latitude that spans the center of the globe), which are based on the sun's position in relation to the earth at two points of the year. The sun is directly overhead at noon on the Tropic of Cancer on June 21 (the beginning of summer in the Northern Hemisphere and of winter in the Southern Hemisphere) and is again overhead at midday on the Tropic of Capricorn on December 21 (the beginning of winter in the Northern Hemisphere and of summer in the Southern Hemisphere).

The Tropic of Cancer lies 23.5° north of the equator and the Tropic of Capricorn lies at 23.5° south, and the following verse has helped many to remember this fact.

CaNcer lies North of the equator.
CapricOrn lies on the Other side of the equator.

Map Reading

Imagine you're a Girl Scout or Boy Scout on an expedition carrying no more than a Hershey bar and a topographical map, or a soldier in the field armed with just a map and a compass. Your map grid reference is 123456. To find your position on the map just think: "Onward and Upward."

Split your map reference into two sets of three figures: 123 and 456.

The 1 is the number of the grid line on the map going across—ONWARD—from west to east. The 2 and 3 give more precise coordinates within that grid.

The 4 is the grid line going up—UPWARD—from south to north. And the 5 and 6 give a more precise location.

The Seven Continents of the World

A continent is defined as a large continuous landmass, and geographers state that the world has seven of them:

Europe Asia Africa Australia
Antarctica North America South America

Although Europe is joined to Asia, the two areas are recognized as separate continents, with the Ural Mountains in Russia dividing the areas that we regard as East and West. Australia is the smallest continent and is also known as Oceania. Australia itself is an island of just under 3 million square miles. Asia is the largest continent at approximately 17 million square miles.

The following phrases are the most popular to remember the continents:

Eat **A**n **A**spirin **A**fter **A** **N**asty **S**andwich.
Eat **A**n **A**pple **A**s **A** **N**ice **S**nack.

The Five Oceans

For a long time, geography teachers categorized four oceans when teaching about the 70 to 75 percent of the earth that is blanketed with water. But in the spring of 2000, the International Hydrographic Organization officially established the Southern Ocean as number five, defining its often frozen perimeters. Now students need to memorize five oceans: Pacific, Atlantic, Indian, Southern, and Arctic (from largest to smallest). Form your own mnemonic to remember the PAISA acronym, such as:

Pacifiers **A**re **I**cky, **S**omeone **A**ttested.

Pick **A**n **I**ndian **S**ummer **A**pple.

The Great Lakes

The five Great Lakes from west to east are: **S**uperior, **M**ichigan, **H**uron, **E**rie, and **O**ntario. As SMHEO is a less than memorable acronym, these short pithy sentences are far more effective:

Sally **M**ade **H**enry **E**at **O**nions.
She **M**akes **H**im **E**at **O**reos.
Super **M**ario **H**eaved **E**arth **O**ut.

From east to west, try:

Old **E**lephants **H**ave **M**uch **S**kin.

An easier and more commonly used mnemonic acronym is HOMES, but this scrambles the correct geographical order.

Niagara Falls

Use the letters LENOR as a reminder of which two Great Lakes surround Niagara Falls. Picture the scene as if looking at a map where north is at the top of the page:

Left—**E**rie—**N**iagara—**O**ntario—**R**ight

Central America

There are seven Central American countries, namely: **G**uatemala, **B**elize, **H**onduras, **E**l Salvador, **N**icaragua, **C**osta Rica and **P**anama. If these names or the letters GBHENCP don't roll easily off your tongue, try using this mnemonic phrase to jog your memory:

Great **B**ig **H**ungry **E**lephant
Nearly **C**onsumed **P**anama.

The World's Longest Rivers

An unusual acronym used to remember the names of the world's longest rivers is NAYY CLAIM. The exact length of the two greatest rivers on Earth—the Nile and the Amazon—varies over time, and geographers disagree on their actual length. Therefore, this acronym is more of an aid to remembering the names of the rivers, rather than their exact pecking order, about which no one seems able to agree. In fact, this list changes significantly when all tributaries are included.

RIVER	CONTINENT	LENGTH
Nile	Africa	4,160 miles (6,695 km)
Amazon	South America	4,150 miles (6,683 km)
Yangtze (Chang Jiang)	Asia	3,964 miles (6,380 km)
Yellow (Huang He)	Asia	3,000 miles (4,830 km)
Congo (Zaire)	Africa	2,880 miles (4,630 km)
Lena	Asia	2,734 miles (4,400 km)
Amur (Heilong Jiang)	Asia	2,703 miles (4,350 km)
Irtysh	Asia	2,640 miles (4,248 km)
Mekong	Asia	2,600 miles (4,180 km)

The three longest rivers in North America, including tributaries, can be recalled using the acronym MMR (think Measles, Mumps, and Rubella):

RIVER	COUNTRY OF ORIGIN	LENGTH
Mississippi–Missouri	United States	3,709 miles (5,970 km)
Mackenzie	Canada	2,635 miles (4,240 km)
Rio Grande	United States and Mexico	1,885 miles (3,034 km)

The Seven Hills of Rome

Rome was built on the seven hills east of the Tiber River. Clockwise from the westernmost hill, they are **C**apitoline, **Q**uirinal, **V**iminal, **E**squiline, **C**aelian, **A**ventine and **P**alatine, and they can be easily remembered with the following phrase:

Can **Q**ueen **V**ictoria **E**at **C**old **A**pple **P**ie?

Alternatively, if you start with the Quirinal, going in a clockwise direction, you could try remembering a slightly more amusing alternative:

Queen **V**ictoria **E**yes **C**aesar's **A**wfully **P**ainful **C**orns.

An even more memorable acronym is **PACE QVC**. *Pace*, the Italian word for "peace," is paired with QVC, the shopping channel.

Italian Geography

If you ever need a reminder of the location of Sicily, here's a verse guaranteed to help:

Long-legged Italy kicked little Sicily
Right into the middle of the Mediterranean Sea.

The Streets of Los Angeles

Mnemonics can be used to help tourists find their way in unfamiliar cities and towns. The following mnemonic mentions 10 primary east to west (actually SE to NW) streets in central LA:

> In LOS ANGELES, you MAINly SPRING onto BROADWAY, go up the HILL to OLIVE with the GRAND HOPE of picking FLOWERs on FIGUEROA.

Grand is actually an avenue not a street, but the idea allows the reader to navigate that part of the city with relative ease by memorizing one simple sentence.

When asked how the Beatles found America on their first U.S. visit:

Just turn left at Greenland....

—John Lennon

5
Animal, Vegetable, Mineral

===

Geological Periods

The list below details the geological classification of rock deposits, starting with the Cambrian, the first period in the Palaeozoic era.

	Approximate number of years ago
Cambrian	570–510 million
Ordovician	510–439 million
Silurian	439–409 million
Devonian	409–363 million
Carboniferous	363–290 million
Permian	290–245 million
Triassic	245–208 million
Jurassic	208–146 million
Cretaceous	146–65 million
Palaeocene	65–56.5 million
Eocene	56.5–35.4 million
Oligocene	35.4–23.3 million
Miocene	23.3–5.2 million
Pliocene	5.2–1.64 million

| Pleistocene | 1,640,000–10,000 |
| Recent (Holocene) | 10,000–present day |

Large mammals flourished and became extinct as recently as the Pleistocene period, during which time anatomically modern humans most likely began to evolve. The Recent period marked the end of the last Ice Age and the start of the development of modern civilization.

Here's a memorable phrase to help you tell your Eocene from the Pliocene period, starting with the Cambrian era from more than 500 million years ago:

Camels **O**ften **S**it **D**own **C**arefully.
Perhaps **T**heir **J**oints **C**reak? **P**ossibly **E**arly **O**iling
Might **P**revent **P**ermanent **R**heumatism.

Components of Soil

When testing the soil for its age, geologists also need to know the main constituents of soil—namely, **A**ir, **H**umus, **M**ineral salts, **W**ater, **B**acteria and **R**ock particles—which can be remembered with this essential saying:

All **H**airy **M**en **W**ill **B**uy **R**azors.

The Hardness of Minerals

The Mohs Scale, devised in 1822 by German mineralogist Friedrich Mohs (1773–1839), lists 10 familiar, easily available minerals and arranges them in order of their "scratch hardness." Scratch hardness involves a mineral's resistance to fracture or its permanent deformation due to friction from a sharp object.

Minerals in order from softest to hardest:

1. **T**alc
2. **G**ypsum
3. **C**alcite
4. **F**luorite (fluorspar)
5. **A**patite
6. **O**rthoclase (feldspar)
7. **Q**uartz
8. **T**opaz
9. **C**orundum
10. **D**iamond

Groups 1–2 can be scratched by a fingernail.
Groups 3–6 can be scratched with a blade.
Groups 7–10 are hard enough to scratch glass.

A couple of useful mnemonics to memorize the Mohs Scale are:

Tall **G**irls **C**an **F**lirt **A**nd **O**ther **Q**ueer **T**hings **C**an **D**evelop.

TAll **GY**roscopes **CA**n **FL**y **AP**art **OR**biting **QU**ickly **TO** **CO**mplete **DI**sintegration.

Types of Fossils

One way of learning the different types of fossils is to remember the acronym IMAP, which stands for:

Imprint
Molds (or casts)
Actual remains
Petrified

Or keep in mind the following apt phrase:

I Marvel **A**t **P**etrification.

Stalactites and Stalagmites

Stalactites form when water containing calcium carbonate dissolves after seeping down through limestone or chalk, then evaporates leaving deposits of carbonates of lime to accumulate over time to form mineral columns in caves. Stalagmites develop in the same way when rain falls onto the floor of caves and minerals build up to form pillars.

The similarity between the spelling and pronunciation of the two words sometimes causes confusion, so several memory aids have been developed to help simplify matters.

The following example relies on the difference in spelling, using the C and the G to relate to the origin of the formation:

StalaCtites are formed on the Ceiling.

StalaGmites are formed on the Ground.

A slightly sillier way is to think of the reaction to having ants (mites) in your pants:

When mites go up, the tights come down!

A couple of other suggestions have been:

Stalactites hang *tight* from the roof;

Stalagmites *might* reach the roof.

Stalactites hang down like *tight*s on a clothesline;

Stalagmites *might* bite if you sit on them.

Camels: One Lump or Two

There are two main types of camel—one has one hump and the other has two. But what's the best way to remember which is which?

A **B**actrian camel's back is shaped like the letter B
—it has two humps.

A **D**romedary's back is shaped like the letter D
—it has only one hump.

Both species of camel come from the dry deserts of Asia and North Africa. The Bactrian, or two-humped, camel inhabits central Asia. The Dromedary, or one-humped camel, is a light and fast breed, otherwise known as the Arabian camel. The name comes from the Greek word *dromas*—to run. The Dromedary is domesticated and no longer lives in the wild.

Elephants Never Forget

How do you tell the difference between an Indian (Asian) elephant and an African elephant? It's all in the size, as this rhyme proves:

India's big, and its elephant there features,
But Africa's bigger with much bigger creatures.

Generally the ears of an African elephant are bigger than those of its Indian counterpart. Imagine that those ears resemble the shape of the larger African continent, while those of the Indian elephant are the shape of India.

Insect Stings

From one of the world's largest creatures to two of the smallest. What home remedies will effectively treat a bee or a wasp sting?

Use **A**mmonia for a **B**ee sting

And **V**inegar for a **W**asp sting.

B follows **A** and **W** follows **V**
(Think of the VW car as well).

This is also a useful mnemonic with which to remember the Latin family classification of bees and wasps:

Apidae are Bees.

Vespidae are **W**asps.

More correctly, the Apidae classification refers to the "superfamily" of bees, while Vespidae is the "family" classification for wasps.

Taxonomic Classifications

Not to be confused with the art of preparing, stuffing and mounting animal skins (taxidermy), alpha taxonomy is the principle of arranging groups of living organisms—that is, plants and animals—into groups based on similarities of structure and origin. To give an example of the classifications, here are the definitions of man or *homo sapiens:*

Kingdom	*Animalia*
Phylum	*Vertibrata*
Class	*Mammalia*
Order	*Primate*
Family	*Hominidae*
Genus	*Homo*
Species	*Sapiens*
Variety	—

To remember the different classifications including "variety," these two phrases supply strong visual memory aids:

Krakatoa **P**ositively **C**asts **O**ff **F**umes
Generating **S**ulphurous **V**apors.

Kindly **P**lace **C**over **O**n **F**resh **G**reen **S**pring **V**egetables

Versions excluding reference to "variety" can be remembered by using the following phrases:

Kids **P**refer **C**heese **O**ver **F**ried **G**reen **S**pinach.
Kim **P**ut **C**heese **O**n **F**rank's **G**reen **S**hoes.
Kings **P**lay **C**hess **O**n **F**ine **G**reen **S**ilk.

Cedar Trees

Evergreen cedar trees in many parks and gardens come in three types:

Atlas has **A**scending branches.

Lebanon has **L**evel branches.

Deodar has **D**rooping branches.

The Cedar tree has a long history, dating back to biblical times. The Cherokee Indians believed that cedar trees held the spirits of ancient ancestors. The Atlas cedar, was first introduced into the United States in 1845, makes a popular specimen tree, and is used today in some aromatherapies. Lebanon cedar trees were coveted in ancient times for their appearance, fragrance, and commercial value, particularly in the building industry and today they are a threatened conifer. The massive Deodar cedar tree can reach approximately 250 feet in its original Himalayan habitat. Deodar, from the Sanskrit *devadaru*, translates into "timber of the gods."

Firewood

If you are building a fire at home or making a campfire, consider this traditional poem on the opposite page to avoid suffocating smoke and flying sparks.

Beech wood fires are bright and clear,
If the logs are kept a year.
Chestnut's only good, they say,
If for long it's laid away.
Birch and fir logs burn too fast,
Blaze up bright and do not last.
It is, by the Irish said,
Hawthorn makes the sweetest bread
Elm wood burns like a churchyard mold,
Even the very flames are cold.
Poplar gives a bitter smoke,
Fills your eyes and makes you choke.
Apple wood will scent your room
With an incense like perfume.
Oak and maple, if dry and old,
Keep away the winter cold.
But ash wood wet and ash wood dry,
A king shall warm his slippers by.

6

Time and the Calendar

Spring Forward, Fall Back

The seasons change, the clocks go back and forth, time waits for no man, and woe betide the person who forgets to reset his or her clock at the beginning of autumn and spring.

Most of the United States now begins daylight saving time at 2:00 A.M. on the second Sunday in March and reverts to standard time on the first Sunday in November. The Energy Policy Act, passed by the U.S. Congress in July 2005, marked the start of this change. This act altered the time-change dates for daylight saving in the United States. The legislation was enacted in the hope that this change would result in energy savings.

Another advantage to daylight saving time is that many fire

departments urge people to change the batteries in their smoke detectors on the same day that they change their clocks. This provides a convenient reminder.

So in the **spring** the clocks move **forward** one hour to herald summer, and in autumn (or **fall**) they are set **back** one hour to welcome winter.

A similar saying to "Spring Forward, Fall Back" adapted to the new system reminds people of the change in time: "Forward March, back November." That is all you need to remember.

Thirty Days Hath September...

The words to this rhyme are possibly the most often-repeated of all memory aids. This verse, first learned in childhood, helps to recall how many days there are in each month.

The origin of the "Thirty Days Hath September" poem is obscure, but the use of "old" English in the verse suggests that it dates back to at least the sixteenth century. Several different endings to the last two lines of the verse have been recorded, two are listed below:

Thirty days hath September,
April, June, and November;
All the rest have thirty-one
Excepting February alone,
And that has twenty-eight days clear,
With twenty-nine in each leap year.

Which hath but twenty-eight, in fine,
Till leap year gives it twenty-nine.

The verse informs the reader that four particular months contain 30 days, and February has either 28 or 29. Therefore, by process of elimination we can work out that the remaining seven months all comprise 31 days. February was the last month in the Julian calendar year; that's the reason it was left to pick up the leftovers.

Days of the Months by Hand

A physical mnemonic trick that can help determine the days of each month is right on the back of your hands. Place your clenched fists together, side by side, and begin with your left hand, naming the knuckle of your little finger as January. The valley or dip between the first two knuckles is February, the knuckle of the ring finger is March, and the next valley is April. July marks the last knuckle on the left hand, and August marks the first knuckle on the right hand, since both months have 31 days. Carry on until you reach the penultimate knuckle on your right hand, representing December. The two thumb knuckles are both excluded from this technique.

All the knuckles represent months with 31 days, and the valleys the shorter months. As in the rhyme, remember that February is the exception. So if you can't remember the famous verse, you can rely on your own hands to jog your memory. A similar memory devise uses the piano keyboard, moving from January, represented by the "F" key, and moving up the keyboard in semitones—the black notes indicate the short months and the white the long months.

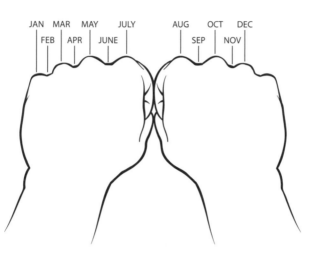

Teaching the Days of the Week

Teaching young children the days of the week poses a challenge for many parents and preschool teachers. The melody to "Clementine" *(Oh, my darlin', oh, my darlin', oh, my darlin', Clementine…)* provides a rhythmic background to the following verse:

> Sunday, Monday,
> Tuesday, Wednesday,
> Thursday, Friday, Saturday,
>
> There are seven days,
> There are seven days,
> There are seven days in a week.

Another musical variation uses the tune to the old TV show *The Addams Family:*

> Days of the week (clap, clap)
> Days of the week (clap, clap)
> There's Sunday and there's Monday
> There's Tuesday and there's Wednesday
> There's Thursday and there's Friday
> And then there's Sat-ur-day.
> Days of the week (clap, clap)
> Days of the week (clap, clap)
> Days of the week, days of the week, days of the week (clap, clap).

Teachers and parents can point to the days on a calendar as the children sing the song, to further help with placement and word identification.

How to Remember Dates

Writer and educator Grace Fleming writes a column on homework and study tips. She claims that an effective way to remember an important date is to think of a silly, visual term that rhymes with the date to imbed the thought into one's consciousness. She offers the following useful examples:

> You can leave off the century, so that 1861, the starting date for the Civil War, becomes 61.

> Example:
>   61 = Sticky gun

Imagine a Civil War soldier struggling with a gun that's been covered with honey. It may sound silly, but the technique works!

1773 was the date of the Boston Tea Party. To remember this, you could think:

> 73 = Heavenly tea

Think of protesters, sipping lovely cups of tea right before tossing them into the water.

This strategy also works for the husband who can't seem to remember his wedding anniversary or wife's birthday:

June 10, I married the hen.
September 15, treat her like a queen.

Time Travel

When traveling long distances throughout the world, it helps to remember EWG and WEL to calculate if you'll be losing or gaining time during a journey:

East to **W**est **G**ains and **W**est to **E**ast **L**oses.

The Caribbean Hurricane Season

The people of the Caribbean and the southern United States are only too aware of the risks of hurricanes, as this mnemonic indicates:

June—Too Soon (first month)

July—Stand By (for any news of a storm)

August—You Must (prepare in case a storm comes)

September—Remember (to stand by)

October—It's All Over (last month)

The Signs of the Zodiac

Aries	The Ram	March 21 – April 20
Taurus	The Bull	April 21 – May 20
Gemini	The Twins	May 21 – June 20
Cancer	The Crab	June 21 – July 22
Leo	The Lion	July 23 – August 22
Virgo	The Virgin	August 23 – September 22
Libra	The Scales	September 23 – October 22
Scorpio	The Scorpion	October 23 – November 21
Sagittarius	The Archer	November 22 – December 21
Capricorn	The Goat	December 22 – January 19
Aquarius	The Water Bearer	January 20 – February 18
Pisces	The Fish	February 19 – March 20

The first letters of the words in this mnemonic sentence provide the signs of the astrological zodiac in order, which can be remembered with these phrases:

All **T**he **G**reat **C**hancellors **L**ive **V**ery **L**ong
Since **S**hops **C**an't **A**lter **P**olitics.

A Tense **G**ray **C**at **L**ay **V**ery **L**ow
Sneaking **S**lowly, **C**ontemplating **A P**ounce.

Alternatively, if starting from January, the order changes:
Capricorn, **A**quarius, **P**isces, **A**ries, **T**aurus, **G**emini,
Cancer, **L**eo, **V**irgo, **L**ibra, **S**corpio, **S**agittarius:

Can **A**ll **P**eople **A**lways **T**ake **G**ood **C**are
Lighting **V**aluable **L**amps **S**urrounding **S**aratoga?

To recall the list with a sense of rhythm instead, use the verse written by preacher, poet and hymn writer Isaac Watts (1674–1748), which starts with Aries:

> The *Ram*, the *Bull*, the Heavenly *Twins*,
> And next the *Crab*, the *Lion* shines,
> The *Virgin* and the *Scales;*
> The *Scorpion, Archer* and *Sea Goat.*
> The *Man* who held the watering out
> And *Fish* with glittering tails.

Or perhaps try this alternative from E. Cobham Brewer's *Dictionary of Phrase & Fable* (1899):

> Our vernal signs the *Ram* begins
> Then comes the *Bull*, in May the *Twins;*
> The *Crab* in June, next *Leo* shines,
> And *Virgo* ends the northern signs.
> The *Balance* brings autumnal fruits,
> The *Scorpion* stings, the *Archer* shoots;
> December's *Goat* brings wintry blast,
> *Aquarius* rain, the *Fish* come last.

The events in our lives happen in a sequence in time, but in their significance to ourselves they find their own order: the continuous thread of revelation.

—Eudora Welty

7
The Sky at Night and by Day

The Order of the Planets

Before August 2006, the planets of the solar system were **M**ercury, **V**enus, **E**arth, **M**ars, **J**upiter, **S**aturn, **U**ranus, **N**eptune, and **P**luto. Their initial letters lent themselves to all sorts of phrases:

My **V**ery **E**asy **M**ethod: **J**ust **S**et **U**p **N**ine **P**lanets.

My **V**ery **E**ducated **M**other **J**ust **S**erved **U**s **N**ine **P**izzas.

Mom's **V**ery **E**arly **M**orning **J**elly **S**andwiches **U**sually **N**auseate **P**eople.

In August 2006, the International Astronomical Union decided to downgrade the status of Pluto, and so some new mnemonic phrases that don't mention poor old Pluto have been devised for the new generation of stargazers:

My **V**ery **E**ducated **M**other **J**ust **S**erved **U**s **N**achos.

My **V**ery **E**nergetic **M**other **J**ust **S**ent **U**s **N**owhere.

My **V**ery **E**ducated **M**other **J**ust **S**ent **U**s **N**uts.

My **V**ery **E**xotic **M**istress **J**ust **S**erved **U**s **N**oodles.

The four planets closest to the sun are **M**ercury, **V**enus, **E**arth, and **M**ars. These are called the "rocky," or "terrestrial," planets. They are small in relation to other planets, and consist of similar materials to Earth:

My **V**isitor **E**ats **M**ice.

My **V**irgin **E**ats **M**en.

My **V**oice **E**xpects **M**ore.

The "gas" planets are **J**upiter, **S**aturn, **U**ranus, and **N**eptune, which all have rings and moons, and consist mainly of hydrogen, helium, frozen water, ammonia, methane, and carbon monoxide:

Jelly **S**andwiches **U**sually **N**eeded

Joyful **S**usan's **U**nder-**N**ourished

John **S**mith **U**psets **N**eighbors

Saturn's Moons

Saturn has a number of moons. The count is currently 59 with three of them unconfirmed. The fifty-seventh (S/2007 S 1) was discovered on April 13, 2007, and the fifty-eighth and fifty-ninth (S/2007 S 2 and S/2007 S 3) on May 1, 2007.

Saturn moon spottings have increased significantly since the advent of the Voyager missions and the Hubble

Space Telescope; therefore, many books and websites are not accurate or up-to-date. A mnemonic, put into practice prior to the discovery of most of these moons, helped students to memorize the following nine moons of Saturn: Mimas, Enceladus, Tethys, Dione, Rhea, Titan, Hyperion, Iapetus, and Phoebe.

MET DR THIP

The Brightest Stars in the Sky

Positioned at the center of the solar system, the closest star to Earth is the sun. The brightest stars visible from Earth are listed below, along with the constellation where each is located:

Sir Can Rig A VCR, PA

Sir	Sirius in Canis Major
Can	Canopus in Carina
Rig	Rigil Kent in Centaurus
A	Arcturus in Boötes
V	Vega in Lyra
C	Capella in Auriga
R	Rigel in Orion
P	Procyon in Canis Minor
A	Achernar in Eridanus

The Earth's Atmospheres

Troposphere: extends from the Earth's surface to approximately 3.72–6.21 miles (6–10 km).

Stratosphere: extends to approximately 6.21–31.06 miles (10–50 km) above the Earth.

Mesosphere: located 31.06–49.7 miles (50–80 km) above the Earth's surface.

Thermosphere: located more than 49.7 miles (80 km) above the Earth.

Exosphere: the outermost layer of the atmosphere at 310.6–621.37 miles (500–1,000 km) above the Earth.

To help recall the order of the Earth's atmospheres, the following phrases may act as helpful reminders:

The **S**trong **M**an's **T**riceps **E**xplode.

The **S**traight **M**an's **T**hrottle **E**xcites.

Men on the Moon

Named after the Greek god of the sun, the Apollo program was a series of manned space flights that aimed to land a man on the moon by the end of the 1960s. On

July 20, 1969, Neil Armstrong accomplished this mission when he became the first man to walk on the moon. Armstrong was a member of the crew of Apollo 11, which we can remember by the double *ll* in "Apollo." The names of Armstrong and his fellow astronauts can be recalled with the simple use of ABC:

Neil **A**rmstrong

Buzz Aldrin

Michael **C**ollins

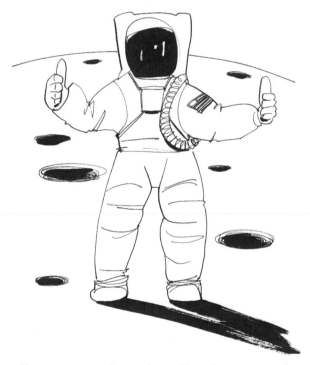

The Apollo program lasted until only 1975, when it was cut short due to rising costs. Only 12 men have ever walked on the moon: Neil Armstrong, Buzz Aldrin, Pete Conrad, Alan Bean, Alan Shepard, Edgar Mitchell, David Scott, James Irwin, John W. Young, Charles Duke, Eugene Cernan, and Harrison Schmitt.

Colors of the Rainbow

When a rainbow appears in the sky as a result of the refraction and dispersion of the sun's rays by light or other water droplets, the seven colors that are said to be visible are: **R**ed, **O**range, **Y**ellow, **G**reen, **B**lue, **I**ndigo, and **V**iolet.

"**R**ichard **O**f **Y**ork **G**ave **B**attle **I**n **V**ain" is the popular mnemonic phrase. It refers to the Battle of Bosworth in 1485, when King Richard III was defeated by Henry Tudor, who became, as Henry VII, the first king of the Tudor dynasty. However, it can also be fun to make up other phrases, such as:

Run **O**ff **Y**ou **G**irls, **B**oys **I**n **V**iew!

Ran **O**ut **Y**esterday, **G**ot **B**lotto **I**n **V**ineyard

Still, other people prefer to recall the colors by making up a man's name: **ROY G BIV**.

Nowadays, however, it is widely believed that indigo does not strictly appear in the spectrum but was merely included by Sir Isaac Newton, the seventeenth-century English physicist and mathematician, because seven colors were considered to be better than six.

Weather Forecasting

A red sky at night; shepherd's delight,
A red sky in the morning; shepherd's warning.

The origins of this rhyme can be traced back to St. Matthew's Gospel in the Bible:

> *When evening comes, you say, "It will be fair weather, for the sky is red," and in the morning, "It will be foul weather today, for the sky is red and overcast."*

Although the words refer to a shepherd who would say that a red sky in the morning would indicate inclement weather to follow, the words could pertain to a sailor's predictions:

Red sky at night, sailor's delight;
Red sky at morning, sailors take warning.

Hundreds of years ago, before any accurate means of weather forecasting became available, people had to rely on those with knowledge and experience, such as sailors and shepherds, whose lives depended on the weather and its changing moods.

Fahrenheit and Celsius

With many countries converting to the metric system, deciding whether to pack a sweater or a coat can get awfully confusing. Here are two basic formulas to help navigate between the two:

> Celsius to Fahrenheit:
> Multiply C by 9
> Divide the answer then by 5
> Next, all you need to do, is to add 32.

> Fahrenheit to Celsius:
> From F, subtract 32
> Divide that by 9, but before you're through
> Multiply that whole by 5
> To Celsius, you will arrive.

8
The World of Science

━━━━━

Chemistry instructors expect their students to have a sound, working knowledge of the names and properties of the 100+ chemical elements of the Periodic Table. It's crucial that students learn not only a chemical's unique properties but also how it reacts with other elements, because getting it wrong can have disastrously flat, fizzy, or fiery consequences.

The Periodic Table of Elements

The Periodic Table was devised in 1869 by Russian chemist Dmitri Mendeleyev. The elements are arranged in increasing order of atomic number from left to right across the table so that elements with similar atomic structures and chemical properties appear in vertical columns. The horizontal rows are called periods, and the vertical rows are known as groups.

Setting a long list of strange names to music is a tried and tested way to remember them. Music has a structure and flow, so if the words fit, they fly off the tongue with ease. Singer-songwriter and mathematician Tom Lehrer concocted his own version of Gilbert and Sullivan's "I Am the Very Model of a Modern Major-General," a song from the comic opera *The Pirates of Penzance.* To hear the ditty sung live, simply type "The element song" into youtube.com.

> There's antimony, arsenic, aluminum, selenium,
> And hydrogen and oxygen and nitrogen and
>   rhenium,
> And nickel, neodymium, neptunium, germanium,
> And iron, americium, ruthenium, uranium,
> Europium, zirconium, lutetium, vanadium,
> And lanthanum and osmium and astatine and
>   radium,
> And gold and protactinium and indium and gallium,
>
> *[Gasp]*
>
> And iodine and thorium and thulium and thallium.
> There's yttrium, ytterbium, actinium, rubidium,
> And boron, gadolinium, niobium, iridium,
> And strontium and silicon and silver and samarium,
> And bismuth, bromine, lithium, beryllium and
>   barium.
> There's holmium and helium and hafnium and
>   erbium,
> And phosphorus and francium and fluorine and
>   terbium,

And manganese and mercury, molybdenum,
    magnesium,
Dysprosium and scandium and cerium and caesium.
And lead, praseodymium, and platinum, plutonium,
Palladium, promethium, potassium, polonium,
And tantalum, technetium, titanium, tellurium,

[Pause for deep breath]

And cadmium and calcium and chromium and
    curium.
There's sulfur, californium, and fermium, berkelium,
And also mendelevium, einsteinium, nobelium,
And argon, krypton, neon, radon, xenon, zinc and
    rhodium,

And chlorine, carbon, cobalt, copper, tungsten, tin
    and sodium.

These are the only ones of which the news has come
    to Harvard,

And there may be many others, but they haven't been
    discavard!

In addition to the 102 elements listed above, there are a
few more that complete the list; namely, lawrencium,
rutherfordium, dubnium, seaborgium, bohrium, hassium,
meitnerium, darmstadtium, iroentgenium, and seven
others, which have yet to be named.

Here are some ways of remembering the first 18 elements in the periodic table, which occupy the first three periods:

Periods 1–2 (Elements 1–10)

H	Hydrogen
He	Helium
Li	Lithium
Be	Beryllium
B	Boron
C	Carbon
N	Nitrogen
O	Oxygen
F	Fluorine
Ne	Neon

Happy **H**enry **L**ikes **B**aking **B**ig **C**akes,
Not **O**mitting **F**loury **N**uggets.

Happy **H**enry **L**ikes **B**eer
But **C**ould **N**ot **O**btain **F**our **N**uts.

Period 3 (Elements 11–18)

Na	Sodium
Mg	Magnesium
Al	Aluminum
Si	Silicon
P	Phosphorus

S	Sulfur
Cl	Chlorine
Ar	Argon

Naughty **M**agpies **A**lways **S**ing **P**erfect **S**ongs **C**lawing **A**nts.

The Most Common Magnetic Material

The four most common magnetic materials are **N**ickel, **I**ron, **C**obalt, and **S**teel, which can be remembered by the clever saying:

Nick **I**rons **C**reased **S**hirts.

Oxidation and Reduction

Oxidation is the loss of an electron by a molecule, an atom, or an ion. Reduction is the opposite; that is, the gain of an electron by molecule, atom, or ion. A simple example of an oxidation—reduction reaction (you can't have one without the other) is the reaction of hydrogen gas with oxygen gas to form water: $2H_2 + O_2 = 2H_2O$.

Many students have found the OILRIG acronym an invaluable method of understanding the process:

Oxidation **I**s **L**oss (of electrons)

Reduction **I**s **G**ain (of electrons)

Parts of an Atom

PEN is possibly the simplest acronym in the history of mnemonics:

Proton, **E**lectron, **N**eutron

CFCs

CFCs have invaded the language and the atmosphere. Thomas Midgley, an organic chemist at General Motors Corporation, discovered chlorofluorocarbons (CFCs) in the 1920s. They are a group of gases believed to contribute to global warming by eroding the ozone layer. The gases that come from leaking air conditioners, refrigerators, and aerosols take 10 to 20 years to reach the stratosphere and remain there for 65 years.

Because the word chlorofluorocarbons doesn't exactly roll off the tongue, some thoughtful soul shortened the word to **CFC**, to keep this vital word in the forefront of our minds.

The Speed of Light

In the same way that it is possible to remember pi to different numbers of decimal places, a simple phrase also enables us to recall the speed of light in meters per second:

We guarantee certainty, clearly referring to this light mnemonic = 299,792,458 m/sec.

Chemistry Experiments: A Warning

And here's a warning to all would-be chemists about the dangers of confusing water with sulfuric acid:

Johnny was a chemist,
But Johnny is no more,
For what he thought was H_2O,
Was H_2SO_4!

The capacity to blunder slightly is the real marvel of DNA. Without this special attribute, we would still be anaerobic bacteria, and there would be no music.

—Lewis Thomas

9
World History

The Greek Philosophers

The names of the three most important Greek philosophers, in order of their dates of birth and also their influence, are:

> **S**ocrates (469–399 BC)
> **P**lato (c. 429–c. 347 BC)
> **A**ristotle (384–322 BC)

Socrates taught Plato, and Plato taught Aristotle. Together they created the foundations of Western philosophy. Use your visual memory and imagine them meditating in a health **SPA**. Or think of the phrase: **S**mart **P**eople of **A**thens.

Roman Emperors

After Julius Caesar, the Roman general and statesman who became dictator of the Roman Empire before his assassination in 44 BC, the first five emperors of Rome were all Caesars. The first emperor was Julius Caesar's adopted son (and great-nephew), Augustus, who handed down the title to his son-in-law Tiberius. From Augustus to Nero, Caesar's descendants, by adoption, marriage, or birth, all inherited the family name:

Augustus	(31 BC–AD 14)
Tiberius	(AD 14–37)
Caligula	(AD 37–41)
Claudius	(AD 41–54)
Nero	(AD 54–68)

Here's a phrase to help remember the names by which they were most commonly known:

Another **T**om **C**at **C**aught **N**apping.

The next six Roman emperors after Nero are **G**alba, **O**tho, **V**itellius, **V**espasian, **T**itus, **D**omitian:

At **T**he **C**at **C**lub **N**ever **G**ive **O**ut
Violent **V**ermin **T**o **D**ogs

The Seven Wonders of the Ancient World

The seven wonders of the ancient world were chronicled in the second century B.C., but a list has been discovered in *The Histories of Herodotus* in the fifth century B.C. The final list of amazing monuments to religion, mythology, and art was compiled in the Middle Ages.

1. **S**tatue of Zeus at Olympia
2. **L**ighthouse (Pharos) of Alexandria
3. **M**ausoleum of Halicarnassus
4. **P**yramids of Egypt
5. **H**anging Gardens of Babylon
6. **T**emple of Artemis at Ephesus
7. **C**olossus of Rhodes

This mnemonic phrase has proved useful in remembering the seven wonders:

Seems **L**ike **M**ata **H**ari **P**icked **H**er **T**argets **C**arefully.

Mythological Matters

Mnemosyne is the Greek goddess of memory, daughter of Gaia and Uranus. She lay with Zeus for nine nights and gave birth to the nine Muses: **C**alliope, **E**uterpe, **C**lio, **E**rato, **M**elpomene, **P**olyhymnia, **T**erpsichore, **T**halia, and **U**rania.

Carol **E**ats **C**runchy **E**ggs,
Mashed **P**otatoes, **T**hen **T**hrows **U**p.

Clarissa **E**ats **C**andy **E**very **M**orning,
Politely **T**aking **T**urns.

In classical art, the Muses are represented by emblems, or mnemonic symbols, of which the masks of comedy and tragedy are probably the most familiar.

Name	Association	Mnemonic symbol
Calliope	Chief of the muses and muse of epic poetry	writing tablet
Euterpe	Muse of music	flute
Clio	Muse of history	scroll and books
Erato	Muse of love poetry	lyre and crown of roses
Melpomene	Muse of tragedy	tragic mask
Polyhymnia	Muse of sacred poetry	pensive expression

Terpsichore	Muse of dance	dancing with a lyre
Thalia	Muse of comedy	comic mask
Urania	Muse of astronomy	staff and celestial globe

Joan of Arc

Also known as the Maid of Orléans, Joan of Arc (c. 1412–1431) a French national heroine, claimed that it was God's mission for her to reclaim her homeland from English domination toward the end of the Hundred Years War. She triumphed at the Siege of Orléans in 1429, which led to Charles VII's coronation at Reims, but was later captured at a skirmish near Compiègne. The English regent John of Lancaster, first Duke of Bedford, had her burned at the stake at Rouen when she was only 19. She was canonized in 1920.

This mnemonic phrase describes the short life of Joan of Arc:

ORLEANS CAMPAIGN RUIN

Orleans – victory – 1429

Compiègne – capture – 1430

Rouen – trial and death – 1431

The Six Wives of Henry VIII

Henry VIII (1491–1547) married six times in a quest to have a son and heir. His decision to divorce his first wife and remarry was the root of the split of the Roman Catholic Church, the dissolution of the monasteries, and the formation of the Church of England. The following is a list of Henry's wives in order of marriage dates from first to last:

1510—Catherine of Aragon (mother of Mary I)
1533—Anne Boleyn (mother of Elizabeth I)
1536—Jane Seymour (mother of Edward VI)
1540—Anne of Cleves
1540—Catherine Howard
1543—Catherine Parr

Use this rhythmic couplet to remember their first names:

Kate & Anne & Jane & Anne & Kate again & again!

Using the initial letters of their surnames gives the phrase:

All **B**oys **S**hould **C**ome **H**ome, **P**lease.

The following memorable rhyme reveals the ultimate fate of these six women:

> Divorced, beheaded, died,
> Divorced, beheaded, survived.

Brief History of the United States

The following verse was devised by American poet and former child prodigy Winifred Sackville Stoner, Jr. (1902–1983). She was best known for writing mnemonic rhymes and poems to help people recall important information, particularly for educational purposes. One of her most famous poems is "The History of the U.S." The poem contains 19 stanzas, but people often remember only the first one or two. It paints an often-unrealistic picture of U.S. history but serves as a clever mnemonic to remember those important historical dates. Below you will find the first five stanzas, which start in 1492, along with the final stanza, which brings the reader all the way to 1918 and the end of WWI.

> In fourteen hundred ninety-two,
> Columbus sailed the ocean blue

And found this land, land of the Free,
beloved by you, beloved by me.

And in the year sixteen and seven,
good Captain Smith thought he'd reach Heav'n,
And then he founded Jamestown City,
alas, 'tis gone, oh, what a pity.

'Twas in September sixteen nine,
with ship, Half Moon, a read Dutch sign,
That Henry Hudson found the stream,
the Hudson River of our dream.

In sixteen twenty, pilgrims saw
our land that had no unjust law.
Their children live here to this day
proud citizens of U.S.A.

In sixteen hundred eighty-three,
good William Penn stood 'neath a tree
And swore that unto his life's end
he would be the Indian's friend.

…Thank God in nineteen eighteen,
Peace on earth again was seen,
And we are praying that she'll stay
forever in our U.S.A.

The Pilgrim Fathers

In 1620 a group of English puritans who had fled to Holland to avoid religious persecution returned to England and sailed on the *Mayflower* from Plymouth to America. After a long, treacherous journey, they landed at Cape Cod, Massachusetts.

Nothing abbreviates this voyage more cleverly than the *Schoolhouse Rock* cartoon from the 1970s, "No More Kings."

> The pilgrims sailed the sea
> To find a place to call their own.
> In their ship, *Mayflower*,
> They hoped to find a better home.
> They finally knocked
> On Plymouth Rock
> And someone said, "We're there."
> It may not look like home
> But at this point I don't care.

The *Schoolhouse Rock* (SHR) revolution began in 1971, when David McCall, chairman of the ad agency McCaffrey & McCall, noticed that his son could sing all the Beatles and Rolling Stones lyrics but couldn't handle simple math. His solution was to link math with contemporary music. Grammar and history were added to the SHR mix, and the fact that many adults can still sing its phrases today solidly establishes video, combined with song, as an effective mnemonic device.

Declaration of Independence

The date 1776 marks the signing of the Declaration of Independence. The number of letters in each word in the following sentence stands for a numeral in the date:

I sighted Thomas's rights.

American poet Winifred Sackville Stoner, Jr.'s take on how to remember the date of the Declaration of Independence goes like this:

> Year seventeen hundred seventy-six,
> July the fourth, this date please fix
> Within your minds, my children dear,
> for that was Independence Year.

The Civil War

And regarding the dark days of the American Civil War, Winifred Sackville Stoner, Jr. wrote:

> In eighteen hundred and sixty-one,
> an awful war was then begun
> Between the brothers of our land,
> who now together firmly stand.

Author and certified holistic counselor Laurel Ann Browne offers the following civil war mnemonic on her parenting website:

> Four Bulls Ate Everything Vicky Grew.

It translates into chronological order the major events of the Civil War.

> **Four**: Fort Sumter, the first shots in the Civil War
> **Bulls**: Battle of Bull Run (First Manassas), the first major battle of the Civil War
> **Ate**: Antietam, the bloodiest battle in Civil War history with over 20,000 casualties
> **Everything**: Emancipation Proclamation, in which Lincoln abolished slavery

Vicky: The battle of Vicksburg, which controlled the Mississippi River for the North
Grew: The Gettysburg Address, four score and seven years ago…

Presidents of the U.S.

To date, 43 U.S. presidents have assumed office, which would make an incredibly long and complicated mnemonic phrase. The names of the first 11 presidents are:

George Washington (1789–1797)
John Adams (1797–1801)
Thomas Jefferson (1801–1809)
James Madison (1809–1817)
James Monroe (1817–1825)
John Quincy Adams (1825–1829)
Andrew Jackson (1829–1837)
Martin van Buren (1837–1841)
William Henry Harrison (1841)
John Tyler (1841–1845)
James Polk (1845–1849)

Here's a question to ponder to help recall the first 11:

Will **A** **J**olly **M**an **M**ake **A** **J**ust
But **H**arshly **T**reated **P**resident?

And if 11 is too many to remember, here's a phrase for the first seven:

Washington **A**nd **J**efferson **M**ade **M**any **A** **J**oke

The names of the middle American presidents are:

Zachary Taylor (1849–1850)
Millard Fillmore (1850–183)
Franklin Pierce (1853–1857)
James Buchanan (1857–1861)
Abraham Lincoln (1861–1865)
Andrew Johnson (1865–1869)
Ulysses S. Grant (1869–1877)
Rutherford B. Hayes (1877–1881)
James Garfield (1881)
Chester Arthur (1881–1885)
Grover Cleveland (1885–1889)
Benjamin Harrison (1889–1893)
Grover Cleveland (1893–1897)
William McKinley (1897–1901)

To recall this eminent list of 14, keep in mind the following phrase:

Taylor **F**elt **P**roud **B**ut Lincoln **J**ust **G**rinned **H**appily, **G**argling, **A**nd **C**ould **H**ardly **C**ontain **M**cKinley

And finally, the presidents of the twentieth century:

Theodore Roosevelt (1901–1909)
William H. **T**aft (1909–1913)
Woodrow **W**ilson (1913–1921)
Warren **H**arding (1921–1923)
Calvin **C**oolidge (1923–1929)
Herbert **H**oover (1929–1933)
Franklin D. **R**oosevelt (1933–1945)
Harry S **T**ruman (1945–1953)
Dwight D. **E**isenhower (1953–1961)
John F. **K**ennedy (1961–1963)
Lyndon B. **J**ohnson (1963–1969)
Richard M. **N**ixon (1969–1974)
Gerald **F**ord (1974–1977)
Jimmy **C**arter (1977–1981)
Ronald **R**eagan (1981–1989)
George H. W. **B**ush (1989–1993)
William J. **C**linton (1992–2001)

Though it's quite a lengthy list, this saying might just make life easier:

Theodore **T**akes **W**ilson's **H**and,
Cool **H**oovering **F**ranklin's **T**rue **E**xperiences.
Ken, **J**ustly **N**oted **F**or **C**andor, **R**uled **B**ut **C**oolly.

The Heads on Mount Rushmore

Mount Rushmore is a world-famous national memorial in South Dakota, which represents the first 150 years of U.S. history with 60-foot-high granite carvings of the heads of four great U.S. presidents: **W**ashington, **J**efferson, **L**incoln, and **R**oosevelt.

We **J**ust **L**ike **R**ushmore.

World War I (The Great War)

Once called the War to End All Wars, this massive military conflict took 20 million lives. Many factors contributed to the outbreak of this global war. The word

ANIMAL assists people in remembering some of the most prominent causes.

Assassination—Archduke Franz Ferdinand of Austria-Hungary and his wife were assassinated on June 28, 1914.

Nationalism—This time period saw a rise in strong patriotic sentiments and loyalty toward home countries.

Imperialism—Colonization was common at the turn of the century, and countries competed for territory and economic advantage.

Militarism—Britain and Germany had well-established military might, and an arms race ensued.

ALliance System—War with any allied nation meant war with the whole alliance. This system was meant to discourage aggressive nations but failed.

We learn from history that we learn nothing from history.

—George Bernard Shaw

10
Musical Interlude

———

Music can be a mnemonic device all by itself: advertisers often use musical jingles to remind us of their products. For example, in just seven fluctuating notes composed by Steve Karmen in 1969 we have: "Nationwide is on your side." Karmen is also notorious for the New York State song "I Love New York." And who could forget the Chock Full O' Nuts song:

Chock Full O' Nuts is that heavenly coffee
A better coffee a billionaire's money can't buy.

Musical Notes

The first seven letters of the alphabet (A, B, C, D, E, F, G) are used in musical notation, which at least helps to keep it simple. In the 1965 film *The Sound of Music*, Julie Andrews's character Maria makes the learning of music seem so easy.

Do–Re–Mi–Fa–So–La–Ti

Do = doe – a female deer

Re = ray – a drop of golden sun
Mi = me – a name I call myself
Fa = far – a long, long way to run
So = sew – a needle pulling thread
La = la – a note to follow "so"
Ti = tea – a drink with jam and bread
Which will bring us back to "Do"

Musical Staves

Learning to read music notation is almost impossible without the use of mnemonic tools. The musical staff is the set of five lines and four spaces on which notes indicate pitch and rhythm. The treble staff (or clef), indicating higher notes, is generally played with the right hand on the piano, and the bass staff (or clef), indicating lower notes, with the left hand.

Treble Clef: Lines

The notes on the lines of the treble clef are, from the lowest, E, G, B, D, F. They can be remembered with the following common:

Every **G**ood **B**oy **D**eserves **F**avor

Favor may be replaced by fruit, fudge, or fun, depending on your taste.

Other variations include:

Every **G**ood **B**oy **D**oes **F**ine.

Every **G**irl **B**uys **D**esigner **F**ashions.

Every **G**ood **B**ird **D**oes **F**ly.

Treble Clef: Spaces

The notes on the spaces on the treble clef are, from the lowest, F, A, C, E. This short rhyme may help with learning the order of notes:

If the note's in a space, together they spell FACE.

Bass Clef: Lines

The order of notes on the lines of the bass clef are G, B, D, F, A. "Good boys" return again in the catchy phrase devised to help musicians remember these basics:

Good **B**oys **D**eserve **F**ruit **A**lways.

"Fruit" can, of course, be substituted for another more suitable f-word if necessary.

Other variations include:

Good **B**oys **D**on't **F**ool **A**round.

Great **B**ig **D**ogs **F**ight **A**lways.

Good **B**ikes **D**on't **F**all **A**part.

Great **B**ig **D**ucks **F**ly **A**way.

Gentle **B**rown **D**onkeys **F**avor **A**pples.

Bass Clef: Spaces

And thus it follows that the notes in the spaces of the bass clef are A, C, E, G. The following sayings act as a useful reminder of the four-note order:

All **C**ows **E**at **G**rass.

All **C**ars **E**at **G**as.

All **C**ats **E**at **G**oldfish.

The Cycle of Fifths

Music theory is not rocket science. There are 12 notes in Western music in one octave, and all you need to do is add, subtract, multiply, and divide. The notes—B, C, C$^{\#}$, D, D$^{\#}$, E, F, F$^{\#}$, G, G$^{\#}$, A, A$^{\#}$—are all half a tone apart.

Major chords are comprised of the root note and the higher third and fifth notes, plus the options of the seventh or eighth. Minor chords are made up of the root note and the minor third and fifth notes of the scale, with the option of the other notes. The cycle of fifths is based on taking the fifth note as the root for the next chord. For example, in an F chord the fifth note is C; therefore, the next chord is C, then G and so on—F, C, G, D, A, E, B:

Father **C**harles **G**oes **D**own **A**nd **E**nds **B**attle.

Other variations include:

Father **C**hristmas **G**ets **D**runk **A**fter **E**very **B**eer.

Fat **C**ats **G**o **D**eaf **A**fter **E**ating **B**ats.

Five **C**ool **G**uys **D**anced **A**way **E**very **B**eat.

And in reverse for the flat keys, the mnemonic can be reversed—B$^{\flat}$, E$^{\flat}$, A$^{\flat}$, D$^{\flat}$, G$^{\flat}$, C$^{\flat}$, F$^{\flat}$:

Battle **E**nds **A**nd **D**own **G**oes **C**harles's **F**ather.

Bottles **E**mpty **A**nd **D**own **G**oes **C**harles's **F**ather.

Be **E**xciting **A**nd **D**aring, **G**o **C**limb **F**ences.

Choral Voices

There are four different voice ranges that one can hear in a quartet, whose initial letters helpfully spell out STAB:

Soprano
Tenor
Alto
Bass

Musical Modes or Scales

The modes as based on the white piano keys beginning at C are:

Ionian mode—the familiar major scale in which most popular music is written.

Dorian mode—most often heard in Celtic music, with a melancholy feel.

Phrygian mode—used especially by guitar soloists in counterpoint to an Ionian mode.

Lydian mode—popular in jazz music, with a mix of major and minor chord progressions.

Mixolydian mode—major feel with minor intervals and popular with soloists as a counterpoint to an Ionian mode.

Aeolian mode—in a minor key and produces a sense of sadness.

Locrian mode—the intervals are considered unsatisfactory and most composers find it unworkable.

Named after Greek cities that are thought to reflect the moods of the seven modes, one way of remembering the order of the modes is to recall this phrase:

I Don't **P**lay **L**ike **M**y **A**unt **L**ucy.

11
Foreign Tongues

French Plurals with an X

Here's a verse to tell you which French nouns require the letter "x" rather than "s" when they are used in the plural:

> *Bijou, caillou, chou,*
> *Genou, hibou, joujou . . .*
> *Pou!*

The English translation of the verse is:

> Jewel, pebble, cabbage,
> Knee, owl, toy . . .
> Flea!

Or commit this rhyme to memory:

> *Mes choux, mes bijoux,*
> *Lassez-vous joujoux,*
> *Venez sur mes genoux!*
> *Regardez ces mauvais petits garçons,*
> *Qui jettent des cailloux a ces pauvres hiboux!*

> My cabbages, my jewels,
> Stop playing with your toys, and come sit on my knees!
> Look at these bad little boys,
> Who throw stones at these poor owls!

Counting to Six in French

The correct words for one to six in French are *un, deux, trois, quatre, cinq,* and *six.* Try to picture the horror of this dark story of how to control the cat population:

> *Un, deux, trois,* cat sank—cease, please!

French Verbs Using *Être*

All French verbs that use *être* in the perfect tense rather than *avoir* indicate a particular kind of movement. The

13 main verbs (and four derivatives) can be recalled using the popular mnemonic phrase **Dr. & Mrs. P. Vandertramp**:

Devenir **R**evenir & **M**onter **R**ester **S**ortir
Passer **V**enir **A**ller **N**aître **D**escendre **E**ntrer
Rentrer **T**omber **R**etourner **A**rriver
Mourir **P**artir

Alternatively, the acronym ADVENT is another useful way to recall the main *être* verbs. Each letter stands for one of the verbs and its opposite, with the thirteenth verb— *retourner*—standing alone.

Arriver—Partir
Descendre—Monter
Venir—Aller
Entrer—Sortir
Naître—Mourir
Tomber—Rester
Retourner

Japanese Vowels

The pronunciation and lexical ordering of the Japanese vowels is AIUEO. Using this short phrase, you can understand the pronunciation of the vowels:

Ah, we soon get old.

Counting to 10 in Japanese

Numeral	Japanese word	Sounds like
1	Ichi	Itchy
2	Ni	Knee
3	San	Sun
4	Shi	She
5	Go	Go
6	Roko	Rocko
7	Shichi	Shi Shi
8	Hachi	Hatchy
9	Kyu	Queue
10	Ju	Jew

Days of the Week in French, Spanish, and Italian

The seven-day week has been the norm for almost 2,000 years. The Romans allocated one of the seven planets to each of the days of the week: the sun, moon and the five planets that shine brightly in the night sky—Mars, Mercury, Jupiter, Venus, and Saturn.

	Planet	French	Spanish	Italian
Sunday	Sun	Dimanche	Domingo	Domenica
Monday	Moon	Lundi	Lunes	Lunedì
Tuesday	Mars	Mardi	Martes	Martedì

	Planet	French	Spanish	Italian
Wednesday	Mercury	Mercredi	Miércoles	Mercoledì
Thursday	Jupiter	Jeudi	Jueves	Giovedì
Friday	Venus	Vendredi	Viernes	Venerdì
Saturday	Saturn	Samedi	Sábado	Sabato

By recalling the planets after which the days were named, it helps to jog the memory when remembering the days of the week in the Latin-based languages.

Since many of the planets were named after the gods, this traditional rhyme borrows some of the characteristics of the planets or gods and pairs them with the corresponding days of the week:

> Monday's child is fair of face,
> Tuesday's child is full of grace,
> Wednesday's child is full of woe,
> Thursday's child has far to go;
> Friday's child is loving and giving,
> Saturday's child works hard for a living,
> But the child that is born on the Sabbath day
> Is bonny and blithe, good and gay.

The Greek Alphabet

To learn the Greek alphabet, you can memorize the order of the 24 letters by singing along to the tune of "Twinkle, Twinkle, Little Star," but if you're no longer a child, it might be better not to practice out loud . . .

> Alpha, Beta, Gamma, Delta,
> Epsilon, Zeta, Eta, Theta,
> Iota, Kappa, Lambda, Mu,
> Nu, Xi, Omicron, Pi,
> Rho, Sigma, Tau, Upsilon,
> Phi, Chi, Psi kai Omega.

NB: *K* (kai) means "and" in Greek.

The Runic Alphabet

The Runic alphabet is also known as FUTHARK, after the first six letters in this alphabet—namely *f, u, th, a, r,* and *k.* Runes were used by Scandinavians, and Anglo-Saxons used runes around the third century. There are 24 letters comprising 18 consonants and six vowels.

The Runic characters comprise a series of glyphs that represent sounds and ideas, based on the hieroglyphs of Ancient Egypt. They were not only used to convey sacred meaning but also mysteries and secrets. It is not known why the letters were ordered in this way, but the word FUTHARK is considered an ancient mnemonic.

12
Religious Matters

For Christians most religious instruction comes from Sunday school or religious-education classes. While children listen to countless Bible stories, many rhymes and sayings help to simplify certain matters of religion, keeping the vast subjects of the Old Testament and New Testament more clearly in their minds.

The Twelve Apostles

The twelve chief followers of Jesus are recalled in a well-known Sunday school rhyme:

> This is the way the disciples run
> Peter, Andrew, James, and John
> Philip and Bartholomew
> Thomas next and Matthew, too.
> James the less and Judas the greater
> Simon the zealot and Judas the traitor.

An alternative shorter method uses the following line:

> Bart And John Fill (Phil) Tom's Matt with 2 Jameses,
> 2 Simons,* and 2 Judases.

> *Peter was originally Simon or Simon-Peter,
> therefore there are two Simons in the second verse.

The Four Gospels

With regard to the first four books of the New Testament (the Gospels), religious leaders and Sunday school teachers have various rhymes to help children remember the names (and their order) more easily.

> Matthew, Mark, Luke, and John
> Went to bed with their trousers on.

The verse is probably derived from the following traditional poem, of which there are two versions:

> Matthew, Mark, Luke, and John
> Bless the bed that I lie on;
> Before I lay me down to sleep,
> I give my soul to Christ to keep.
>
> Matthew, Mark, Luke, and John
> Bless the bed that I lie on;
> Four corners to my bed,
> Four angels round my head;
> One to watch, one to pray,
> And two to bear my soul away!

The Ten Commandments

The Ten Commandments are a list of rules for living an honest and moral life. According to the Old Testament, they are the word of God, inscribed on two stone tablets and given to Moses on Mount Sinai. James Muirden, author of *The Rhyming Bible*, has cleverly compiled them into an unforgettable verse comprising six rhyming couplets:

> The First Law set by God in stone
> reads *Worship me, and me alone!*
> The next says Idols are profane;
> the Third, don't take my Name in vain;

the Fourth says keep the Seventh Day free;
the Fifth, treat Parents properly;
the Sixth says Murdering is wrong
(you knew the Seventh all along*);
the Eighth is crystal clear on Thieving,
as is the Ninth, on Not Deceiving;
and now the last of all His laws—
don't Covet things that are not yours.

*The Seventh, of course, forbids adultery.

Another way of remembering the commandments is the following:

One idle damn Sunday, Dad killed cheating thief
and lied to cover it.

That is, one God; no idols; don't swear; keep the Sabbath; honor your father (and mother); don't kill; don't commit adultery; don't steal; don't bear false witness; and don't covet.

Books of the Old Testament

Although there are a total of 39 books in the Old Testament (King James Bible), this memorable verse has made it much easier to remember them all in order:

That great Jehovah speaks to us,
In Genesis and Exodus,

Leviticus and Numbers see,
Followed by Deuteronomy,
Joshua and Judges sway the land,
Ruth gleans a sheaf with trembling hand;
Samuel and numerous Kings appear,
Whose Chronicles we wondering hear.
Ezra and Nehemiah now,
Esther, the beauteous mourner show.
Job speaks in sighs, David in Psalms,
The Proverbs teach to scatter alms.
Ecclesiastes then come on,
And the sweet Song of Solomon.
Isaiah, Jeremiah then,
With Lamentations takes his pen,
Ezekiel, Daniel, Hosea's lyres,
Swell Joel, Amos, Obadiah's.
Next Jonah, Micah, Nahum come,
And lofty Habakkuk finds room.
While Zephaniah, Haggai calls,
Rapt Zechariah builds his walls,
And Malachi, with garments rent,
Concludes the Ancient Testament.

The 10 Biblical Plagues of Egypt

From Exodus 7:14–12:36, these are the 10 catastrophes that God inflicted upon Egypt:

River to blood

Frogs

Lice

Flies

Murrain (disease)

Boils

Hail

Locusts

Darkness

Firstborn

If the list proves too tricky to remember, the following sentence is a memorable means of recalling the order and initial letter of each plague:

Robert **F**rost **L**ikes **F**udge **M**ilk
Brownies **H**aving **L**ot of **D**ouble **F**udge

or

Flow **L**ike **F**resh **M**ilk
Behind **H**arry **L**ong's **D**eer **F**ence

The Seven Deadly Sins

There are seven days of the week, seven colors in the rainbow, seven wonders of the world, and for those who have not taken their Bible studies to heart, there are seven deadly sins:

Anger, **P**ride, **C**ovetousness, **L**ust, **S**loth, **E**nvy, **G**reed

To help make the list of sins easier to memorize, some God-fearing person devised the following mnemonic phrase:

All **P**rivate **C**olleges **L**eave **S**erious **E**ducational **G**aps.

Or to put it another way:

Pride, **E**nvy, **W**rath, **S**loth, **A**varice, **G**luttony, **L**ust
PEWS 'Ave GLu

The 10 States of Mind

In the Buddhist construct there are 10 states of mind:

1. **H**ell, the state of suffering
2. **H**unger, the state of base needs
3. **A**nimalism, the state of beastly power
4. **A**nger, the state of loathing
5. **N**eutrality, the state of neither one thing or another
6. **R**apture, the state of joy
7. **L**earning, the state of being mentally open
8. **R**ealization, the state of receiving/living wisdom
9. **B**odhisattva, the state of compassion
10. **B**uddha, the state of perfection

All of that mental agony and ecstasy gives us:

Has **H**annah **A**rranged **A**ll **N**ovices **R**unning **L**ate, **R**equired **B**efore **B**uddha?

13
The Human Body

Young medics often face masses of dull and lengthy lists of complicated words, which represent the workings of the human body. Without a wide range of useful and often-amusing memory aids, it would be impossible for them to remember everything.

The Vital Processes of Life

Collectively, these are known as **MRS. GREN**:

Movement, **R**espiration, **S**ensitivity,
Growth, **R**eproduction, **E**xcretion, **N**utrition

The Human Brain

The brain is the most complex structure at the nub of all human decisions, communications, and activities. The cerebral cortex is divided into four sections, or lobes:

Frontal, **P**arietal, **O**ccipital, **T**emporal

First **P**lace **O**ften **T**rounces.

Cranial Bones

Occipital, **P**arietal, **F**rontal, **T**emporal,
Ethmoid, **S**phenoid

Old **P**eople **F**rom **T**exas **E**at **S**piders

Cranial Nerves

How many medical students learned the 12 cranial nerves sung to the tune of "The Twelve Days of Christmas?"
    The first and second verses start off:

I (Olfactory)

On the first nerve of the cranium,
my true love gave to me:
My sense olfactory.

II (Optic)

On the second nerve of the cranium,
my true love gave to me:
Two eyes a-looking,
And my sense olfactory.

The song gets quite lengthy, so the final verse is:

XII (Hypoglossal)

On the twelfth nerve of the cranium,
my true love gave to me:
Twelve lovely lickings, (Hypoglossal)
Eleven heads a-tilting, (Spinal accessory)

Ten heartbeats a minute, (Vagus)
Nine quick swallows, (Glossopharyngeal)
Eight sounds, and balance, (Auditory)
Seven funny faces, (Facial)
Six sideways glances, (Abducens)
Mas-ti-ca-tion! (Trigeminal)
Four superior oblique muscles, (Trochlear)
Three cross-eyed glances, (Oculomotor)
Two eyes a-looking, (Optic)
And my sense olfactory. (Olfactory)

In addition to the song, there is also a catchy phrase to recall when remembering the names of the cranial nerves:

On **O**ld **O**lympus's **T**owering **T**op,
A **F**at-**A**ssed **G**erman **V**iewed **S**ome **H**ops.

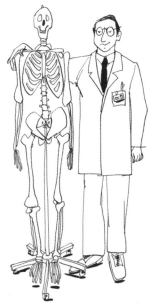

Bones of the Human Body

BONES OF THE UPPER LIMB OR ARM:
Scapula, Clavicle, Humerus, Ulna, Radius, Carpals,
Metacarpals, Phalanges

Some Crooks Have Underestimated Royal Canadian
Mounted Police.

BONES OF THE LOWER LIMB OR LEG:
Hip, Femur, Patella, Tibia, Fibula, Tarsals,
Metatarsals, Phalanges

Help Five Police To Find Ten Missing Prisoners.

BONES OF THE WRIST (CARPAL):
Scaphoid, Lunate, Triquetrum, Pisiform, Trapezium,
Trapezoid, Capitate, Hamate

Some Lovers Try Positions That They Can't Handle.

VERTEBRAE OR BONES OF THE SPINAL COLUMN
(SUPERIOR TO INFERIOR):
Cervical, Dorsal,* Lumbar, Sacrum, Coccyx

Canned Tuna Looks So Cramped.

* Dorsal vertebrae are also known as Thoracic—
therefore, the alternative phrase.

SHOULDER MUSCLES OR ROTATOR CUFF
Teres minor, Infraspinatus, Supraspinatus, Subscapular

Time Is Standing Still.

Bone Fracture Types

Once medical students learn the specific bones, they can use the **GO C3PO** acronym to learn the ways in which the bones can get broken.

Greenstick, **O**pen, **C**omplete/**C**losed/**C**omminuted, **P**artial, **O**thers

Skin Layers

Mnemonic sentences help medics to remember the order of skin layers or nerves so that when they become surgeons and start brandishing scalpels, they can identify which bit to cut through first. They use the aptly named **SCALP** acronym:

Skin, **C**onnective tissue, **A**poneurosis, **L**oose areolar tissue, **P**eriosteum

Excretion

For the excretory organs of the body, think **SKILL**:

Skin, **K**idneys, **I**ntestines, **L**iver, **L**ungs

The Properties of Bile

Here's a catchy ditty to keep the properties of bile in mind:

Bile from the liver emulsifies greases
Tinges the urine and colors the feces
Aids peristalsis, prevents putrefaction
If you remember all this, you'll give satisfaction.

Doctors dealing with a patient who is a possible suicide risk will find the **SAD PERSONS** checklist quite handy:

Sex (male or female)

Age (old or young)

Depression

Previous suicide attempts

Ethanol and other drugs

Reality testing/**R**ational thought (loss of)

Social support lacking

Organized suicide plan

No spouse

Sickness/**S**tated future intent

Signs of Mania

Medics have to **DIG FAST** to identify key symptoms of manic behavior:

Distractibility
Indiscretion (excessive involvement
in pleasurable activities)
Grandiosity
Flight of ideas
Activity increase
Sleep deficit (decreased need for sleep)
Talkativeness (pressured speech)

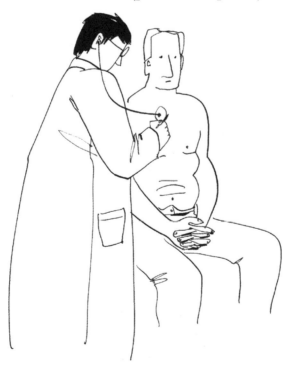

Signs of Schizophrenia

If doctors suspect a patient may have schizophrenia, they will check for **WHID**:

Withdrawn, **H**allucinations,
Inappropriate emotional response, **D**elusions

Signs of Anxiety Disorder

Your doctor will test for **MR FISC** if you're suffering from GAD—General Anxiety Disorder:

Motor tension
Restlessness
Fatigue
Irritability
Sleep disturbances
Concentration difficulty

The Heart

The signs of heart failure are ABCDE:

Acidosis, **B**lue skin, **C**old skin, **D**ilated heart,
Edema

Doctors' Shorthand

Doctors-to-be develop their sense of humor as students and refine it throughout their careers. Consequently, doctors have been known to write F BUNDY on patients' notes if the prognosis is grim:

F*ed **B**ut **U**nfortunately **N**ot **D**ead **Y**et

Fever Facts

Your doctor will check the **FACTS** to diagnose influenza or just "man flu"; that is, a cold:

Fever
Aches
Chills
Tiredness
Sudden symptoms

Vitamins Are Healthy

Vitamins help maintain health. This rhyme reminds us of
the important qualities of each and every vitamin:
Vitamin **A** keeps the cold germs away
And tends to make meek people nervy,
B's what you need
When you're going to seed,
And **C** is specific in scurvy.
Vitamin **D** makes the bones in your knee
Tough and hard for the service on Sunday,
While **E** makes hens scratch
And increases the hatch
And brings in more profits on Monday.
Vitamin **F** never bothers the chef
For this vitamin never existed.
G puts the fight in the old appetite
And you eat all the foods that are listed.
So now when you dine remember these lines;
If long on this globe you will tarry.
Just try to be good and pick out more food
From the orchard, the garden, and dairy.

14
Lifesaving Tips

———

Learning and reviewing lifesaving techniques might be the best thing you ever do, so pay attention and refresh your memory regarding the many first-aid-related acronyms in existence.

The main aim of First Aid is the **3 Ps**:

Preserve life
Prevent deterioration in the patient's condition
Promote recovery

ABC is the traditional and essential way to remember what to check when administering cardiopulmonary resuscitation on a casualty:

Airways

Breathing

Circulation

Here are two groups of **3 Bs** to remember when dealing with an accident victim:

Check **B**reath **B**efore **B**lood (flow)
And then **B**lood **B**efore **B**ones

Keep calm in an emergency, and think **AMEGA**:

Assess the situation
Make the area safe
Emergency aid
Get help
Aftermath

How alert is your casualty? Check for **AVPU**:

Alert
Voice
Pain
Unconscious

Is the victim in circulatory shock? Look for **PCFATS**:

Pale
Cold and **C**lammy skin
Fast pulse
Anxious
Thirsty
Sick

Assess the injuries. Look at areas of soft tissue and bones, and think **RICE**:

Rest
Ice/**I**mmobilize
Compression
Elevation

If your victim is lucid, ask these **AMPLE** questions:

Allergies—do they have any?
Medication—are they taking any?
Past history—do they have any prior medical
problems?
Last meal—what/when did they last eat?
Environment—do they know where they are?

If the injured party is in a coma, it could be caused by any of the following **MIDAS** problems:

Meningitis
Intoxication
Diabetes
Air (respiratory failure)
Subdural/**S**ubarachnoid hemorrhage

Or by **COMA**:

CO_2 (carbon dioxide) and **CO** (carbon monoxide) excess
Overdose: drugs, such as insulin, paracetamol, etc.
Metabolic: BSL (blood sugar level), Na+ (sodium),
K+ (potassium), Mg^2+ (magnesium), urea, ammonia, etc.
Apoplexy: stroke, meningitis, encephalitis,
cerebral abscess, etc.

Keep the word **FAST** in mind when assessing the condition of a possible stroke victim:

Face: is one side of the face drooping downward?
Arm: can the person raise both arms?
Speech: is the person's speech slurred or confusing;
is the person unable to speak?
Time: time is critical.
Call an ambulance immediately.

If you witness a person collapsing, what could have caused it? Think **I'VE FALLEN**:

Illness
Vestibular (balance problem)
Environmental
Feet or **F**ootwear
Alcohol and/or drugs
Low blood pressure
Low oxygen status
Ears or **E**yes
Neuropathy

Is the patient in shock? If so, he or she might be suffering from any one of the **R**egistered **N**urse **CHAMPS** range of shocks:

Respiratory
Neurogenic
Cardiogenic
Hemorrhagic
Anaphylactic
Metabolic
Psychogenic
Septic

Survival Techniques

If it's a case of personal survival out in the wilds, use extreme survival expert Ray Mears's word **STOP**:

Stop
Take inventory
Orientate
Plan

In the event of discovering a fire, think **FIRE**.

Find the fire
Inform people by shouting out
Restrict the spread of fire (*if it is safe to do so*)
Evacuate the area/**Ex**tinguish the fire
(*if it is safe to do so*)
And don't forget to **S**top, **D**rop, and **R**oll to stay clear of
the rising smoke.

Driving a Car

Mirror **S**ignal **M**aneuver is an essential phrase drummed into all student drivers, but it's one that drivers should never forget. Say it to yourself before you start, turn, change lane, reverse, and stop. It's a motorist's way of applying the "Look Before You Leap" principle.

Don't forget to buckle up, too:

Click it or Ticket

Road Safety

When learning to cross the road, children of all ages have been strongly advised to remember these life-saving lines:

Look Right, Look Left, Then Right Again
Stop, Look and Listen

You may also remember the useful public-service
announcement from the 1970s, which featured people
from different walks of life, saying, "Cross at the green,
not in between," in many different languages. In between
their statements, the announcer firmly urges:

> No matter how you say it,
> it always means the same thing.
> Cross at the green, not in between.
> It means cross at the corner,
> never in the middle of the block;
> don't walk until the light turns green;
> always cross at corners
> where motorists expect you
> and where you can see them.
> Cross at the green, not in between
> In any language, it's a way of life.

15
The World of Work

━━━━━

The world of business and employment can be a cut-throat one, which is why it helps to be ahead of the game and gain an advantage over competitors whether individuals or entire companies.

Business Internet Domain Names

As with all aspects of selling yourself, choosing a name for your website is as vital as any other way of making sure people notice your business and, most important, remember it.

Here's the list that the UK Freeserve website defines as the key to success: **RAIL**

Recall	Will the name be easy to remember?
Aesthetics	How will the name look on the screen or on paper?
Impressions	First impressions always count.
Length	Keep it short and sweet. Less is definitely more.

Business Presentations

In any type of public meeting, seminar, or lecture, never forget your **ABC** and always be:

Accurate, **B**rief, and **C**lear

PPPPP

To give a good presentation, plan ahead and remember the **5 Ps**:

Proper **P**lanning **P**revents **P**oor **P**erformance.

PRIDE

Whatever line of work you're in—take **PRIDE** in what you're doing:

Personal **R**esponsibility **I**n **D**aily **E**fforts

To B or Not to B

Be **B**rave and **B**elieve; and don't be **B**oring or **B**ashful.

KISS

No matter how you earn a living, never forget to:

Keep **I**t **S**imple, **S**tupid.

The **KISS** acronym is applied to principles of business, advertising, computer operating systems to science and learning. Albert Einstein's maxim was: "Everything should be made as simple as possible, but no simpler."

SWOT Analysis

SWOT is a study of four crucial elements of a business's planning process:

Strengths, **W**eaknesses, **O**pportunities, **T**hreats

Never ASSUME Anything

Every business person knows that making assumptions is the mother of all screwups:

To assume makes an **ASS** out of **U** and **ME**.

Office Egos

In the world of employment and life in general, it's sometimes wise to keep your ego under control to avoid making enemies of at least half the population. Stick to the **FASTA** technique:

Focus on your goals, not just on yourself.
Ask for other people's opinions.
    You can learn from others.
Say thank you. Always a good idea in any situation.
Treat everyone as your equal.
    Other people know stuff that you don't.
Allow yourself to fail.
    You learn from your mistakes.

Sales Techniques

If you have something to sell, always **PLAN** in advance:

Prepare with research (don't forget your 5 Ps)
Lose time, lose all
Analyze the situation
Never just call (always have a viable reason)
    to make contact if you are making a "cold call."

During a sales pitch, meeting, or presentation, these should be your **AIMS**:

> **A**rrest the senses
> **I**nterest by questions and novelty
> **M**ove by proof and demonstration
> **S**ucceed in getting a "yes."

Think **ETC** after the pitch has been made:

> **E**valuate the outcome
> **T**each yourself and others
> **C**heck for results.

How to Interview

The first mnemonic a journalist learns is the five Ws and the H. The worst moment during an interview is when the subject gives only *yes* or *no* answers. Phrasing a question with these words gets people talking and should prevent single-word replies.

Who? **W**hen? **W**here? **W**hat? **W**hy? **H**ow?

SMART

Use this mnemonic for setting goals. It's a powerful tool for personal planning and kick-starting your career. Setting goals is all about knowing what you want to achieve and where to concentrate your efforts. You have to be **SMART**! Your daily "to do" list must be:

Specific, **M**easurable, **A**ttainable, **R**elevant, **T**ime bound

AIDA

Advertisers need to urge people to buy their products, so they design arresting images and messages for consumers. The key principles of advertising are:

Attract **A**ttention—"Look at that!"
Arouse **I**nterest—"Mmm, that looks interesting!"
Create **D**esire—"I want it!"
Urge **A**ction—"Now!"

Job Interview Techniques

Preparing for meetings is vital in business, and job interviews are possibly the most important meetings in your business life. Your aim at an interview is to sell yourself—you are the product. Hence the need for the **STAR** system:

Situation—Describe your previous experience regarding situations that you have managed successfully.

TAsk—Give details of exactly how you managed the situation. What was your contribution to the task? A tip from the professionals—don't make it up, and don't exaggerate, because you'll be found out!

Result—Congratulations. You're hired!

16
Other Favorites

Champagne Bottles

Name	Capacity	No. of Bottles
Quarter	18.75 cl	—
Half-bottle	37.5 cl	—
Bottle	75 cl	1
Magnum	1.5 l	2
Jeroboam	3 l	4
Rehoboam	4.5 l	6
Methuselah	6 l	8
Salmanazar	9 l	12
Balthazar	12 l	16
Nebuchadnezzar	15 l	20

One way to recall the names of different-sized bottles of champagne is to think of a detective in the company of some ancient men:

Magnum—1980s TV private detective
(or gun)

Jeroboam—Founder and first king of Israel,
931–910 BC
Rehoboam—Son of Solomon, king of Judah,
922–908 BC
Methuselah—Biblical patriarch who lived
to the age of 969
Salmanazar—King of Assyria, 859–824 BC
Balthazar—Son of Nabonide, Regent of Babylon, 539 BC
Nebuchadnezzar—King of Babylon, 605–562 BC

Otherwise this rude mnemonic could jog your memory:

My Joanna Really Makes Splendid Burping Noises.

Alcohol Tips

Few people need tips on drinking alcohol, but some drinkers swear by the advice offered in this rhyme:

> Beer on whisky? Very risky!
> Whisky on beer, never fear . . .

Mixing drinks isn't a wise thing to do, but the warning quote below says it succinctly and honestly:

> Never mix grape with the grain.

Steering a Boat

If you find yourself behind the wheel of a boat, it helps to recall which side of the boat is port (the left side with red lights) and starboard (the right side with green lights). Fortunately, there are several ways to jog one's memory:

> PORT has four letters and so has LEFT.
> P (port) comes before S (starboard) in the alphabet,
> as L (left) comes before R (right).
> PORT wine should be LEFT alone when it is RED
> (therefore starboard is RIGHT).
> There's a little RED PORT LEFT in the bottle.

Five Sailing Essentials

This handy phrase reminds the crew of a boat of the "Five Essentials" of sailing:

Can **T**he **B**oat **S**ail **C**orrectly?

Course to steer—the course might be a particular bearing (as, say, 250 degrees) or at a particular angle to the apparent wind.

Trim—the fore and aft balance of the boat. The movable ballast on the boat is of course the crew, and the aim is to achieve an even keel.

Balance—the port and starboard balance. This is also about adjusting the weight inboard or outboard.

Sail—this is to ensure the sails are set correctly until they fill with wind. The front edge, or luff, of the sail should be in line with the wind.

Centerboard—if the boat has a movable centerboard, it should be lowered when sailing close to the wind. It is raised on a downwind course to reduce drag.

Left and Right

An oft-heard criticism of some organizations is that the right hand doesn't know what the left hand is doing, which is a bit of a problem if you can't even tell the difference.

A quick physical mnemonic you can use to remember is to place your left-hand palm down, rotate your left thumb 90 degrees clockwise so that the forefinger and thumb make the shape of L for Left.

Interest Rates

Every city slicker knows this one:

> When rates are low
> Stocks will grow.
> When rates are high
> Stocks will die.

A Game of Bridge

The order of suits from highest to lowest are:

Spades, **H**earts, **D**iamonds, **C**lubs

If the order of suits just won't stick in your mind, try remembering the following fact:

Sally **H**as **D**irty **C**hildren.

Basic DIY Techniques

So you've found the screwdriver, climbed the ladder, but you don't know which way to turn the screw, because it was secured so tightly the last time round? This invaluable expression will guarantee that you don't waste precious minutes trying to unscrew a screw the wrong way:

> Righty-tighty,
> Lefty-loosey.

Or how about:

> Right on; left off.

And the mantra of every smart woodworker:

> Measure twice,
> Cut once.

The Great Outdoors

If you're invited on a huntin', shootin' and fishin' weekend with the boss, remember the following acronym: **BRASS**.

Breathe, **R**elax, **A**im, **S**ight, **S**queeze

By keeping this sequence in mind, it might help you to shoot a rifle without missing your targets by a mile, or at least make you seem as if you know what you're doing ... .

Setting a Table

When preparing for your next holiday or dinner party, remember that items to the left of the plate have EVEN letters, like the word LEFT (4) FORK (4) and NAPKIN (6). Items to the right of the plate have ODD letters, like the word RIGHT (5), KNIFE (5), SPOON (5), GLASS (5).

Under the
Covers and
between
the Sheets

The inside story behind
classic characters, authors,
unforgettable phrases,
and unexpected endings

C. ALAN JOYCE
& SARAH JANSSEN

Introduction

⌘

Admit it: Even though you're a ravenous reader today, you probably still wince and shudder when someone mentions *The Scarlet Letter,* and you are overcome by memories of that high school English teacher who slowly squeezed the life out of what *technically* should have been a fun read for a 16-year-old. Seriously: It's got sin, adultery, revenge, self-flagellation, mysterious astronomical portents…what's not to like?

We've all been there. No matter how much you love literature, there's probably a roomful of authors and a mountain of books you would go out of your way to avoid reading again. But just because you studied the dickens out of Dickens in high school, that doesn't mean you know the whole story—or even the most intriguing parts if it.

Wouldn't *David Copperfield* have seemed a tiny bit more interesting if you knew the author had a strange fascination with human corpses? And wouldn't it have been mildly reassuring to know that even the gentlemanly Mark Twain, upon opening *Pride and Prejudice,* was overcome with the urge to dig up Jane Austen and "beat her over the skull with her own shin-bone"?

On the other hand, maybe you adore every last scrap of "serious" literature—but you think science fiction is second-class writing and the exclusive province of pocket-protector–wearing men. If so, you probably didn't know that 2007 Nobel Prize winner Doris Lessing has been churning out fantastic sci-fi for years… or you've overlooked Octavia Butler, the first science fiction writer to win a MacArthur "Genius" Grant.

Think that the James Bond novels are a far-fetched waste of time? Some of Ian Fleming's real-life WWII experiences directly inspired Bond's daring exploits. And all those preposterously sexy romance novels? They're kid stuff, compared to the steamy personal lives of their authors, complete with broken homes, illegitimate children, and seductive handymen. We will admit that not every book has a silver lining, but even the dreariest prose can provide a few laughs—so toward that end, we've rounded up the worst of the worst writing of all time, both intentional and embarrassingly unintentional.

Speaking of kid stuff, we've unearthed little-known facts about classic children's authors that cast their lives and books in a whole new light, such as the long, strange trip that turned Fifi the monkey into Curious George, and some decidedly child-unfriendly works by authors like Shel Silverstein, who penned a pop song about venereal disease.

Or maybe you read any fiction you can get your hands on, while nonfiction feels like homework? There's a reason that the phrase "stranger than fiction" is cliché—sometimes the true story is more interesting than the imagined tale. You never know what you'll find inside someone's diary...especially if it belonged to Albert Einstein's last girlfriend, who documented his relatively curious treatment for avian depression.

And when you're tired of all the curious facts that lie under the covers, there's more to be found off the page—from the poet who once worked as a "prostitute manager" to pay the bills to a 1940s precursor to TV's *Big Brother,* where a gaggle of oversexed authors and artists (and a legendary stripper) set up house in Brooklyn.

There's much more to be found between the sheets that follow, including publishers' rejection letters for now-classic works of fiction; the original vampire craze, 200 years before *Twilight*; a concise guide to the greatest chain-smoking, pistol-packing private eyes in crime fiction; the most offensive books you've ever loved; and the secret rock & roll lifestyle of some of the biggest best-selling authors of all time. We hope you'll enjoy discovering these secrets as much as we did.

1

SHOT OUT OF THE CANON

Most of the authors and works profiled here stand among "serious" literature's all-time greats, but don't let that scare you away. We've rounded up all the stories your English Lit teacher didn't tell you about—the authors who almost succeeded in destroying their greatest works, addictions that fueled the creation of classic novels, and some of the downright *weirdest* books ever written. Want to seem like an instant literary expert (without really trying)? It's all right here.

THE GREATEST BOOKS NEVER WRITTEN

In the words of poet John Greenleaf Whittier: "For of all sad words of tongue or pen, / The saddest are these: 'It might have been!'" These writers left behind unfinished writing that—had they lived to see it through—might have surpassed even their greatest published works.

A REAL COOL DROOD

Charles Dickens serialized many of his works in popular magazines, ending each installment with a cliff-hanger ending that left readers wanting more. It's a great system . . . unless the author dies in the middle of the project, as Dickens did while writing *The Mystery of Edwin Drood*. At the time of his death in 1870, Dickens had completed only 6 out of 12 planned installments and left few notes or clues about his plans for the rest of the story. The question "Who killed Edwin Drood?" has engaged Dickens scholars and fans practically since the day of his death. In 1914 members of the Dickens Fellowship, a group that included G. K. Chesterton and George Bernard Shaw, staged a mock trial of John Jasper, the character most often believed to be the murderer (Shaw, as foreman of the jury, said that the evidence was scant but that Jasper should be found guilty of manslaughter . . . if only to spare the jury from the possibility of being murdered in their sleep). At least four films and dozens of theatrical versions have run the story out to various conclusions, and a 1985 Broadway musical gave audience members the chance to vote on the identity of the murderer. And Drood-mania shows no sign of subsiding: As recently as 2009, two new novels (Dan Simmons's *Drood* and Matthew Pearl's *The Last*

Dickens) used the unfinished manuscript as a jumping-off point for murder mysteries of their own.

A GREATER GATSBY?

F. Scott Fitzgerald's *The Great Gatsby* (1925) is routinely held up as one of the greatest works of American fiction. His three other complete novels (*This Side of Paradise,* 1920; *The Beautiful and the Damned,* 1922; and *Tender Is the Night,* 1934) are held in high regard, but generally pale in comparison to Fitzgerald's great Jazz Age portrait. Had he completed his final novel, *The Last Tycoon* (1941), many believe it could have surpassed even *Gatsby:* According to a *New York Times* review from 1941, "...uncompleted though it is, one would be blind indeed not to see that it would have been Fitzgerald's best novel and a very fine one." The chapter Fitzgerald was working on, on the day before he died, brought it roughly halfway to completion, at 60,000 words; it has been rumored that Fitzgerald asked his friend Nathaniel West (author of *Day of the Locust*) to help him finish it if he died before he could complete the task...but tragically, West and his wife were killed in a car crash one day after Fitzgerald's death. (The book was re-released in 1994 under Fitzgerald's original title, *The Love of the Last Tycoon.*)

PHILIP MARLOWE AND THE MARITAL MYSTERY

When mystery master Raymond Chandler died in 1959, he left behind one of the toughest unsolved cases of his career: How in the world would legendary gumshoe Philip Marlowe cope with marriage to *The Long Goodbye*'s femme fatale, Linda Loring? Chandler completed only four first-draft chapters (about 40 typed pages) of the book that would ultimately become *Poodle Springs*

Mystery (1989) with a little help from detective novelist Robert Parker, creator of the Spenser series. Chandler himself offered little help in solving the case, noting in a 1958 letter: "I don't know whether the marriage will last or whether [Marlowe] will walk out of it or get bounced."

....

"I finished the thing; but I think I sprained my soul."

—KATHERINE ANNE PORTER, ON HER NOVEL *SHIP OF FOOLS*

....

THE HAND THAT FEEDS YOU

After ingratiating himself to the leading lights of New York City high society for decades, *Breakfast at Tiffany's* scribe, Truman Capote, took a startling turn with his final, unfinished book, *Answered Prayers*: He turned his sharp eye (and pen) back toward the glamorous jet-setters who had shared all their secrets with the diminutive, oddly mannered writer. Capote hyped the unseen book for years, promising it would be his "Remembrance of Things Past," and finally bowed to public pressure by publishing three chapters in *Esquire* in 1975 and 1976. The response from his so-called friends was swift and harsh: According to legendary New York gossip columnist Liz Smith, "Never have you heard such gnashing of teeth, such cries for revenge, such shouts of betrayal and screams of outrage." In response, Capote defended his actions: "I'm a writer, and I use everything. Did all those people think I was there just to entertain them?" The rest of the manuscript has never surfaced—to the relief of scores of New York "ladies who lunch," no doubt—though Capote claimed the complete novel was finished and stored in a safe-deposit box...whose key has yet to be found.

NOTHING IS CERTAIN BUT DEATH AND TAXES

David Foster Wallace showed few signs of scaling back his infamously verbose style in his follow-up to the heady, footnote-laden *Infinite Jest* (1996). Within a year of its publication, Wallace had begun working on a manuscript about IRS employees and the nature of boredom, for which he dove into a deep study of accounting and tax procedures. Wallace had expressed a desire to make his next work more accessible, but as the text ran up to several hundred thousand words, Wallace began calling the new book simply "The Long Thing." In 2008 after years of struggling with depression, he organized his computer files, neatly stacked the unfinished manuscript for his wife, and hanged himself; the unfinished manuscript was later published under the title *The Pale King*.

> *"This book is an agglomeration of lean-tos and annexes and there is no knowing how big the next addition will be, or where it will be put. At any point, I can call the book finished or unfinished."*
>
> **—ALEXANDER SOLZHENITSYN, IN *THE OAK AND THE CALF***

WASTE NOT, WANT NOT

As the adage goes, "If you want something done, you've got to do it yourself." For whatever reason, some famous authors requested that their papers and manuscripts be destroyed upon their death; lucky for us, their literary executors weren't always so good at following orders.

AN INCOMPLETE HISTORY

Virgil, the preeminent poet of the Roman Empire, is said to have written the *Aeneid* at the request of Caesar Augustus, who wanted a chronicle of Rome's greatness under his rule. Virgil died with the work still incomplete in 19 B.C. and had instructed his literary executor, Varius, to destroy the existing text. Fortunately for us (and, we suppose, Augustus), Varius didn't comply, and Virgil's 11 years of work on the *Aeneid* still stands as one of the great works of classical literature.

Augustus's request may have been influenced somewhat by Virgil's *Eclogues:* In the fourth pastoral poem, Virgil prophesied that a child, presumed to be Augustus (maybe only by Augustus?), had been born to bring a golden age of peace, order, and prosperity. For what it's worth, readers of the same poem in the Middle Ages interpreted it as a prophesy of the birth of Jesus.

A TRILOGY IN ONE PART

Somewhat lesser known to American readers than Russian contemporaries like Tolstoy and Dostoyevsky, writer Nicolai Gogol nonetheless exerted a huge influence on the development of the novel—Dostoyevsky once remarked that every Russian realist to follow actually emerged "from under Gogol's greatcoat."

Unfortunately, we have no idea just how great (or overrated) more of his work might have been. Gogol was attempting to expand his novel *Dead Souls* into a trilogy in line with Dante's *Divine Comedy*, but he inexplicably destroyed the nearly completed second part, then died nine days later.

WITH FRIENDS LIKE THIS . . .

Emily Dickinson was an enormously productive poet, writing nearly 1,800 poems before her death in 1882. Of course, no one knew that until after she died: She published fewer than a dozen poems in her lifetime. Dickinson's work would have been lost forever had her sister Lavinia not half-broken her promise to Emily. A prolific letter writer, Emily had made Lavinia promise to burn all her papers following her death. But when Lavinia discovered the trove of poems that no one knew existed, she refused to burn the verses. She did destroy Emily's letters, so perhaps Dickinson only half turned over in her grave.

BETTER OFF DEAD

Most people wouldn't look kindly on a person who disobeyed their friend's dying wish—but would most likely make an exception for Max Brod, who saved Kafka from the incinerator. Much of Kafka's work wasn't published until Brod championed it after Kafka's death, completely disregarding a stipulation in Kafka's will that his work be burned. Though Brod was ultimately overshadowed by his friend's posthumous successes, he had been a much more successful writer than Kafka was in his lifetime and ended up editing or appending much of the work Kafka left behind.

The Castle, for instance, stopped in midsentence, and *Amerika,* Kafka's story about a visitor in a country he would never himself have visited, was originally titled "The Man Who Disappeared" (the phrase was resurrected as a subtitle for some editions).

HIS BETTER HALF

Even when Vladimir Nabokov was alive, his wife, Vera, had to stop him from destroying his manuscripts: She once ran out of the house and snatched pages of what would become *Lolita* from a backyard bonfire. But a dying Nabokov made it clear that he wanted his final, fragmentary manuscript—consisting of about 50 handwritten index cards—destroyed after his death, which occurred in 1977. Instead, Vera placed them into a Swiss safe-deposit box for safekeeping while she decided what to do. Upon her death more than a decade later, responsibility for the decision—destroy or preserve? publish or not publish?—fell to Dmitri Nabokov, the couple's son. After seesawing over the decision for years, Nabokov announced in 2008 that he would publish *The Original of Laura*; he claimed that his father appeared to him in a dream and announced, "You're stuck in a right old mess—just go ahead and publish!" We'll believe it when we see it.

....

"Paper is cheap, and authors need not now erase one book before they write another."

—Henry David Thoreau

....

WRITING UNDER THE INFLUENCE

It's no secret that many writers have had substance abuse issues—some have practically made whole careers of it. Alcoholism, drug abuse, and writing don't always go hand in hand, but for these writers addiction was equal parts inspiration and albatross.

....

"An alcoholic is someone you don't like, who drinks as much as you do."

—DYLAN THOMAS

....

GENTLY INTO THAT GOOD NIGHT

The Welsh poet Dylan Thomas (1914–53) spent many of the final days of his alcohol-soaked life traveling in the United States on college reading tours. As he became more widely known, the tours also afforded Thomas opportunities to hobnob (and drink) with celebrities. On one besotted occasion, Thomas was seen urinating on a plant in Charlie Chaplin's house. Of course, Thomas's career as a poet and a drinker ended tragically early. One night, at the age of 39, the story goes, he bragged about consuming 18 whiskeys, calling it a record, then fainted and died in the hospital several days later. In actuality, Thomas died of pneumonia—and despite his affinity for whiskey, an autopsy showed his liver to be remarkably clear of cirrhosis.

> ## LAUDABLE LAUDANUM?
>
> **Just a few of the writers who enjoyed this common opium-based drug in the 19th century included Charles Dickens, Elizabeth Barrett Browning, and Sir Walter Scott. Allusions to Barrett Browning's habit can be found in the infamous Barrett Browning love poems, in the form of red poppies.**

AT WIT'S END

After her stinging one-liners, acerbic critic and writer Dorothy Parker (1893–1967) may be best known for three-martini lunches with the Algonquin Round Table in the 1920s. Along with alcoholism, however, came the complications; Parker attempted suicide several times before dying of natural causes. With no children or other close relatives, she left her entire estate to Martin Luther King Jr., who would be assassinated the next year.

....

"I hate to advocate drugs, alcohol, violence, or insanity to anyone, but they've always worked for me."

—Hunter S. Thompson

....

UNSAFE AT ANY SPEED

Jean-Paul Sartre's (1905–80) longtime companion, Simone de Beauvoir, catalogued his use of amphetamines (up to 200 mg per day) and sleeping pills, which he often washed down with whiskey (presumably to take the edge off all those amphetamines). Sartre began work on *Saint Genet* (1952) as a 50-page introduction to a book collecting Jean Genet's writings, but, overstimulated, the work grew to 800 pages.

Science fiction author Philip K. Dick (1928–82) was also a heavy user of amphetamines and countless other drugs, both recreationally and because he believed they enhanced his productivity. He eventually suffered permanent pancreatic damage because of his many Schedule I pursuits, but he may not have been as prolific without them. In one year (1963–64), he produced 11 novels and innumerable essays, short stories, and plot treatments.

SPEED BUMP

W. H. Auden, who took amphetamines daily for 20 years beginning in 1938, called the pills a "labor-saving device" in the "mental kitchen"—"very crude, liable to injure the cook, and constantly breaking down."

FEAR AND LOATHING AND WILD TURKEY

From Chivas-drinking and Dunhill chain-smoking, to varying levels of abuse of just about every psychedelic or psychotropic controlled substance, Hunter S. Thompson's (1937–2005) drug use was as much a part of his writing as was his politics (though he once managed to share a limo with Richard Nixon, on the condition that they talk only about football). His drug use could sometimes be a detriment to his productivity: In one cocaine-fueled episode, Thompson, in Africa to cover the 1974 "Rumble in the Jungle" between Muhammad Ali and George Foreman, gave away his tickets so he could go for a swim in the hotel pool.

> *"There is no such thing as bad whiskey. Some whiskeys just happen to be better than others. But a man shouldn't fool with booze until he's fifty; then he's a damn fool if he doesn't."*
>
> —William Faulkner

DRINKS OF A DIRTY OLD MAN

Charles Bukowski (1920–94) began drinking at the age of 13 as a defense mechanism against an abusive father. In his novels, alter ego Henry (Hank) Chinaski binges in barrooms in reflection of Bukowski's own liver-abusing days and nights, whether while working for the postal service—as Bukowski did for 12 years—or gambling at the horse track (a favorite Bukowski hobby). Bukowski finally left his odd jobs behind when John Martin, publisher of Black Sparrow Press, promised his life savings, in $100-a-month increments for life, if Bukowski would write full time. The money was enough to keep him in rent, smokes, and booze—though Bukowski eventually made a little money from the actual sale of his writing, too.

WILLIAM TELL

Drunk and possibly high at a Mexico City party in 1951, William Burroughs (1914–97) suggested to Joan Vollmer—the mother of his son—that they do their "William Tell" act. Burroughs accidentally shot Vollmer in the process, killing her. Burroughs said many times that he never would have become a writer if not for the incident. In *Queer*, which he began writing while awaiting his trial, he wrote, "So the death of Joan brought me in contact with the invader, the Ugly Spirit, and maneuvered me into a lifelong struggle, in which I have had no choice except to write my way out." (He was given a two-year suspended sentence.)

MISERY

Acclaimed horror writer Stephen King (1947–) struggled with addiction to drugs and alcohol frequently during his writing career—to the point where he doesn't remember finishing or revising some of his best-known books, including *It* (1986). His wife, Tabitha, held an intervention in 1987, pouring out the contents of his trash can in front of friends and family, including "cocaine in gram bottles and cocaine in plastic Baggies, coke spoons caked with snot and blood, Valium, Xanax . . ." King stayed off drugs for many years, until he became addicted to Oxycontin after he was hit by a van in 1999. "I had to kick it the way a junkie kicks heroin . . . I didn't sleep for two weeks. My feet twitched uncontrollably—that is why it is called kicking the habit; your feet literally kick out. It was horrible."

THE ORIGINAL "COFFEE ACHIEVER"

Compared to some of the addictions of his fellow literary legends, Honore de Balzac's (1799–1850) principal addiction—to coffee!—seems downright tame. Who hasn't relied on a few extra cups to get through an all-night study session or to polish off a particularly irksome piece of prose? But Balzac took it much, much further: He practically couldn't breathe without the stuff. The corpulent writer is said to have downed 50 cups a day of thick Turkish coffee…and when he couldn't wait for the next cup to brew, he would chomp on a handful of raw beans to keep the buzz alive. Mainlining caffeine helped him maintain an incredibly prolific output, but it also drove him to an early grave: Balzac succumbed to a constellation of ailments, including high blood pressure, at age 51.

BRAVE NEW WORLD

Author Aldous Huxley, an advocate of psychedelic drug use, reportedly had his wife inject him with LSD as he was dying of cancer.

UNDER THE INFLUENCE

British poet Samuel Taylor Coleridge (1772–1834) was known to disappear on opium binges for days at a time, during which he could produce astonishing work: He said that the images of his great poem *Kubla Khan* came to him in a vivid opium dream. But not all of his efforts under the influence were so successful…or at least, so scholars used to think. In 1814 Coleridge was commissioned to translate Goethe's poem *Faust* into English, but he never delivered a completed manuscript and presumably spent the advance to feed his growing addiction. But in 2007 a new translation of *Faust* emerged, purportedly written by Coleridge; according to Professor James McKusick, who studied the text since the 1970's, Coleridge did complete the translation, but for *another* publisher—and probably insisted that it be published anonymously (in 1821) to prevent the original publisher from coming after him to recoup its advance.

THE METHODS OF THEIR MADNESS

The writing tools, rituals, and obsessions that fueled the world's best-known authors, from nudity and rented typewriters to … visits to the morgue?

UNDER A "SENTENCE" OF DEATH

In 1959 Anthony Burgess received some life-changing news: Doctors told him that he had an inoperable brain tumor and that he had one year left to live. Driven by a need to provide for his wife after his supposedly inevitable demise, Burgess wrote five novels in an incredible rush over the next year … and then published *A Clockwork Orange* in 1962 … and kept on churning out novels until 1993 (outliving his wife in the process), when he finally succumbed to *lung* cancer, with more than 30 novels to his name.

THE ORIGINAL "DIME NOVEL"?

In the late 1940s, Ray Bradbury became fascinated with the history of book burning in different civilizations. Gradually, the seed of an idea began to form about firemen who burned books, but with a vocal newborn daughter at home, Bradbury had trouble focusing on the text. He didn't have enough money to rent an office, but one day, while wandering around the UCLA campus, he found a basement room full of typewriters that could be rented for 10 cents per half hour. He promptly rounded up a bag of dimes and holed up in that room for nine days, tapping out a novella called *The Fireman* that he later expanded into *Fahrenheit 451*. Total cost for writing the story? $9.80.

THEY TOOK IT LYING DOWN

Though Marcel Proust, Mark Twain, and Truman Capote were all ambitious and prolific writers, you wouldn't necessarily have known it from observing them at work: Each was famously fond of lying down on the job. Proust's housekeeper noted that she "never saw him write even the shortest note standing up...He didn't even prop himself up on the pillow." Twain rebuked authors who complained about the difficulty of writing, saying "Writing is the easiest thing in the world...Just try it in bed sometime. I sit up with a pipe in my mouth and a board on my knees, and I scribble away." And Capote claimed, "I can't think unless I'm lying down"— especially with a cigarette and coffee. One imagines that Capote must have gone through a lot of cigarettes and coffee in bed, since his strict writing ritual also required him to produce two full drafts in longhand before he ever approached a typewriter (where revisions had to be typed on "a very special kind of yellow paper").

STAND UP AND BE COUNTED

Many authors—including Ernest Hemingway, who reportedly wrote *A Moveable Feast* at a stand-up desk—went the opposite route, preferring to do most of their writing on their feet. Philip Roth has said that he stands and paces almost continuously while working and that each page of his books probably represents about one-half mile of walking (which makes his National Book Award–winning first book, *Goodbye, Columbus,* roughly equal to a 100-mile trek). Charles Dickens also wrote on his feet and found inspiration by putting one in front of the other...but while strolling, he sometimes heeded a very peculiar call: "Whenever I am in Paris," he once said, "I am dragged by invisible force into the Morgue." Ah, Paris!

LITERATURE "BUFFS"

The bloggers of today didn't invent the practice of writing in their pajamas (or even less): Some of the greatest writers in history were known to write *au naturale*. Playwright Edmond Rostand (*Cyrano de Bergerac*) cooled his heels in the bathtub while working; D. H. Lawrence found inspiration by climbing trees in the nude (a kink that, to the best of our knowledge, never found its way into his books); and on at least one occasion, Victor Hugo is said to have conquered writer's block by giving a servant his clothes, locking himself in his room, and making the servant promise not to return until Hugo had finished his day's writing.

THE LIGHT AT THE END OF THE TUNNEL

Unlike many authors who let the narrative flow where it may, John Irving always likes to know where he's going. He has claimed that whenever he starts a new book, he tries "to write the last sentence first, even the last several paragraphs."

DO HIS PARTICIPLES DANGLE, TOO?

Leave it to best-selling author Dan Brown to think outside the box, even when it comes to his writing habits: When he hit a block trying to write anagrams for the book *Angels & Demons,* he got the creative juices flowing by hanging upside-down in gravity boots—a habit he carried through his work on *The Da Vinci Code,* along with frequent breaks for push-ups, sit-ups, and stretching.

THE BLIND READING THE BLIND

Legend has been built around Beethoven composing after he lost his hearing completely—but, likewise, many classic texts were written by authors who couldn't read the words on their pages.

- It *would* figure that the so-called "Blind Bard" probably wasn't vision-impaired in the slightest, wouldn't it? Homer—the author of the preliterate epics *The Odyssey* and *The Iliad*—didn't exactly leave a written record of his life, so Homer's reputation as a blind, itinerant poet may have developed as a figment of history's collective imagination. The theories on why history put Homer down as blind range from the literal (in some dialects, variations on the word "homer'"were defined as "one who does not see") to the presumed (*The Odyssey* features a blind man telling stories about Troy—it doesn't take a huge leap to wonder if that character was self-referential).

- Argentine writer Jorge Luis Borges began his career as a librarian but was "promoted" to the post of poultry inspector as a presumed punishment for his criticism of Juan Peron's authoritarian regime (he didn't take the job). When Peron was removed from office, Borges was appointed director of Argentina's National Library—but he had already lost his sight. Borges called the circumstances proof of "God's splendid irony, in granting me at once 800,000 books and darkness."

- John Milton "sacrificed his sight, and then he remembered his first desire, that of being a poet," according to Borges. After focusing for years on his philosophical tracts, the newly blind Milton returned to his attempts at the

masterpiece epic *Paradise Lost.* He did all his "writing"—
that is, composing—at night; the next day, he dictated the
mentally honed verses.

• *All the King's Men* author and poet-laureate Robert Penn
Warren had been preparing to enter the Naval Academy
at age 16, but his brother forced a change of plans when
he threw a stone that blinded Warren in one eye. Warren
instead attended college at Vanderbilt University, and there
he attempted suicide when he mistakenly began thinking
that he was also losing sight in the other eye as a result of
"sympathy syndrome."

• Pulitzer Prize–winner Alice Walker also lost an eye to sib-
ling hijinks: Walker and two brothers were playing a game
of cowboys and Indians using all-too-real B.B. guns as
weapons, and Walker was struck in the eye. Like Warren,
Walker feared for decades losing her sight completely,
which she attributed to a doctor casually telling her as a
five-year-old, "Eyes are sympathetic . . . the other will likely
become blind, too."

• James Joyce was essentially blind by the time he began
work on *Finnegan's Wake,* so he relied on a pool of friends
and aspiring writers to take dictation. One of these assistants was a young Samuel Beckett; during one of their
sessions, Joyce heard a knock at the door and said "Come
in," which Beckett dutifully wrote down. Upon hearing the
text read back to him, Joyce questioned the odd phrase . . .
but then decided to "let it stand" in the final manuscript,
yet another curious puzzle for scholars to decode.

YES, BUT IS IT ART?

You thought *Moby Dick* was tough reading? Try these on for size: These are works of serious literature, where some are written without verbs, without punctuation . . . or even without the letter "e."

James Joyce, *Finnegan's Wake* (1939): Joyce said that this opaque and multilayered text was meant "to keep the critics busy for three hundred years" (so check back with us in 2239, when all its secrets will presumably have been uncovered). The text draws inspiration from the historical theories of Italian philosopher Giambattista Vico; forms a closed narrative loop, with the first sentence of the book completing the final sentence; and makes liberal use of invented words, derived from dozens of languages. Among these are a collection of hundred-letter words representing "thunderclaps," which announce the start of each age of history. (Example: Bababadalgharaghtakamminarronnkon nbronntonnerronntuonnthunntrovarrhounawnskawntoo- hoohoordenenthurnuk.) What could be simpler?

Ernest Vincent Wright, *Gadsby: Champion of Youth* (1939): Though many writers had written shorter works under similar conditions, Wright challenged himself to write a complete novel without using the letter "e": The 50,110-word *Gadsby* is the staggering result. The preface notes that as he wrote, "a whole army of little E's gathered around my desk, all eagerly expecting to be called upon." Years later, Georges Perec accepted the same challenge, producing *La Disparition* (A Void) in 1969. The French original and English translation also omitted the letter "e"—but the Spanish translation omitted "a," the most common letter in that language, instead.

Jerzy Andrzejewski, *Bramy Raju* (*Gates of Paradise*) (1961): Andrzejewski's serious novella about the Children's Crusade of 1212 clocks in at 40,000 words...but only one sentence, with no punctuation except commas.

Vladimir Nabokov, *Pale Fire* (1962): The ostensible "text" of Nabokov's peculiar book is a 1,000-line narrative poem (entitled "Pale Fire") by the fictional poet John Shade—but the real story is told through accompanying commentary and footnotes that overwhelm the poem and comprise the bulk of the book.

William Gaddis, *JR* (1975): Twenty years after publication of his über-challenging *The Recognitions,* Gaddis returned with this story about an 11-year-old who creates a business empire from a pay phone in his school—told in more than 700 pages of nearly pure dialogue, creating a symphony (or cacophony, depending on your attention span) of interweaving voices and conversations.

Michel Thaler, *Le Train de Nulle Part* (*The Train from Nowhere*) (2004): Thaler's 233-page novel offers plot, character, action...but not a single verb. According to Thaler, "The verb is like a weed in a field of flowers. You have to get rid of it to allow the flowers to grow and flourish. Take away the verbs and the language speaks for itself." In June 2004, the author (whose real name is Michel Dansel) even held a ceremony to "bury" the verb at Paris's Sorbonne University.

Mark Z. Danielewski, *House of Leaves* (2000): This bizarre book—which seems to be equal parts horror novel, film analysis, memoir, and collage—is about a house with more space inside than outside, hiding an unseen and presumably evil force. One of the book's multiple narratives analyzes a film about the house, another analyzes that analysis...and in the meantime, text flows in all directions on the page, interspersed with meandering footnotes and eye-straining layout tricks.

Hannu Luntiala, *Viimeiset Viestit* (*The Last Message*) (2007): If a novel like this was going to be written, it was inevitably going to come from Finland, the home of Nokia: Luntiala's book is written entirely in text messages—about 1,000 of them, covering more than 300 pages. We just hope that the main characters had bargain-basement rates on their cell-phone service.

DOGGONE IT

The original manuscript for *On the Road* was written on a 119-foot-long scroll of paper. Literature lovers have long been able to visit the scroll at exhibitions in museums and libraries across the country. However, no one knows exactly how long the manuscript was when Kerouac completed it or what the treatise's original ending lines were. Kerouac's handwriting appears at the end of the scroll, noting that a cocker spaniel belonging to Lucien Carr, a friend (and the father of writer Caleb Carr), had eaten the last lines.

YOU DON'T SAY?

Many commonly used words, phrases, and proverbs were coined or popularized in classic works of fiction, though they didn't always mean what we think they do today. Find out more than you ever cared to know about the ones you've used (and possibly abused) for years.

TOO MUCH OF A GOOD THING

So many common expressions (including the title of this section) originated in Shakespeare's work that it would be impossible to name them all. Here are a few of the more familiar turns of phrase for which the Bard deserves credit:

All's well that ends well	*All's Well That Ends Well* (1602)
All the world's a stage	*As You Like It* (1600)
Fair play/foul play	*The Tempest* (1610–11), among others
Give the devil his due	*Henry IV, Part I* (c. 1597)
Green-eyed monster	*Othello* (1603)
Love is blind	*The Merchant of Venice* (1597)
Neither a borrower nor a lender be	*Hamlet* (1603)
Rhyme nor reason	*Comedy of Errors* (1590)
Send him packing	*Henry IV, Part I* (c. 1597)
There's a method in my madness (literally, "Though this be madness yet there is method in it.")	*Hamlet* (1603)
The long and short of it	*The Merry Wives of Windsor* (c. 1597)
We have seen better days	*Timon of Athens* (1607)
Wear your heart on your sleeve	*Othello* (1603)
Wild-goose chase	*Romeo and Juliet* (1592)

> ## ISN'T IT IRONIC?
> "Sweets to the sweet" isn't exactly the corny-yet-well-intentioned expression it appears to be, so you might want to pick a different phrase for your next candygram. Spoken by Hamlet's mother over Ophelia's grave, the phrase actually refers to the "sweet"-smelling funeral flowers she brought to cover the "sweet" smell of a decaying body.

AUTHOR! AUTHOR!

There are countless words based on author's names, but most of those words simply add an adjectival suffix to the author's name and are used to describe something that relates to the style of the writer referenced (Shakespearean stands as a good example). A handful, however, are elevated to meanings beyond "in the style of":

Bowdlerize: He couldn't have been the only one to find Shakespeare's bawdier bits offensive, but Thomas Bowdler—a writer and editor—is the only one who did something about it, sparing prudish readers everywhere. His 10-volume *Family Shakespeare* (1818) cut out anything that might disturb the sensibilities of readers—creating a collection that was reprinted many times. He also thought enough of himself to edit and publish censored versions of the Old Testament (1822) and Gibbon's *History of the Decline and Fall of the Roman Empire* (1826). So Bowdler is justly honored with an original eponym of his very own—*bowdlerize* now refers to any instance of removing or censoring indelicate references or vocabulary from a text.

Orwellian: Thank goodness George Orwell had the presence (or prescience?) of mind to write *1984* and *Animal Farm*, or we wouldn't have a quick term to describe grim, totalitarian dystopias. Fortunately, whenever something reminds us of a threat to a free society—especially if some form of misinformation, propaganda, or truth denial is involved—we can describe it thusly. Especially if there's some sort of ominous Big Brother–style overseer involved (another term we can thank Orwell for).

Kafkaesque: Much like Kafka's work itself, the meaning of Kafkaesque is somewhat amorphous, but one good catch-all definition is Merriam-Webster's: "Having a nightmarishly complex, bizarre, or illogical quality." The disorienting feeling this definition implies would, of course, be quite familiar to Gregor Samsa.

CLEARING THROUGH THE RED TAPE

A fact of modern life, bureaucratic red tape was once tangible rather than metaphorical—lawyers and government officials in England bound documents together with actual red tape made of cloth or ribbon. Charles Dickens was the first writer to use the term metaphorically in *Bleak House* (1852–53): "[We] think to keep away the Wolves of Crime and Filth by our…gentlemanly handling of red tape."

WHAT A CHARACTER!

Some characters are just so memorable that their names become synonymous with their most outstanding personality traits. Of course, sometimes that means the new word describes a trait that has less-than-flattering associations. (How many girls have you met named Lolita?)

What the Dickens? We can only guess what Charles Dickens had in mind when he named the miserly focal character Ebenezer Scrooge in *A Christmas Carol* (1843)—especially given the fact that there is no evidence that Scrooge was an established English surname. But what do we care? It comes in handy now and then in describing the cheapskates and misanthropes among us—and not just during the holiday season.

"They Misunderestimated Me" Centuries before President George W. Bush became the admitted modern master of misspeaking, Richard Sheridan's *The Rivals* (1775) coined the word malapropism with the character Mrs. Malaprop. Of course, there was already a Latin word for these bumbling turns of phrase (*acyrologia,* for what it's worth), but Mrs. Malaprop made it her own by sheer virtue of opening her mouth, describing one person as "the very *pineapple* of politeness." Hopefully, fans of the play, in Mrs. Malaprop's own words, "might *reprehend* the true meaning of what she is saying."

Elementary, My Dear Eponym It may be most commonly used as sarcasm against the not-so-observant, but Sherlock Holmes's first name is still listed in dictionaries today as a synonym for detective. So ease up on your unperceptive friends (they may just take you seriously, anyway).

Sunny-Side Up The more cynical probably shudder at the notion of playing the "Glad Game," invented by Eleanor Porter's titular *Pollyanna* (1913). But at least when someone tells them to turn those lemons into lemonade, they have a better word for describing the irrepressibly optimistic, in several parts of speech—Pollyanna, Pollyannaism, and Pollyannaish are technically all words. And for those who revel in appreciating a glass half full, there's always Littleton, New Hampshire's, Official Pollyanna Glad Day, an annual June festival.

It Isn't Nice to Call Names He probably didn't set out to expand the list of synonyms for a sexually precocious young girl, but Vladimir Nabokov's memorable title character in *Lolita* (1955) and his character Humbert Humbert's own term nymphet are listed in Merriam-Webster's dictionary with that definition.

DOUBLE BIND

Catch-22 is one of those terms that is more often misused than not. As described in Joseph Heller's 1961 novel of the same name, Catch-22 is a rule or set of circumstances that inherently denies a solution to a problem, usually by employing circular logic. It appears most notably as the rule that keeps mentally ill WWII pilots from grounding themselves: "Orr would be crazy to fly more missions and sane if he didn't, but if he was sane he had to fly them. If he flew them he was crazy and didn't have to; but if he didn't want to he was sane and had to."

MAKE IT WORK

'Generation X'—from Douglas Coupland's 1991 novel *Generation X: Tales of an Accelerated Culture*—originally referred to those born in the late 1950s and 1960s. Though those identified today as members of Generation X are a few years younger than the characters Coupland described, certain generic characteristics are the same. One of Coupland's Gen-Xers admits to working a "McJob"—a term that Coupland didn't coin but is credited with forcing into the popular vernacular. A McJob was defined by Coupland as "a low-pay, low-prestige, low-dignity, low-benefit, no-future job in the service sector." Needless to say, the term is a nod to a popular fast-food franchise that shall remain nameless: The company threatened to sue when McJob was added to Merriam-Webster's dictionary and has formally campaigned to have it redefined to reflect "a job that is stimulating, rewarding . . . and offers skills that last a lifetime."

SCIENCE NONFICTION

Sci-fi giant Isaac Asimov is too often credited with inventing the word robot, which was actually coined by Czech playwright Karel Capek in *R.U.R.* (*Rossum's Universal Robots,* 1920). Technically, you could argue that Asimov gets a half credit on this one, though, because he was the first to use the term robotics in reference to the science of robots, in 1941—and Asimov *does* deserve full credit for his three laws of robotics.

Many other scientific concepts were originally named in fictional works:

Zero gravity/zero-G: Jack Binder first described zero gravity as a concept in 1938, though he wasn't referring to outer space: Binder was describing the center of the Earth's core.

Sci-fi savant Arthur C. Clarke coined zero-G in *Islands in the Sky* (1952), when his protagonist had to adapt to the physical effects when visiting a space station in Earth's orbit.

EAT IT AND WEEP

You can thank Robert Burns for giving us the most commonly sung holiday song (after "Happy Birthday," of course) when you're warbling to "Auld Lang Syne" on New Year's Eve. But unless you live in Scotland, you're probably missing out on Burns Night—for some, an equally boozy tradition. Across Scotland the week of January 25, highly structured "Burns suppers" honor the birth of the 18th century bard, complete with a recitation of Burns's poem "Address to a Haggis," which toasts the much-maligned main course for the evening. (Haggis, the unofficial national dish of Scotland, is a sheep's stomach stuffed with a mixture of sheep organs, oatmeal, onion, and other spices.) And, of course, Burns Night also concludes with a singing of "Auld Lang Syne."

Deep space: E. E. Smith is credited with using the term first in 1936, to refer to space far removed from one's home planet, in his seminal *Lensman* series. Outside of science fiction, its definition has changed since then to refer to something far more local—most scientists use the term to refer to space outside the Earth's atmosphere.

Pressure suit: Worn to maintain consistent pressure levels in space, the pressure suit was another product of E. E. Smith's imagination. Fortunately for Buzz Aldrin and his pals at NASA, their suits didn't follow Smith's sartorial design exactly—sparing us the sight of U.S. astronauts floating in fur-covered space suits.

THE DARK SIDE

David Gerrold was the first to call a self-replicating computer program a "virus" in 1972, in *When HARLIE Was Won,* which was nominated for Hugo and Nebula awards in 1972. But he's probably more famous for another self-replicating creation: Gerrold wrote the infamous *Star Trek* episode "The Trouble with Tribbles."

Ion drive: Imagined and named by Jack Williamson in *The Equalizer* (1947), more than a few spacecraft since have been powered in the same way—propulsion created by charged-particle emission.

THE OTHER FINAL FRONTIER

The term *cyberspace* first appeared in William Gibson's short story "Burning Chrome" (1982), and much of Gibson's seminal *Neuromancer* (1984) takes place in that same virtual plane of data, or "consensual hallucination experienced daily by billions of legitimate operators." Gibson said later that cyberspace—combining the words "cybernetics" and "space"—was conceived of as a buzzword—"evocative and essentially meaningless" with "no real semantic meaning."

....

"Individual science fiction stories may seem as trivial as ever to the blinder critics and philosophers of today— but the core of science fiction, its essence . . . has become crucial to our salvation if we are to be saved at all."

—Isaac Asimov

....

EVERYONE'S A CRITIC

Some writers were famously friendly and supportive of each other's work—Herman Melville even dedicated *Moby-Dick* to his friend Nathaniel Hawthorne "in token of my admiration for his genius." But it's equally likely that they hate other writers' work (or just despise the writers themselves). In fact, it's probable that no one critiques writers as cruelly as their own kind. Here are a few of the more revered, on the writers they despised the most:

- "I cannot stand Tolstoy, and reading him was the most boring literary duty I ever had to perform, his philosophy and his sense of life are not merely mistaken, but evil, and yet, from a purely literary viewpoint, on his own terms, I have to evaluate him as a good writer." —AYN RAND

- "Poor Faulkner. Does he really think big emotions come from big words? He thinks I don't know the ten-dollar words. I know them all right. But there are older and simpler and better words, and those are the ones I use." —ERNEST HEMINGWAY, having been informed that William Faulkner believed that Hemingway "had no courage" and "had never been known to use a word that might send the reader to the dictionary."

- "That's not writing, that's typing." —TRUMAN CAPOTE on Jack Kerouac's *On the Road*

- "This is not at all bad, except as prose," —GORE VIDAL on Herman Wouk's *The Winds of War*

- "At certain points, reading the work can even be said to resemble the act of making love to a three-hundred-pound woman. Once she gets on top, it's over. Fall in love, or be asphyxiated." —**NORMAN MAILER,** on Tom Wolfe's *A Man in Full*

- "No more than the greatest mind ever to stay in prep school." —**NORMAN MAILER,** on J. D. Salinger

- "Every word she writes is a lie, including 'and' and 'the'." —**MARY MCCARTHY** on Lillian Hellman

- "The characters are nearly indistinguishable. A man in a wheelchair cannot just be a man in a wheelchair; he must be a vehicle to help a lame metaphor get around. Such is the method of the Well-Crafted Short Story." —**COLSON WHITEHEAD** on Richard Ford's short-story collection *A Multitude of Sins* (Two years later, Ford responded by spitting on Whitehead.)

CAN'T NOT PUT IT DOWN?

You can stop feeling guilty for giving up halfway through George Eliot's *Middlemarch* or Marcel Proust's *In Search of Lost Time* (nee *Remembrance of Things Past*). Turns out many fancy-pants authors do the same thing. Canadian short-story doyenne Alice Munro admitted as much in a 2001 interview with *The Atlantic*, noting that she was rereading Dostoyevsky's *The Brothers Karamazov*—not necessarily because she enjoyed it so much, but because she missed so much the first time around, when she skipped "the parts about money."

JUST SAY NO

Even the most-lauded writers have received a rejection letter or two from publishers or agents before they were awarded their Pulitzers and Nobels, but thankfully many persist. The excerpts below—including text from rejection letters, as well as publishers' "reader's reports" on submitted manuscripts—might have any aspiring writer rethinking his vocation.

James Baldwin (1924–87)	*Giovanni's Room* (1956) was called "hopelessly bad."
Jorge Luis Borges (1899–1986)	Submissions said to be "utterly untranslatable."
Pearl Buck (1892–1973)	Pulitzer Prize–winning *The Good Earth* (1931) was rejected because Americans are "not interested in anything on China."
William Faulkner (1897–1962)	Of *Sanctuary* (1931), which Faulkner claimed to have "deliberately conceived to make money," his editor said, "Good God, I can't publish this. We'd both be in jail."
Anne Frank (1929–45)	The reader found Frank's diary to be "a dreary record of typical family bickering, petty annoyances, and adolescent emotions," commenting that it wouldn't sell due to a lack of familiar or appealing characters. "Even if the work had come to light five years ago, when the subject was timely," the reader wrote, "I don't see that there would have been a chance for it."
Tony Hillerman (1925–2008)	Hillerman was told by an agent to "get rid of all that Indian stuff."
Jack Kerouac (1922–69)	"His frenetic and scrambling prose perfectly express the feverish travels of the Beat Generation. But is that enough? I don't think so."
John le Carré (1931–)	A publisher sent his submission to a colleague with a note: "You're welcome to le Carré—he hasn't got any future."

Ursula K. Le Guin (1929–)	*The Left Hand of Darkness* (1969) was "endlessly complicated by details of reference and information, the interim legends become so much of a nuisance despite their relevance, that the very action of the story seems to be to become hopelessly bogged down and the book, eventually, unreadable."
Vladimir Nabokov (1899–1977)	*Lolita* (1955) was considered "…overwhelmingly nauseating, even to an enlightened Freudian… the whole thing is an unsure cross between hideous reality and improbable fantasy. It often becomes a wild neurotic daydream…I recommend that it be buried under a stone for a thousand years."
Anaïs Nin (1903–77)	"There is no commercial advantage in acquiring her, and, in my opinion, no artistic."
George Orwell (1903–50)	*Animal Farm* (1945) was declined because it is "impossible to sell animal stories in the U.S.A."
Sylvia Plath (1932–63)	"There certainly isn't enough genuine talent for us to take notice."
Marcel Proust (1871–1922)	One editor said in response to the tome *In Search of Lost Time,* also known as *Remembrance of Things Past* (published in English, 1922–31), "My dear fellow, I may be dead from the neck up, but rack my brains as I may I can't see why a chap should need 30 pages to describe how he turns over in bed before going to sleep."

HORTON HEARS A "NO!"

Dr. Seuss's (1904–91) *And to Think That I Saw It on Mulberry Street…* (1937) was rejected by publishers 27 times before Vanguard Press agreed to publish it. His subsequent success as a children's author didn't make him immune to rejections, though. Random House rejected Seuss's proposal for a book on how to write for children in 1949, saying, "Some of them would feel an author-artist of picture books could hardly qualify as an expert in the field of juvenile writing."

Guilty Pleasures

Airport books, whodunits, page-turners, bodice rippers, potboilers, best sellers.... There are many names for so-called genre fiction, but that last one is the most important. And even though you'll find some bad books in any of these genres, you'll find there are a lot of "classics" on these shelves as well, from Jane Austen to H. G. Wells. So here's to dusting off that Georgette Heyer or reading your Tom Clancy in public again—there is no shame in that.

THE ROOTS OF PULP FICTION

In the early years of the 20th century, pulp fiction came into its own. Given this moniker because pulp's stories and serialized novels were printed in magazines on cheap pulpwood paper, pulp fiction created or evolved many of the genre fictions as we know them today. Pulp fiction was the ultimate in populist literature, priced at less than half the cost of weightier magazines. It introduced American readers to writers as diverse as Edgar Rice Burroughs, Raymond Chandler, Dashiell Hammett, H. P. Lovecraft, and Tennessee Williams, in monthly pulps. Initial general-interest pulps like *Argosy* (established in 1896), and *All-Story* (1905) eventually ceded the market to specialized titles like *Black Mask* (detective stories from 1927 on), *Weird Tales* (1923), and *Western Trails* (1938).

....

"I have been a soreheaded occupant of a file drawer labeled 'Science Fiction'. . . and I would like out, particularly since so many serious critics regularly mistake the drawer for a urinal."

—KURT VONNEGUT (1922–2007)

....

SCIENCE FICTION, SCIENCE FACT

These science-fiction writers didn't just write about spaceships and little green men: Some were eerily prescient about future technology, while others left a mark on pop culture that extended well beyond the printed page. And a surprising number of women writers proved that they could "geek out" as well as any man.

THE FUTURE IS NOW

Sir Arthur C. Clarke (1917–2008) is perhaps best known as the author of the novel *2001: A Space Odyssey*. Unlike most book-to-film adaptations, the novel was written during the production of the film, in close collaboration with director Stanley Kubrick, and published after the movie was released. If you've seen only the film, you may be surprised to learn that the alien monoliths of Kubrick's film have something in common with Dorothy's ruby slippers in *The Wizard of Oz*. Those slippers were gleaming silver in L. Frank Baum's book, but they were changed to ruby red in the movie version to better showcase Technicolor film stock. Similarly, the monoliths in Clarke's book were translucent crystal but became solid black in Kubrick's film.

If alien monoliths are ever found on the Moon, the safer bet is that they would be translucent crystal; Clarke is celebrated for making accurate predictions of various technologies years ahead of their time. In 1945 he predicted that geostationary satellites would make ideal relays for television and other communication signals—and to this day, the geostationary orbit (22,369 miles [36,000 km] above the Earth) is known as a "Clarke Orbit."

Clarke is in good company: A surprising number of modern-day inventions and technologies were predicted decades ahead of their time by science-fiction writers.

AUTHOR PREDICTED	BECAME REALITY IN
Jules Verne (1828–1905) Lunar travel, in *From the Earth to the Moon* (1865)	**1969:** *Apollo 11* crew walks on the moon
Edward Bellamy (1850–1898) Credit cards, in his novel *Looking Backward* (1888)	**1950:** First modern credit card (Diner's Club) is introduced
H. G. Wells (1866–1946) Automatic sliding doors, in the story *When the Sleeper Wakes* (1899)	**1954:** Invented by Dee Horton and Lew Hewitt; triggered by stepping on a mat
Hugo Gernsback (1884–1967) Individualized news reports, in *Ralph 124C 41+* (1925)	**2002:** Google News goes live in September
Aldous Huxley (1894–1963) Test-tube babies, in *Brave New World* (1932)	**1978:** Louise Joy Brown, the first test-tube baby, is born in England
Ray Bradbury (1920–) Full-wall, flat-screen TVs, in *Fahrenheit 451* (1953)	**1971:** First LCD panels shown to the public; as of 2009, LCD and plasma screens more than 100 inches (254 cm) across are available
Douglas Adams (1952–2001) Electronic books, in the form of the eponymous *Hitchhiker's Guide to the Galaxy* (1979)	**1990s:** Early handheld e-book readers on sale; first Amazon Kindle, with built-in wireless connection, available in 1997

THE FIRST LADY
OF SCIENCE FICTION

Though its many movie adaptations and derivatives have fallen more within the horror genre, Shelley's *Frankenstein* (originally subtitled "The Modern Prometheus") is more accurately viewed as science fiction—and one of the earliest examples of the genre, made all the more notable for being written by a teenage girl. The genesis of the book is almost as weird as the story itself. On a rainy evening in 1816 at the poet Lord Byron's villa in Geneva, a group of guests (including Mary and her husband, Percy Shelley) participated in a challenge to see who could write the best ghost story. Byron gave up after a few pages, and Percy wrote a fragment of verse . . . but Mary took the challenge seriously. Within a few days, she had begun the text of *Frankenstein*, partly inspired by recent scientific experiments performed by Erasmus Darwin (Charles's grandfather).

MAN ON THE MOON

Jules Verne (1828–1905) predicted lunar travel with particularly uncanny accuracy in *From the Earth to the Moon* (1865). In Verne's book and in reality, the United States launched the first manned spacecraft (with a three-man crew) to land on the moon. The craft was launched from Florida and splashed down in the Pacific Ocean. His spacecraft was even similar in size to *Apollo 11*: 8,730 kg for Verne's *Columbiad* versus 11,920 kg for *Apollo 11*. But Verne's capsule had the advantage in creature comforts: On the return flight, Verne's astronauts unwound with a bottle of fine wine.

IT'S A MAN'S WORLD BUT A WOMAN'S UNIVERSE

**Think sci-fi is mainly a playground for nerdy boys
(and the men they grow into)? Think again.
These women rank among the giants of the genre:**

Author	Recommended Reading	Noteworthy Facts
Gertrude Barrows Bennett	*The Citadel of Fear* (1918)	Published under the name "Francis Stevens"; one of H. P. Lovecraft's major influences
Andre Norton (Alice Mary Norton)	*Witch World* (1963)	Named a Grand Master of the Science Fiction Writers of America
James Tiptree Jr. (Alice Bradley Sheldon)	"Love Is the Plan the Plan Is Death" (1973)	Award is given in her (Tiptree's) name each year for a new sci-fi work that best explores gender issues
Doris Lessing	*Shikasta* (1979)	Winner of the 2007 Nobel Prize in Literature
Joan Vinge	*The Snow Queen* (1980)	Robert Heinlein dedicated his novel *Friday* (1982) to Vinge, Le Guin, and other notable women in sci-fi
Octavia Butler	*Bloodchild* (1995)	First sci-fi writer to win a MacArthur Genius Grant
Ursula K. Le Guin	*The Dispossessed* (1974)	Received Library of Congress Living Legend award

GROUND CONTROL TO MAJOR JON

Literary wunderkind Jonathan Lethem made his reputation with *Motherless Brooklyn* and *Fortress of Solitude,* but his first four published novels (*Gun, with Occasional Music*; *Amnesia Moon*; *As She Climbed Across the Table*; *Girl in Landscape*) were all well within the conventions of traditional sci-fi. Anyone who knew the teenage Lethem could have seen this coming: He cites his earliest "novel" as a 125-page unpublished work entitled *Heroes* (named for the David Bowie song), which he wrote over summer vacation at age 15.

REACHING FOR THE STARS

Sci-fi writers have too many surprises up their sleeves to limit themselves to one medium. In some cases, they wrote their really fantastic (and cinematic) stories specifically to be told on-screen, instead of on a page.

Theodore Sturgeon: Sturgeon was Kurt Vonnegut's inspiration for the character Kilgore Trout (see pages 278 and 303–304) and was a prolific sci-fi writer. Though his written work didn't reach a very wide audience, he did pen scripts for several curious episodes of the original *Star Trek* television series. In "Amok Time," the stoic Dr. Spock is afflicted with "Pon Farr," a hormonal condition that will kill him unless he returns to his home planet to mate; the episode also introduced the Vulcan salute, "Live long and prosper." In "Shore Leave," the *Enterprise* crew confronts an assortment of bizarre characters on the surface of an unexplored planet—including a samurai, a medieval knight, and characters from *Alice in Wonderland*. And in a third, unproduced episode, Sturgeon introduced one of the central tenets of the *Star Trek* universe: the Prime Directive, which dictates non-interference with alien cultures encountered by Federation ships.

Harlan Ellison: Ellison ranks as one of classic sci-fi's elder statesmen, with scores of stories and essays to his name; he also ranks as perhaps its most litigious representative. In 2009 he sued Paramount Home Entertainment for licensing revenue based on his award-winning script for the *Star Trek* episode, "The City on the Edge of Forever." Said the colorful Ellison in his own press release: "Am I doing this for other writers, for Mom (still dead), and apple pie? Hell no! I'm doing it for the 35-year-long disrespect and the money!"

William Gibson: Cyberpunk originator William Gibson (see page 209) and fellow author Tom Maddox wrote two episodes of *The X-Files*—dealing, naturally, with artificial intelligence, computers, and other common Gibsonian themes—as well as an early version of the movie *Alien 3*. But even Gibson's sci-fi cred couldn't save that script, which did away with series star Ripley (Sigourney Weaver) and turned the famously face-hugging aliens into an ebola-like airborne virus.

SPEAK GEEK?

GTW/CS/L/MD d-- s:+ a? C++++$ UL++++$ UC++$ US+++$
P++++$ L+++$ E--- W+++$ N+++ o+ K+++ !w--- O- M+ V-
PS+++ PE Y++ PGP+ !t 5? X-- !R(+++) tv-- b+++ DI++++/++ !D
G+ e+++ h++/-/--- r++ z?

That's how über-brainy sci-fi writer Charles Stross describes
himself in "geek code" on his website. The code, created by Robert
Hayden in 1993, translates various personal attributes into brief
codes. For example, Stross's code identifies him as a geek of technical writing, computer science, literature, and medicine (GTW/
CS/L/MD), who is of average height and above-average round-
ness (s:+), has no interest in *The X-Files* (X--), and reads several
books a week (b+++).

....

*"When people talk about genre, I guess they men-
tion my name first, but without Richard Matheson,
I wouldn't be around. He is as much my father as
Bessie Smith was Elvis Presley's mother."*

—STEPHEN KING

....

SCARE TACTICS

Who doesn't love a good scare? From vampire legends to the zombie apocalypse (it's coming, we swear!), these authors are guaranteed to send a shiver through your reading list.

NOT IF YOU WERE THE LAST MAN ON EARTH

According to the poet Robert Frost, "Some say the world will end in fire, some say in ice." How (and when) has it ended in other writers' apocalyptic works?

BOOK	THE END OF THE WORLD
Mary Shelley, *The Last Man* (1826)	**2090–2100:** Plague of natural origin decimates England (and presumably, the human race)
Richard Matheson, *I Am Legend* (1954)	**1976–79:** Bacterial plague transforms humans into bloodthirsty vampires
Stephen King, *The Stand* (1978)*	**1980:** Plague of man-made origin decimates the human race
Paul Auster, *In the Country of Last Things* (1987)	**Year unknown:** Cause unknown
Tim LaHaye & Jerry B. Jenkins, *Left Behind* (1995)	**Any day now:** Rapture, tribulation, second coming of Christ
Cormac McCarthy, *The Road* (2006)	**Year unknown:** Unspecified disaster covers planet with ash and destroys all plant and animal life

* King revised the second edition to take place in 1990. At the time of this publication, he doesn't seem to have received more recent information about the end of the world.

BLOODY GOOD FUN

If you thought the frenzy over Stephenie Meyer's *Twilight* series was intense, you must not have lived through the vampire crazes of the 18th and 19th centuries (and thus—phew—you're probably not a vampire yourself!). In the early 1700s, a fascination with blood-sucking monsters was fueled by reports of people exhuming corpses in Eastern Europe and "killing" them again, after those people supposedly rose from the grave and killed others in their region.

The word vampire officially entered the English language in 1734, according to the *Oxford English Dictionary,* though the vampires of the time weren't quite what we imagine today. Fear of crosses and holy water were common to many early vampire stories, as was the ability to transform into animals or mist. But not all vampires had pointy teeth: Many sucked blood through their victims' skin or suffocated them in their sleep. The vampires' lack of a shadow or reflection was mostly limited to German legends, while Romanian versions added sensitivity to garlic as a characteristic.

Most 18th-century vampire literature was in verse (even Goethe penned a poem about the undead), but in the 19th century it came into its own as one of the great types of horror fiction. Here are some notable bloodsuckers from that era, up to and including the greatest of them all:

John Polidori's *The Vampyre* (1819) was technically born on the same night in 1816 as Shelley's *Frankenstein* (see page 218). When Byron abandoned his horror-story idea, Polidori (Byron's personal physician) picked it up and produced the first vampire novel in English. Polidori reportedly couldn't stand Byron and made the title character a thinly veiled portrait of the great poet as a bloodthirsty ghoul. Ironically, Polidori's publishers attributed early printings of the novel to Byron to increase sales.

James Malcolm Rymer's *Varney the Vampire* **(1845–47)** was a popular "penny dreadful" (a cheap, illustrated work of fiction published as a series of slim pamphlets) that had a strong influence on later vampire fiction. Rymer had a curious fascination with blood-letting protagonists: He was also the author of the best-known penny dreadful, *Sweeney Todd*.

Carmilla **(1872),** by the Irish ghost-story writer Joseph Sheridan le Fanu (nicknamed "The Invisible Prince" for his reclusive nature and nocturnal writing habit), is viewed by some as the first lesbian vampire novel. Echoes of the book can be found in Stoker's work, notably in Count Dracula's vampiric female attendants, and in the fact that the vampire's bite didn't automatically turn victims into vampires themselves.

Bram Stoker's *Dracula* **(1897)** wasn't the first, but is certainly the most influential vampire novel of all time. Stoker drew inspiration from 18th-century legends, earlier vampire verse and novels . . . and his boss, Sir Henry Irving, a famous actor and manager of London's Lyceum Theatre. Stoker idolized Irving and served as his personal assistant and business

---

BAD DECISION

While traveling in America, Stoker and Irving met Mark Twain and agreed to invest in one of Twain's many doomed mechanical enterprises (see page 316). When the business began to sour, an embarrassed Twain wrote to Stoker, asking him to tell Irving that "when the wreckage floats ashore, he will get a good deal of his $500 back; and a dab at a time, I will make up to him the rest."

manager for 27 years, and many of the Count's mannerisms and physical characteristics are said to be based on his flamboyant employer. Some modern scholars have even claimed that Stoker harbored a repressed love for Irving; an allegedly heartbroken Stoker suffered a stroke a few weeks after Irving died in 1905, though he continued to write, with some impairment, until his death in 1912.

FAMOUS FIRST WORDS

"It is a truth universally acknowledged that a single man in possession of a good fortune, must be in want of a wife."

—Jane Austen, *Pride and Prejudice* (1813)

"It is a truth universally acknowledged that a zombie in possession of brains must be in want of more brains."

—Seth Grahame-Smith,
Pride and Prejudice and Zombies (2009)

THE WRITING DEAD

Much as the early 1700s were marked by a vampire craze, so too may the first years of the 21st century be remembered as a kind of "zombie renaissance" in the literary world, with a surprising flood of titles about the brain-devouring undead—some of them even appropriate for timid types who couldn't stomach *Night of the Living Dead*. For readers who want to check "zombie apocalypse" off their disaster-preparedness list, there's *The Zombie Survival Guide* (2003) by "preeminent zombie expert" Max Brooks, which covers such essential knowledge as the relative merits of rifles and flamethrowers when defending against zombie hordes. Or for the classically minded (and anyone who ever wished there were more zombie romance novels), there's Seth Grahame-Smith's *Pride and Prejudice and Zombies* (2009), which mashes up liberal chunks of Austen's original text with plenty of "ultraviolent zombie mayhem," and adds "martial arts master" to the list of qualities that draw Mr. Darcy to heroine Elizabeth Bennet. We imagine this is one Austen book that Mark Twain may have enjoyed (see page 289).

KUBRICK AND KING'S "SHADOW" WRITER

Love it or loathe it, Stanley Kubrick's adaptation of King's *The Shining* ranks as one of the most memorable horror films of all time. But for his big stab (pun intended) at making a scary movie, Kubrick almost adapted Diane Johnson's novel *The Shadow Knows*. Although he chose to film King's novel, Kubrick was dissatisfied with King's own screenplay; instead, Kubrick enlisted Johnson as his co-screenwriter for the film. Their script ultimately diverged from King's text in significant ways—to King's great disappointment—most notably with the addition of the now-iconic hedge maze scene.

....

"There's a lot to like about it. But it's a great big beautiful Cadillac with no motor inside. You can sit in it, and you can enjoy the smell of the leather upholstery—the only thing you can't do is drive it anywhere."

—STEPHEN KING, ON STANLEY KUBRICK'S
ADAPTATION OF *THE SHINING*

....

THE THRILL OF A LIFETIME

Action! Intrigue! Suspense! Some readers just can't resist a rollicking good thriller, and these authors have mastered the genre. From the courtroom to the operating room, here are (Shocking! Heart-pounding!) facts about some of the greatest suspense novelists around.

THE PEN IS MIGHTIER THAN THE SCALPEL

Best-selling thriller novelist Tess Gerritsen dreamed of writing Nancy Drew books as a child, but she ended up becoming a doctor. When a patient gave her a sack of romance novels, Gerritsen was bitten by the writing bug again and ended up writing her own romantic suspense thriller while on maternity leave. She later shifted to medical thrillers—including the rather un-Nancy-Drew-like *Harvest,* which featured Russian criminals stealing organs from orphans—even as she continued to work as a physician. Medical-thriller master Robin Cook has also kept up his Boston medical practice while churning out a new book almost every year since he wrote *Coma* (1977) during a medical residency. But his first book, 1972's *Year of the Intern,* was written onboard a U.S. Navy research submarine in 75 days.

....

"Hospital autopsies aren't so bad, because the bodies are very fresh."

—TESS GERRITSEN

....

SECRET AGENT MEN

John le Carré and Ian Fleming are often held up as polar opposites in the spy fiction genre: Le Carré's hero, George Smiley, is a brilliant but physically average agent in a morally complex world, while Fleming's dashing James Bond knocks back cocktails, beds beautiful women, and operates in a world where good and evil are clearly defined. After a glance at their respective creators' resumés, it's not hard so see why.

Le Carré (the pen name of David John Moore Cornwell) wrote his first book, *Call for the Dead,* while working for British military intelligence (MI5) in West Germany. He later transferred to foreign intelligence (MI6) and wrote *A Murder of Quality* and his best-known novel, *The Spy Who Came in from the Cold.* All three starred world-weary spymaster George Smiley, whose skills were mostly psychological and bureaucratic—an appropriate hero for Le Carré, who claims he spent most of his time in intelligence sitting behind a desk.

In contrast to Le Carré, Ian Fleming came from a life of wealth and privilege (Winston Churchill wrote the obituary for Fleming's father) and had a career in intelligence that wasn't far from the exploits of action hero Bond. In fact, a climactic moment in *Live and Let Die* was inspired by a real-life training exercise, when Fleming had to swim underneath a tanker and attach a mine to it. Fleming worked as assistant to British spymaster Admiral John Godfrey, planning intelligence operations for a commando team named "30 Assault Unit" (30 AU). He later settled in Jamaica in a house he named Goldeneye—after an operation he had planned during World War II.

HAIR OF THE DOG

Bond buffs have ordered their vodka martinis shaken, not stirred, ever since Sean Connery did the same in 1962's *Dr. No*—but they may have been thrown for a loop by the elaborate libation Bond knocked back in 2006's *Casino Royale*. But the recipe for "the Vesper" was taken practically verbatim from the first Bond novel: "Three measures of Gordon's, one of vodka, half a measure of Kina Lillet. Shake it very well until it's ice cold, then add a large thin slice of lemon peel." Later Bond ghostwriter (and legendary drinker) Kingsley Amis remarked that Kina made the Vesper too bitter and recommended Lillet vermouth in its place. And the morning after downing a few Vespers, true Bond fans would no doubt turn to 007's own preferred hangover cure: brandy with club soda and two tablets of phensic (a mixture of aspirin and caffeine).

WORLD'S TOP-EARNING AUTHORS, 2008

Most of them may write "guilty pleasures," but we doubt they feel much guilt about the money they rake in.

Author	Worth (U.S. dollars in millions)
1. J. K. Rowling	$300
2. James Patterson	$50
3. Stephen King	$45
4. Tom Clancy	$35
5. Danielle Steel	$30
6. (tie) John Grisham	$25
6. (tie) Dean Koontz	$25

....

"He loves cooking—he's done the Cordon Bleu exams—and it's great fun to sit with him in the kitchen while he prepares a meal and see that he's as happy as a clam."

—LITERARY AGENT MORT JANKLOW,
ON HANNIBAL LECTOR CREATOR THOMAS HARRIS

....

LEGAL EAGLES

Courtroom-thriller masters John Grisham and Scott Turow really are lawyers (though Grisham is retired), but please don't make them the butt of any lawyer jokes: Both men have used their considerable success and legal skills to do some truly good work. One of Turow's highest-profile cases occurred in 1995 when he represented Alejandro Hernandez, who was ultimately released from death row after serving 11 years for a crime he didn't commit. Grisham has churned out one novel almost every year since 1989 but also serves on the board of The Innocence Project, a national organization dedicated to reforming the criminal justice system and exonerating people falsely convicted of crimes. Ironically, he was sued in 2007 for his nonfiction book *The Innocent Man* (about two men falsely accused of murder) by the attorney who prosecuted the case Grisham described.

ROMANCING THE TOME

For someone who wrote only six novels—and was credited anonymously as "A Lady" on the books' title pages—Jane Austen left her mark not only on romantic literature but on literature in general. Just as Bridget Jones owes a debt of personality to Elizabeth Bennet, so do most characters envisioned in what we today call romance novels. Jane Austen didn't live in an era in which Fitzwilliam Darcy could appear bare chested on the cover of a paperback, but she did lay the groundwork for thousands of bodice rippers to come—and the basis for Fabio's career, we suppose.

Any romance fan also owes a debt of gratitude to Harlequin, the pioneering publisher of bodice rippers everywhere. The 60-year-old Toronto-based company—whose titles spend hundreds of weeks on best-seller lists annually—brought the romance novel to new audiences and popular heights in the early 1970s. Booksellers had shied away from selling the mass-market paperbacks, so Harlequin put the books on shelves in supermarkets and drugstores, where their potential readers were more likely to see them.

TOPPLING THE WALL

When the Berlin Wall fell, Harlequin distributed 720,000 paperbacks to border checkpoints to get an edge on the newly available Eastern European romance readership.

LUSTY LADIES

If romance novelists write fiction, why do their own lives sometimes seem more salacious than their latest plotlines?

Danielle Steel, author of more than 60 novels, is pretty familiar with the *New York Times* best-seller list, appearing on it, with one romantic tome or another, for years at a stretch (381 consecutive weeks, at one point, earning her placement in the *Guinness Book of World Records*.) Married (and divorced) five times—twice to convicted felons—the mother of five (and stepmother to two) has at least a few books' worth of material from her own life.

Steel's scandalous personal life was made only worse by her fame as an author. An unauthorized 1993 biography revealed, among other details, that one of her sons had a different biological father (husband No. 3) than most of the family thought (current husband, No. 4). Steel sued the book's writers futilely, then blamed the stress of the situation on the later failure of that marriage. However, she did get another book out of it—the plot of *Malice* shows how tabloid gossip destroys her characters' happy marriage.

Grace Metalious's novel, *Peyton Place,* which revealed the sex and scandal lurking in the shadows of a fictional New England town, was based on a true story of small-town intrigue and caused some scandals of its own. Metalious based one of *Peyton Place's* seamy secrets on the story of a local New England girl who had killed her father after years of sexual abuse and buried him in a barnyard pen.

After *Peyton Place* was published, Metalious's neighbors and fellow townspeople recognized other similar characters and plots in her melodramatic novel. Tomas Makris, who worked with Metalious's husband at the local school, went so far as to sue the author for libel, claiming the character Michael Kyros was based on him. An out-of-court settlement for $60,000 was agreed to, but later editions of the book had to rename the character—the seductive Michael Kyros was rechristened Michael Rossi.

Nora Roberts, the best-selling author of more than 100 romance novels—and mysteries, under the pseudonym J. D. Robb—partially blames her divorce on the initial fame that came with becoming a writer. In Roberts-like fashion, though, things worked out in the end. She ended up getting married again, to the carpenter who came to build her new bookshelves—presumably to hold the hundreds of best sellers she would later publish.

In an incident that certainly didn't do anything to dissuade critics who think that romance novels are all the same, Nora Roberts accused Janet Dailey—herself the author of more than 90 romance novels—of replicating more than a dozen of Roberts's passages in her work. The plagiarism allegations, which Roberts melodramatically labeled "mind rape," were scattered throughout several of Dailey's novels. The lawsuit was settled out of court in 1998 for an undisclosed sum, and Dailey—a friend of Roberts's before the falling out—said in a statement that the "essentially random and nonpervasive acts of copying are attributable to a psychological problem that I never even suspected I had."

> **THANKS, BUT NO THANKS**
>
> Long before her successful newspaper column was adapted to become the best-selling novel *Bridget Jones's Diary,* Helen Fielding tried her hand at traditional romance writing and was summarily rejected by one of Harlequin's U.K. imprints.

MR. RIGHT

Mr. Romance—a reality show on the Oxygen Network, produced by Gene Simmons (yes, the serpent-tongued bass player from KISS)—sought to find Harlequin's next face (and naked chest) of romance in 2005. New Jersey truck driver Randy Ritchwood won the steamy title. No word on whether Simmons tried to enter himself in the running.

....

"Her books were put down by most critics, but readers would not put down her books."

—*Today* SHOW CRITIC GENE SHALIT
EULOGIZING *VALLEY OF THE DOLLS* (1966)
AUTHOR JACQUELINE SUSANN

....

IT'S CRIMINAL

The great detectives of fiction—Sherlock Holmes, Philip Marlowe, Easy Rawlins—all possess character flaws, from arrogance to alcoholism. Perhaps flaws are necessary for the creators of crime fiction, too. How else would they be able to imagine the devious twists and turns that are so important to their stories?

CRIMINAL MINDSET

Though widely considered a master of horror, Edgar Allan Poe (1809–49) is also credited with the creation of the now ubiquitous "detective story" with his short story, "The Murders in the Rue Morgue" (1841). That investigation into the deaths of a mother and daughter also introduced C. August Dupin—widely considered the first detective in fiction—and the familiar tropes of the unwitting sidekick-narrator and mostly clueless police investigators.

NEVER MORE

It's unlikely that Poe borrowed much from his own life for "Rue Morgue," if only because people in 19th-century America were rarely exposed to straight-razor wielding "Ourang-Outangs" (that's orangutan in our 21st-century vernacular). Much has been written about Poe's own troubles, especially his reported alcoholism. And as a West Point cadet, Poe was court-martialed and charged with gross neglect of duty and disobeying orders. Found guilty on all counts, he was kicked out of the Army in 1831. Poe's personal life also tended toward the nefarious. He married his 13-year-old cousin, Virginia Eliza Clemm, in 1836 (though she was listed as 21 years old on the marriage registration); the 27-year-old Poe was more than double her age.

....

"No doubt you think that you are complimenting me in comparing me to Dupin," he observed. "Now, in my opinion, Dupin was a very inferior fellow."

—SHERLOCK HOLMES,
IN SIR ARTHUR CONAN DOYLE'S *A STUDY IN SCARLET* (1887)

....

NARCOTICS, MY DEAR MAN

Characteristically, Sherlock Holmes thought himself superior to the brilliant Dupin. But his habits leave some doubt in the reader's mind. Sir Arthur Conan Doyle (1859–1930), as narrator Dr. Watson, often wrote of iconic investigator Sherlock Holmes's drug use, especially his injections of "cocaine, a seven percent solution." Watson's response to Holmes's drug use—legal at the time and generally considered harmless—is more prescient than Holmes's sharply honed investigation skills. Dr. Watson describes making valiant efforts to wean Holmes off drugs in the short story "The Adventure of the Missing Three-Quarter" (1904). In the manner of a latter-day Narcotics Anonymous pamphlet, he speaks of how, even off drugs, Holmes's habit "was not dead, but sleeping."

MISQUOTED

Sherlock Holmes's presumed catchphrase, "Elementary, my dear Watson," is not actually uttered by Holmes in any of Conan Doyle's stories. The nearest dialogue is from the short story "The Crooked Man" (1893):

"Excellent!" I cried.

"Elementary," said he.

BLESSING IN DISGUISE?

Actor Alec Guinness claimed that he converted to Catholicism in part because of his experiences playing G. K. Chesterton's (1874–1936) priest-detective Father Brown in the eponymous film.

THE CASE OF THE DISAPPEARING AUTHOR

Agatha Christie's imagination seemed to get the best of her when she abruptly disappeared from her Berkshire, England, home in 1926. Christie (1890–1976), at the time, was reeling from her mother's death and the news that her husband was being unfaithful. For 11 days Christie fans speculated over her disappearance, theorizing that her adulterous husband had murdered her or that she had drowned herself; others conjectured that it was merely a publicity stunt. Sir Arthur Conan Doyle even took one of her gloves to a medium.

Christie, the creator of beloved detectives Miss Marple and Hercule Poirot and the best-selling author of all-time, was found at a health spa. She had registered as South African tourist Teresa Neele (borrowing the surname from her husband's mistress). Perhaps Christie was exacting revenge on her husband, or as more recently theorized, was genuinely in a fugue state—a psychogenic trance. But Christie never explained her disappearance and omitted the episode from her autobiography altogether. Frankly, Miss Marple would never have left the mystery unsolved.

HARD-BOILING OVER

The innovation of mystery-specific pulp magazines in the early 20th century introduced the now familiar—and sometimes cliché—hard-boiled private investigator, which is usually cred-ited to Carroll John Daly. But it was Sam Spade, a creation of Dashiell Hammett (1894–1961) in a serial (1929–30) for *Black Mask,* who became the prototype for the street-savvy, hard-and-shifty private eye. Spade wasn't above sullying himself by sleeping with his partner's wife, but he adhered to his own indistinct yet stringent moral code, as would be the case with some of these later hard-boiled gumshoes:

- Philip Marlowe, introduced to the detective canon by Raymond Chandler, shares many of the characteristics of earlier hardened private investigators, with his enthusiasm for women and whiskey and a tendency toward talking back (for which he was fired from his job with the Los Angeles district attorney). Chandler's own job history was just as colorful—before he began writing short stories for *Black Mask,* he was fired for absenteeism and on-the-job drunkenness from his work as a Los Angeles oil company executive. His first novel, *The Big Sleep* (1939), wasn't published until Chandler was 51 years old.

- Best known for creating Perry Mason, Erle Stanley Gard-ner (under the pseudonym A. A. Fair) also created one of the first female private eyes in the hard-boiled genre, Bertha Cool, in 1939. A 200-pound widow eschewing the Miss Marple tradition for female matron-sleuths, Bertha chain-smoked, drank, used profanity, and generally behaved like her more notorious male counterparts.

- Hoping to earn enough for a down payment on a house, Mickey Spillane (1918–2006) wrote *I, the Jury* (1947) in just three weeks, introducing Mike Hammer—the macho, ultraviolent private dick—to the world. Of all of the hard-boiled gumshoes, Hammer probably racked up the highest body count. In his mind, solving the crime meant eye-for-an-eye justice, carried out by him. In the first five Hammer books alone, 48 people are killed—34 of them by Mike Hammer, in a lurid, sadistic fashion. Unfortunately for fans of graphic violence, Spillane became a Jehovah's Witness in 1951 and didn't write for more than 10 years after that; his later books were said to lack Hammer's signature panache for the art of maiming and killing.

- Matthew Scudder, the ex-NYPD detective created by Lawrence Block (1938–) in 1976, is more flawed than most—he is introduced as an alcoholic who accidentally shot a little girl, quit the police force, and abandoned his family. Though Scudder joins Alcoholics Anonymous in later books, Block himself nominated his character as the most overrated fictional detective when asked by *American Heritage* magazine in 2000:

  I'll tell you, if I were going to hire a private eye, Scudder's the last one I'd pick. He's either drunk or going to AA meetings, which leaves him with precious little time for work. His girlfriend's a hooker, and his best buddy is a career criminal and multiple murderer. And he does weird things: In one book he clears his client of a murder the man really did commit, then frames him for one he didn't have anything to do with. Who in his right mind would have anything to do with a guy like that?

THE SINCEREST FORM OF FLATTERY

Before he created Spenser or Jesse Stone, prolific crime author Robert B. Parker (1932–) wrote his 1971 Ph.D. dissertation on the private detectives depicted by Dashiell Hammett, Raymond Chandler, and Ross Macdonald. Less than two decades later, he published *Poodle Springs* (1989), adapted from an unfinished manuscript of Chandler's, and *Perchance to Dream* (1991), a sequel to Chandler's *The Big Sleep.*

GOOD ADVICE

Western and detective novel author Elmore Leonard (1925–) contributed his rules on writing to the *New York Times* in 2001. His sensible advice included: "Never open a book with weather," and "Never use a verb other than 'said' to carry dialogue" (and never modify said with an adverb). On exclamation points: "No more than two or three per 100,000 words of prose."

....

"The weapon should always be appropriate to the murderer. For example, elderly ladies, however murderous, are unlikely in the U.K. to have access to guns."

—P. D. JAMES

....

THE BAD AND THE UGLY

Of course, even as we appreciate oft-maligned genres and writers, there are some that deserve praise for work that is so very bad that it's good. Endorsed by writers no less esteemed than Aldous Huxley and Mark Twain, Irish writer Amanda McKittrick Ros's texts were so purple, it was as though they had been beaten to a bruising by a bad-writing stick. (And that sentence is in tribute to her.)

KEEP A STRAIGHT FACE

The alliteration-adoring Amanda McKittrick Ros (1860–1939) was so famous for her corpulent prose and poetry that J. R. R. Tolkien and C. S. Lewis competed against each other to see who could read the most without laughing. How bad was it? Read this verse and decide for yourself:

Beneath me here in stinking clumps
Lies Lawyer Largebones, all in lumps;
A rotten mass of clockholed clay,
Which grown more honeycombed each day.
See how the rats have scratched his face?
Now so unlike the human race;
I very much regret I can't
Assist them in their eager 'bent'

Americans can claim one of the world's worst writers as their own, too—one so beloved that independent publishing house McSweeney's in 2005 decided to reprint one of his works, *The Riddle of the Traveling Skull,* just to make the world aware of its sheer awfulness. Often referred to as the Ed Wood of detective fiction, Harry Stephen Keeler (1890–1967) wrote *Traveling Skull* and other titles that practically beg you not to read them: *The Man with the Magic Eardrums, Finger! Finger!*, and *The Case of the Transposed Legs*. Not convinced? Keeler writes in the *The Steeltown Strangler*:

> …We can eat up-town at an air-cooler place—rather half-way deluxe, too, for a town like this—or we can eat at a joint outside the gates where a hundred sweat-encrusted mill-workers, every one with a peeled garlic bean laid alongside his plate, will inhale soup like the roar of 40 Niagras, and crunch victuals like a half-hundred concrete mixers all running at once.

You have to give Keeler a hand for his creativity, though. In *X. Jones, of Scotland Yard,* the main suspect is a killer midget (disguised as a baby, naturally) that stalks his victims in a helicopter. He is known as "the Flying Strangler-Baby."

THE WORST FIRST

In the tradition of "It was a dark and stormy night . . . " the Bulwer-Lytton Fiction Contest, sponsored by San Jose State University has challenged writers to construct the worst possible first sentence for a novel since 1983. Here are some of our favorite winners:

- The lovely woman-child Kaa was mercilessly chained to the cruel post of the warrior-chief Beast, with his barbarous tribe now stacking wood at her nubile feet, when the strong, clear voice of the poetic and heroic Handsomas roared, "Flick your Bic, crisp that chick, and you'll feel my steel through your last meal."
—Steven Garman, Pensacola, Florida (1984)

- The countdown had stalled at T minus 69 seconds when Desiree, the first female ape to go up in space, winked at me

243

slyly and pouted her thick, rubbery lips unmistakably—the first of many such advances during what would prove to be the longest, and most memorable, space voyage of my career. —Martha Simpson, Glastonbury, Connecticut (1985)

• She wasn't really my type, a hard-looking but untalented reporter from the local cat box liner, but the first second that the third-rate representative of the fourth estate cracked open a new fifth of old Scotch, my sixth sense said seventh heaven was as close as an eighth note from Beethoven's Ninth Symphony, so, nervous as a tenth grader drowning in eleventh-hour cramming for a physics exam, I swept her into my longing arms, and, humming "The Twelfth of Never," I got lucky on Friday the thirteenth. —Wm. W. "Buddy" Ocheltree, Port Townsend, Washington (1993)

• Paul Revere had just discovered that someone in Boston was a spy for the British, and when he saw the young woman believed to be the spy's girlfriend in an Italian restaurant he said to the waiter, "Hold the spumoni— I'm going to follow the chick an' catch a Tory." —John L. Ashman, Houston, Texas (1995)

• She resolved to end the love affair with Ramon tonight...summarily, like Martha Stewart ripping the sand vein out of a shrimp's tail...though the term "love affair" now struck her as a ridiculous euphemism...not unlike "sand vein," which is after all an intestine, not a vein...and that tarry substance inside certainly isn't sand...and that brought her back to Ramon. —Dave Zobel, Manhattan Beach, California (2004)

BETTER LEFT UNSAID

Samuel Wesley may have been a clergyman by trade (and his sons John and Charles Wesley would later be credited with founding the Methodist movement), but you can't say that he was a stereotypical dour preacher. At least we hope he wasn't too serious when he composed *Maggots: Poems on Several Subjects, Never Before Addressed* (1685). The collection of poems was so resoundingly bad that for more than a century afterward, certain kinds of terrible writing were referred to as "maggoty." Just how bad was it? Judge for yourself; his poems' titles included:

- "On two Souldiers killing one another for a Groat"

- "A Dialogue, Between Chamber-pot and Frying Pan"

- "On a Supper of a Stinking Ducks"

- "An Anacreontique on a Pair of Breeches"

- "A Tame Snake, left in a Box of Bran"

- "A Pindarique, on the Grunting of a Hog"

LIKE PULLING TEETH

Referred to in his day as the "poet laureate of dentistry," Solyman Brown published "Dentalogia, a Poem on the Diseases of the Teeth," in 1833. Perhaps the only epic poem on the subject of dental hygiene, the surprisingly well-received volume was 54 pages long.

YOUNG AT HEART

From Winnie the Pooh to Nancy Drew, your favorite children's characters—and their creators—were often more complex than they seemed. Which universally beloved writer and illustrator moonlighted as a propagandist for the U.S. Army? Which renowned "authors" were really pseudonyms for a virtual army of anonymous writers? Which fairy tale originally ended not with a happily-ever-after wedding but with a 300-year curse on a dead girl? Revisit some of those old favorites that you thought you knew from cover to cover.

GRUESOMELY EVER AFTER

If you've ever revisited one of your favorite childhood stories as an adult, you've probably noticed that the story seems...different. (We're looking at you, *The Lorax!*) There are nuances you missed as a child, details you've forgotten, and things that just may not have been in the edition you owned back then.

This is especially true with traditional stories that are adapted year after year: Sometimes the stories change to match shifting generational attitudes, and other times they are simplified to keep an animated feature film under 90 minutes long. These bowdlerized adaptations are so ubiquitous that the original versions of some of the world's most cherished children's tales, such as *Snow White* and *Cinderella,* are completely unfamiliar—and more disturbing—than you might ever imagine.

THE BROTHERS GRIMM

Brothers Jacob (1785–1863) and Wilhelm (1786–1859) Grimm created collections of popular European myths, legends, and folklore in their native German. Their volumes of fairy tales introduced characters that became familiar to children in every subsequent generation. Many of their stories were later adapted to animated films, from *Snow White* to *Hansel and Gretel,* but the Grimms' stories have more in common with modern horror films than Disney cartoons.

> *Snow White:* The Grimms' version is full of twisted detail. Snow White is exiled by her evil stepmother, the Queen, who commands a hunter to kill Snow White and bring her heart back as proof. Taking pity on her, the hunter brings the Queen the heart of a bear instead—which she

eats. The Queen is repaid violently at the end of the tale, when she is forced to dance in red-hot iron slippers until she dies.

Cinderella: The cruel stepsisters—who cut off parts of their own feet in an attempt to trick the prince and fit into the golden (that's right: golden, not glass) slipper—are gruesomely killed at Cinderella's wedding. In a different Grimm edition, they are allowed to live…but charmed pigeons use their beaks to poke out the sisters' eyes, cursing them with blindness.

Rumpelstiltskin: After his plot is foiled, the title character stomps his foot on the ground in a fit of rage, burying his body up to his waist. When he tries to extricate himself, he tears himself in half.

THE OTHERS GRIM

The Grimms' grim imaginings aside, there are a lot of other dark stories out there—tales that many parents would think twice about reading to their children before bedtime.

Pinocchio: This story was first imagined in Carlo Collodi's (1826–90) *The Adventures of Pinocchio* (1883). Most remember the animated Disney feature best, with the delightful Jiminy Cricket, some darkness inside the belly of a whale, and its pro-truth (and anti-big-nose) morality. Collodi's fairy tale, on the other hand, opens with Pinocchio yelping in pain as he's being carved and sanded. He then proceeds to get Geppetto arrested and kills the talking cricket by throwing a hammer at it—all by the end of Chapter 4.

The Little Mermaid: Hans Christian Andersen (1805–75) also had an aversion to the "happily ever after." The Disney adaptation of *The Little Mermaid* was wrapped up with a happy ending, but in Andersen's 1837 version, the little mermaid is forced to watch the prince she loves marry another woman. The sea witch gives her a choice: Stab the prince to death in his sleep or die herself. So, logically, she throws her now-finless self into the sea and, in keeping with the Victorian-era moralizing of so many contemporary fairy tales, will eventually be able to earn her soul back by doing good deeds for 300 years. Maybe.

THE KID-GLOVE TREATMENT

Nathaniel Hawthorne's *The Scarlet Letter* is usually not assigned to students until they are old enough to understand what exactly that scarlet "A" stands for. But 19th-century readers were introduced to Hawthorne at much younger ages—not via bowdlerized (see page 203) editions of *The House of Seven Gables* or *The Scarlet Letter,* but in a handful of children's books, which he wrote both before and after his successful novels were published. Several of the books retold Greek myths and legends in the voice of a young college student entertaining his cousins; another tells the childhood stories of notable figures such as Isaac Newton, Benjamin Franklin, and Oliver Cromwell. Though Hawthorne tried not to, in his words, "write downward" to children, the themes of his children's books were quite different. As Hawthorne wrote in the introduction to his *Biographical Stories for Children,* "The author regards children as sacred, and would not, for the world, cast anything into the fountain of a young heart that might imbitter [sic] and pollute its waters."

SHORT BUT NOT SO SWEET

Of course, traditional children's reading material isn't always a complete story—sometimes it's just a few verses. *Mother Goose's Melodies* (published in the United States in various editions by the early 19th century) catalogued familiar nursery rhymes with origins reaching back hundreds of years.

Those origins weren't necessarily pretty, no matter how catchy the sing-song rhyme scheme or how adorable the accompanying pantomime. The theory that "Ring a Ring o' Roses" (or "Ring Around the Rosie") was about the bubonic plague has been debunked by many historians, but many "innocent" rhymes really were inspired by sordid or grotesque events in history. If you're reading a rhyme for the umpteenth time, it's more fun to imagine that some of the content may not be suitable for minor children.

"Mary, Mary, Quite Contrary"
Mary, Mary, quite contrary,
How does your garden grow?
With silver bells and cockleshells
And pretty maids all in a row.

"Mary" is thought to be Bloody Mary (Queen Mary I), who executed hundreds of Protestant dissenters. The "silver bells and cockleshells" are thought to be implements of torture: thumbscrews and genital clamps. And those pretty maids? Probably a reference to the "Scottish maiden," an early guillotine.

"Georgie Porgie"
Georgie Porgie pudding and pie
Kissed the girls and made them cry
When the boys came out to play
Georgie Porgie ran away.

More royal hijinks: Historians believe that "Georgie" refers to George Villiers, First Duke of Buckingham and rumored homosexual, whom King James I honored as "Gentleman of the Bedchamber" until a disapproving Parliament "came out to play."

"Jack and Jill"
Jack and Jill went up the hill
To fetch a pail of water.
Jack fell down and broke his crown,
And Jill came tumbling after.

These origins are quite disputed, but one hypothesis is that "Jack and Jill" refers to King Louis XVI and his wife, Marie Antoinette. The guillotine undoubtedly broke Louis XVI's crown (and Marie Antoinette's shortly thereafter).

LIONS AND TIGERS AND BEARS (OH MY!)

Furry and feathered friends have always had a place in our favorite stories. For every Alice (in Wonderland) and Dorothy (of Kansas), there's a Cheshire Cat or a Toto. These mostly four-legged creatures have many of the same quirks as their two-legged counterparts in fiction, but the idea of a toad driving a motorcar or a monkey taking the subway to his job as a window washer is somehow infinitely more appealing.

Most writers didn't just pull their anthropomorphized creatures out of thin air. Some of their real-life inspirations almost served in World War I, some were born out of annoyance with older relatives, and some were based on the author's own children.

EXOTIC LEADING CREATURES

Some Pig: E. B. White may often be remembered as a cosmopolitan *New Yorker* writer, but his children's books showed an affinity for the animal kingdom that went beyond the Central Park Zoo. Most fans of the original porcine leading man, Wilbur in *Charlotte's Web* (1952), believe that the tale was in part a natural continuation of White's 1948 essay "Death of a Pig." White had tried, unsuccessfully, to save a pig (originally purchased to be eaten) from an illness. "I found myself cast suddenly in the role of pig's friend and physician—a farcical character with an enema bag for a prop," he wrote. The pig didn't make it to White's dinner table that winter.

Monkey See, Monkey Do: H. A. (Hans Augusto) Rey and Margret Rey, both German-born Jews, married in Brazil in 1935 and sailed to Europe for a honeymoon, bringing their two pet marmoset monkeys along with them. Unfortunately, the sweaters Margret had knit for the simian twosome were not warm enough, and they died during the voyage. The Reys settled in Paris and signed a contract in 1939 with a French publisher for *The Adventures of Fifi*—a book about a troublemaking monkey. With the manuscript, they escaped wartime Paris ahead of approaching Nazi soldiers and sailed to New York in 1940. There "Fifi" became "Curious George": The American publisher believed that no mischievous male monkey should be named Fifi.

A PARTICULARLY PORCINE PROBLEM

William Steig used lots of anthropomorphized animals in his children's books, which included *Shrek!* (1990) and *Doctor De Soto* (1982)—the latter about a mouse-dentist who treats (and tricks) a fox with a toothache. But another animal selection landed him in hot water in 1970, when he was boycotted by the International Conference of Police Associations because his book *Sylvester and the Magic Pebble* (1969) depicted police officers as pigs.

Grin and Bear It: Winnie—short for Winnipeg—the Pooh was a brave Canadian soldier, of sorts, during World War I. Purchased for $20, the black bear cub was adopted as a mascot by a Canadian infantry brigade and traveled with the soldiers to England. While the infantry was fighting in mainland Europe, Winnie was left in the London Zoo, where he became a favorite attraction. One of his frequent visitors was A. A. Milne's son, Christopher Robin Milne. Christopher Robin's interactions with his toys—which included a teddy bear, a tiger, a pig, a baby kangaroo, and a donkey with no tail—became the basis for Milne's stories.

A Monster in the Family: Maurice Sendak had intended to create wild horses for a new book, originally titled *Where the Wild Horses Are.* But he quickly became frustrated with how difficult horses were to draw. So he began drawing monsters—griffins, gargoyles, and other creatures. But the monsters became satisfying to him only when he turned them into caricatures of his uncles and aunts, whom he so disliked as a child, because "they were rude, and because they ruined every Sunday, and because they ate all our food."

Toad in a Hole: The inspiration for Disneyland's "Mr. Toad's Wild Ride" attraction, Toad of Toad Hall in *Wind in the Willows* (1908), came out of a series of letters that author Kenneth Grahame wrote to his son Alastair, who was possibly as unruly as Toad. Alastair was a disobedient child, known to attack other children in London's Kensington Gardens or to lie down in front of traffic, forcing cars to stop.

FINDING INSPIRATION IN DARKNESS

The Dementors introduced in *Harry Potter and the Prisoner of Azkaban* (1999)—hooded creatures that feed on human happiness—were inspired by J. K. Rowling's bout with clinical depression following the birth of her daughter.

Not So Cuddly Bunny: With his wife, Debbie, James Howe began writing *Bunnicula*—the story of a stealthy, vegetarian vampire rabbit—in the late 1970s. The couple was inspired by their longtime devotion to vampire movies on late-night TV, which they considered more silly than scary. "It came from asking the question, what's the silliest, least likely vampire I can imagine?" Howe said.

IT'S RAINING CATS AND DOGS (AND OTHER PETS AND PESTS)

A miscellany of tidbits about our most beloved—or loathed—animal characters and their creators.

Clifford the Big Red Dog (1963), Norman Bridwell	Named after Bridwell's wife's childhood imaginary friend, Clifford was imagined as a giant dog like the one Bridwell himself had wanted as a child (he wanted to be able to ride it).
The Incredible Journey (1961), Sheila Burnford	Burnford didn't intend for her story to become a children's book; her animals don't speak. A human narrator follows two dogs and a Siamese cat (who hates cats) on their trip through northwestern Ontario in search of their masters.
The Cat in the Hat (1957), Dr. Seuss	Dr. Seuss (Theodor Geisel) was attempting to create a book that would be accessible to beginning readers. He whittled a list of 400 early vocabulary words down to 223, adding 13 additional words. "Cat" and "Hat" were the first two rhyming words on the list.
The Poky Little Puppy (1942), Gustaf Tenggren, illustrator	One of the first Little Golden Books, *The Poky Little Puppy* is one of the best-selling children's picture books of all time. Tenggren was also a successful animator who had worked on Disney classics such as *Bambi*, *Snow White and the Seven Dwarfs*, and *Fantasia*.

....

"She will probably be played by a boy, if one
clever enough can be found, and must never be
on two legs except on those rare occasions when
an ordinary nurse would be on four."

—J. M. Barrie (Stage direction for Nana,
the Darlings' nursemaid, in *Peter Pan*)

....

BACK IN THE USSR

Robert McCloskey's Caldecott award–winning *Make Way for Ducklings* (1941) chronicled the march of Mrs. Mallard and her eight ducklings from their birthplace, an island in Boston's Charles River, to their new home in Boston's Public Garden, assisted by kindly police officers. (McCloskey's duckling illustrations owed their realism to six live duckling models he had living in his studio at the time.) Mrs. Mallard and the ducklings made the move to the Public Garden permanent when they were immortalized in bronze on cobblestones by sculptor Nancy Schön in a life-sized statue installed there in 1987.

A replica of the "Ducklings" statue also played a minor role in ending the cold war. On the occasion of the START treaty signing in 1991, Barbara Bush presented the statue to Raisa Gorbachev as a gift "given in love and friendship to the children of the Soviet Union, on behalf of the children of the United States."

TELL ME A STORY

Many "children's" authors didn't *always* limit themselves to writing at a fifth-grade reading level. Whether they were writing songs about venereal disease, illustrating manuals for orgasmic-energy machines, or penning tales about murderous, meat-wielding wives, one thing is for certain: Some of your favorite children's authors churned out plenty of work that is not for underaged eyes.

SISTER, CAN YOU SPARE A DIME?

Louisa May Alcott (1832–88) first began making money as a writer by publishing stories in magazines and newspapers—much like her fictional *Little Women* counterpart, Jo March—though none of the publication titles were so cuttingly named as March's *Daily Volcano.* Alcott's stories were as full of wily heroines, sexual intrigue, and pure evil as the era allowed. These tall tales were published anonymously, but dozens of stories are attributed to her now. "Pauline's Passion and Punishment," "Behind a Mask, or A Woman's Power," and "Betrayed by a Buckle," among others, bear witness to the purplish prose that put food on her family's table during their lean years. (Her transcendentalist-philosopher father had once returned from a long lecture tour with a mere dollar in earnings.) In her own words, Alcott was "the goose that laid the golden egg," but she was curiously as contemptuous of her best-selling novels as she was of the thrillers, calling *Little Women* "moral pap for the young."

ALTERNATIVE ENERGY

Shrek! creator William Steig (1907–2003) may be remembered best for his children's books, but he didn't even start illustrating for children until he was in his 60s. Steig was a well-known *New Yorker* cartoonist for years and, later in life, said that he turned to children's books only to avoid having to supplement his income by drawing advertisements. Steig's strangest illustrations, though, are probably those found in psychoanalyst Wilhelm Reich's *Listen, Little Man!* Reich was the creator of "orgone therapy," which promised to harness orgasmic energy. Steig was a great believer in Reich's theories and even dedicated a book to him; he sat in his orgone box—a telephone booth–like structure made of cardboard, wire, and metal—daily for most of his life.

IN THE ARMY NOW

Readers of Dr. Seuss's work (or, more accurately, their parents) have long identified political allegory in his children's books, from *How the Grinch Stole Christmas* (materialism) to *The Butter Battle Book* (nuclear proliferation). It's probably no surprise to those on-the-ball readers that Theodor Geisel also penned political cartoons in the years surrounding World War II—and spent several years during the war making propaganda films for the U.S. Army.

SHEL SHOCKED

Shel Silverstein (1932–99) fans usually cite his poetry collections, *Where the Sidewalk Ends* and *A Light in the Attic,* or his children's story, *The Giving Tree,* as favorites. But only a superfan would know to read those books while listening to Johnny Cash sing "A Boy Named Sue"—the song for which Silverstein won a songwriting Grammy. Silverstein also wrote other popular songs, including "The Cover of the Rolling Stone" and "Don't Give a Dose to the One You Love the Most" (a song about venereal disease) for Dr. Hook & the Medicine

Show. Silverstein's randiness wasn't limited to songwriting either: His illustrations have appeared in *Playboy* and his "Buy One, Get One Free," a short-sketch play, featured two prostitutes making their sales pitch entirely in rhyme.

RATED R

Long before the success of *Charlie and the Chocolate Factory* (1964), Roald Dahl's earliest writing appeared in the pages of *Playboy* and in other adult magazines. In fact, Dahl didn't even begin writing for children until he had children of his own to write for. From the twisted title story in *Switch Bitch* to "Lamb to the Slaughter"—a tale about a woman who kills her husband by beating him with a frozen leg of lamb, which she then serves to the detectives that come to investigate—Dahl's short stories are definitely not anything you'd read to a child before bedtime, unless you were trying to give him nightmares.

....

"I'm probably more pleased with my children's books than with my adult short stories. Children's books are harder to write. It's tougher to keep a child interested, because a child doesn't have the concentration of an adult. A child knows the television is in the next room. It's tough to hold a child, but it's a lovely thing to try to do."

—ROALD DAHL

....

....

*"You cannot write for children ... They're much too
complicated. You can only write books that are of
interest to them."*

—MAURICE SENDAK

....

LONGSTOCKING LAWS

Astrid Lindgren's (1907–2002) free-spirited Pippi Longstocking (Pippilotta Delicatessa Windowshade Mackrelmint Efraim's
Daughter Longstocking, to be exact) may have thought Lindgren
became a little too serious in later years. The Swedish writer
sparked controversy in 1976 when a newspaper published her
satirical adult fairy tale "Pomperipossa in the World of Money."
The story protested the marginal tax rate for self-employed artists,
which had ballooned to an impossible-seeming 102 percent (the
artist was required to pay payroll taxes and employer's fees). She
also wielded her pen as a political sword in protest of the treatment of farm animals: "Every pig is entitled to a happy pig life,"
said Lindgren in an open letter to the prime minister, published
in major Swedish newspapers. A law that ensured farm animals
were treated humanely was passed in Sweden in 1988; it was
informally named after Lindgren.

HEAL THYSELF

Generations of children will always remember Judith Viorst
(1931–) as the author of *Alexander and the Terrible, Horrible,
No Good, Very Bad Day*—which she based on her own sons.

But Viorst, a research graduate in psychology, also wrote poetry and nonfiction books—mostly of the self-help variety. In fact, one of her children's books, *The Tenth Good Thing About Barney,* which deals with getting over the death of a pet, could be said to be part of a children's self-help genre if (shudder) there were such a thing.

PART-TIME AUTHOR

The first time he ever wrote a book for children, Sherman Alexie (1966–) won the National Book Award (2007) for young people's literature. In the semiautobiographical novel *The Absolutely True Diary of a Part-Time Indian,* Alexie wrote about his decision to attend an off-reservation high school, where "he was the only Indian, except for the school mascot." Alexie's other writing, including poetry, short stories, and the celebrated independent film *Smoke Signals,* may also have won him awards, but Alexie was most gratified by the response to *Part-Time Indian,* saying of his book tour, "The response from the road is larger than anything in my career. My wife and I are calling it the hug-and-run tour. People are coming up in tears, and hugging me and running. There is no jaded literary response among the audience. It's so validating."

....

"When I was a kid, I would much rather have been a good baseball player or a hit with the girls. But I couldn't play ball. I couldn't dance. So I started to draw and to write."

—SHEL SILVERSTEIN

....

PARENTAL GUIDANCE SUGGESTED

Reading is a good thing for kids, right? Books introduce knowledge and light and new perspectives that open the eyes of our little ones…don't they?

To some, books look more like a threat, chock-full of smut and subversive ideas. The presence of many, many children's books and young adult novels in libraries and classrooms are challenged each year by individuals and parent organizations. If you're thinking that only the worst, most age-inappropriate titles are ever questioned, think again: Even those long-deemed classics by teachers and young readers alike have been thrown off of curricula and plucked from library shelves in towns across North America.

CRITICAL MASS

The Adventures of Huckleberry Finn (1884): No less a writer than Ernest Hemingway flatters Mark Twain's novel as the font of more than a century of literature. But despite its early and frequent placement on English class reading lists, *The Adventures of Huckleberry Finn* may be as talked about outside of classrooms as in them. In a letter written the year after his book's publication, Mark Twain (b. Samuel Clemens, 1835–1910) wrote, "The Committee of the Public Library of Concord, Mass., have given us a rattling tip-top puff which will go into every paper in the country. They have expelled Huck from their library as 'trash and suitable only for the slums.' That will sell 25,000 copies for us sure."

The leading target of literary censorship efforts everywhere, *Huck* remains controversial to this day, mostly due to the language—in keeping with the age—of its racial references. As recently as 2007, it was challenged in schools in Minnesota, Texas, and Connecticut, the latter "because the 'N' word is used in the book 212 times." Let's just hope that they didn't make a student do the counting.

....

"All modern American literature comes from one book by Mark Twain called Huckleberry Finn.... *American writing comes from that. There was nothing before. There has been nothing as good since."*

—ERNEST HEMINGWAY

....

The Catcher in the Rye (1952): J. D. Salinger's young adult classic is another challenged list mainstay. Alienated antihero Holden Caulfield quickly found a place on high school reading lists and just as quickly found his placement challenged by those he would undoubtedly deem phonies. Complaints against the book ranged from antiwhite and obscene in Selinsgrove, PA, in 1975, to violations of the Morris, Manitoba, school libraries' guidelines regarding "excess vulgar language, sexual scenes, things concerning moral issues, excessive violence, and anything dealing with the occult" in 1982. Poor Holden found himself expelled, yet again.

Judy Blume: *Huckleberry Finn* may have the record for longest-running on the banned/challenged books list, but Twain isn't the most-banned author. That dubious honor probably goes to Judy Blume (1938–), who took up five slots (out of 100) on the American Library Association's most recent ranking of banned or challenged books. The *Are You There God? It's Me, Margaret* author has responded to critics by becoming active in anticensorship organizations. In 1999 she published *Places I Never Meant to Be*, a volume of short stories by other well-known children's authors who had seen their work removed from library and classroom shelves, including Katherine Paterson (*Bridge to Terabithia*), Walter Dean Myers (*Fallen Angels*), and Paul Zindel (*The Pigman*).

That same year Blume also rose to defend *Harry Potter* author J. K. Rowling against rising calls for boycotts of the series and upcoming films in a *New York Times* editorial, writing, "At the rate we're going, I can imagine next year's headline: '*Goodnight Moon* Banned for Encouraging Children to Communicate with Furniture.' And we all know where that can lead, don't we?"

PHOTO FINISHED

Judy Blume's jest about Margaret Wise Brown's bedtime classic *Goodnight Moon* (1947) wasn't entirely off the mark. In 2005, Harper Collins made a small but significant change to the book to stop it from sending a potentially "harmful message" to kids. The change? The publisher digitally altered a back-cover photograph of illustrator Clement Hurd—to remove a cigarette that had dangled between his fingers for nearly 60 years.

READ AT YOUR OWN RISK

What's all the fuss about? Here's why some concerned citizens wanted to ban classic books.

Brave New World
(1932), Aldous Huxley

Makes promiscuous sex "look like fun" (1980); centers "around negative activity" and opposes the health curriculum (1993); contains "orgies, self-flogging, suicide" and characters with "contempt for religion, marriage, and the family" (2000).

Of Mice and Men
(1937), John Steinbeck

"Steinbeck is known to have had an antibusiness attitude" and "he was very questionable as to his patriotism" (1989); contains "profane language, moral statement, treatment of the retarded, and the violent ending" (1993); "takes God's name in vain 15 times and uses Jesus's name lightly" (1998).

Lord of the Flies
(1954), William Golding

Is "demoralizing inasmuch as it implies that man is little more than an animal" (1981).

To Kill a Mockingbird
(1960), Harper Lee

Contains the words damn and whore lady (1977), "profanity and racial slurs" (1985); causes "psychological damages to the positive integration process" and "represents institutionalized racism under the guise of good literature" (1981).

**One Flew Over the
Cuckoo's Nest**
(1962), Ken Kesey

"Glorifies criminal activity, has a tendency to corrupt juveniles and contains descriptions of bestiality, bizarre violence, and torture, dismemberment, death, and human elimination" (1974).

Slaughterhouse-Five
(1969), Kurt Vonnegut

Contains "foul language, a section depicting a picture of an act of bestiality, a reference to 'Magic Fingers' attached to the protagonist's bed to help him sleep, and the sentence: 'The gun made a ripping sound like the opening of the fly of God Almighty'" (1985).

In the Night Kitchen
(1970), Maurice Sendak

"The little boy pictured did not have any clothes on and it pictured his private area" (1994) so the book "could lay the foundation for future use of pornography."

The Golden Compass (1995), Philip Pullman	The main character drinks wine and ingests poppy with her meals (Kentucky, 2007); the trilogy is "written by an atheist where the characters and text are anti-God, anti-Catholic, and antireligion" (Ontario, 2007).

NEWS FLASH: SATAN LOVES HARRY POTTER!

Many of the most zealous *Harry Potter* critics have been fooled by a bizarre story, spread via email, message boards, and blogs, that originated in the satirical newspaper *The Onion*—but was passed around by church and parents' groups who mistook it for factual journalism. The article, *"Harry Potter* Books Spark Rise in Satanism Among Children" appeared just after the fourth volume in the series was published, and contained the publication's signature tongue-in-cheek, AP-style news parody:

> "Harry is an absolute godsend to our cause," said High Priest Egan of the First Church of Satan in Salem, MA. "An organization like ours thrives on new blood—no pun intended—and we've had more applicants than we can handle lately. And, of course, practically all of them are virgins, which is gravy."

....

> *"You have got to be very careful of banning. What you ban is not going to hurt anybody, usually. But the act of banning is."*
>
> —MADELEINE L'ENGLE (1918–2007)

....

PARENTAL ADVISORY

After being challenged over its antireligious themes, *The Golden Compass,* the first book in Philip Pullman's frequently challenged His Dark Materials trilogy (see page 101), was allowed to remain in the libraries of a publicly funded Catholic school district in Mississauga, Ontario, in 2008—but with a disclaimer. The district added a sticker to the inside cover of each book, which warned readers that "representations of the church in this novel are purely fictional and are not reflective of the real Roman Catholic Church or the Gospel of Jesus Christ."

TREE'ED OFF

Dr. Seuss (Theodor Geisel) was challenged in Laytonville, CA—redwood territory—in 1989, after logging-equipment wholesaler Bill Bailey's second-grader "came home and labeled [him] a criminal" after reading *The Lorax.* Local residents began buying ads in the local paper in protest, one of which read, "To teach our children that harvesting redwood trees is bad is not the education we need."

> *"Censorship is telling a man he can't have a steak just because a baby can't chew it."*
>
> —MARK TWAIN

NANCY DREW AND HER MANY MOMMIES

Ever read anything by Mildred Wirt Benson? Harriet Stratemeyer Adams? If you ever read any of Carolyn Keene's original Nancy Drew novels, you likely have: Adams and Benson were the primary authors behind the pseudonymous Carolyn Keene. The not-so-hidden dirty secret behind many children's books is that the author listed on the front cover—even if he or she actually exists—may not have written a word of what the reader finds inside. Whether you grew up on Tom Swift and the Bobbsey Twins or the Baby-Sitters' Club and Fear Street, the series stayed the same, but the author rarely did.

The Stratemeyer Syndicate perfected the process of the ghostwritten children's series in the early 20th century. Syndicate creator Edward Stratemeyer—who shied away from the idea that children's books necessarily had to contain moral instruction—began publishing the Rover Boys series in 1899, followed by Tom Swift and the Bobbsey Twins. The process of creating the books evolved into an assembly line process, in which Stratemeyer himself (or someone else at the syndicate) would outline the basic story and pass it off to a ghostwriter for development. To maintain the appearance that each book was written by the same author, Stratemeyer chose a pen name when he created a new series.

Canadian author Leslie McFarlane is thought to have been primarily responsible for turning the idea of the Hardy Boys into the behemoth detective series it was to become, writing at least 20 of the first 25 books credited to Franklin W. Dixon. McFarlane was initially contracted for the first three books in the series, which were to be released all at once, in keeping with Stratemeyer's "breeder" theory: A new series always launched the first three books at the same time (a practice many book packagers continue to this day). Hence, the characterizations in the original series, such as the lovably tough Aunt Gertrude and the clumsy prankster Chet Morton, were all creations of McFarlane. McFarlane, who would go on to work on the TV show *Bonanza* and create more than 50 films for Canada's National Film Board, was paid as little as $85 per book and no more than $165.

EVERYTHING OLD IS NEW AGAIN

Of course, even a beloved series loses its relevance over time. The Hardy Boys books were first given heavy revisions in 1959 to remove dated references to "roadsters" and racially insensitive language and stereotypes. Nancy Drew also received a number of makeovers through the years, as her hair went from blond to "titian"—initially the result of a printer's color error on the cover—to strawberry blond.

Then-syndicate boss and sometime Nancy Drew author Harriet Stratemeyer Adams chafed under the publisher's revision requests, which took place over 20 years beginning in 1959, often writing defensively to Grosset and Dunlap editor Anne Hagan. According to Nancy Drew scholar Jennifer Fisher, Harriet did not find the following comments to be "top-quality editing":

> "Ned is doltish," "McGinnis sounds like a dumb cop," "This is icky," "Nancy sounds like a nasty female." Harriet pondered, "Anne, are your remarks intended to mend story holes or do you get some sadistic fun out of downgrading and offending me? It will take me a long time to live down the remark, 'Nancy sounds like a nasty female.'"

SWEET VALLEY'S TUMMY-TUCK

The Sweet Valley High series, starring identical twins Jessica and Elizabeth Wakefield, was given a 21st-century revamp of its own, complete with references to texting and Internet dating. No word yet on whether they'll update the insane plots to make them more in touch with reality, too.

Old Sweet Valley High (c. 1983)	New Sweet Valley High (c. 2008)
Elizabeth and Jessica share a Fiat convertible	The twins tool around in a red Jeep Wrangler
The twins have "perfect size 6 figures"	Elizabeth and Jessica shrunk down to a size 4
Elizabeth writes the "Eyes and Ears" gossip column in the SVH newspaper *The Oracle*	Elizabeth edits the school newspaper website and has a secret blog
Student band "The Droids" plays school dances	"The Droids" are now "Valley of Death"
Attractive boys described as "handsome"	At least two mentions of boys being "Abercrombie-hot"

A "GHOST" NO LONGER

In his salad days, acclaimed fiction writer Tom Perrotta *(Election, Little Children)* was a ghostwriter for R. L. Stine's Fear Street series.

STRANGER THAN FICTION

Sometimes the truth really is strange—and supposedly true stories often turn out to have more than a dash of fiction in the mix. Here we present the true stories behind the most memorable literary hoaxes of all time; surprising facts about memoirists who claim to lay it all on the line; tantalizing private thoughts from the diaries and correspondence of great writers; and essential information about books that truly changed the world.

THE LONG CON

If you're an avid reader (and if you're not, what are you doing here?), you probably know at least a little bit about James Frey—the gritty, compelling, once-Oprah-beloved memoirist—whose down-and-dirty *A Million Little Pieces* turned out to be filled with a million little lies. Frey's fiasco looms large in recent publishing history, but he's far from the first (or the worst) perpetrator of nonfiction fraud. Here we present a rogues' gallery of literary liars through the ages.

WHEN FRAUD IS ALL IN THE FAMILY

Less widely known but far stranger than Frey's debacle is the tale of J. T. LeRoy, whose first published book (*Sarah,* 1999) presented the supposedly semi-autobiographical story of a teen boy whose mother had pimped him as a cross-dressing prostitute at truck stops across America. A cult following had been building around LeRoy for years, but he never appeared in public, and even his agent and editors never met him in person: Interviews were conducted over the phone, and public readings of his work were performed by other people. After *Sarah* hit the shelves, LeRoy started making public appearances, albeit disguised in wigs, hats, and sunglasses—supposedly to help him cope with the near-crippling shyness and insecurity caused by his damaged youth.

But a 2006 *New York Times* exposé (triggered by, of all things, a LeRoy-penned travel story about Disneyland Paris for the *Times'* travel supplement) revealed the bizarre truth: The 25-year-old LeRoy's works were actually written by 40-year-old musician Laura Albert, who had also given all of LeRoy's phone interviews; LeRoy was played in person by Savannah Knoop, the half-sister of

Albert's partner, with Albert always standing nearby pretending to be "Emily," LeRoy's close friend and "outreach worker."

A THOUSAND LITTLE REFUNDS

Despite the controversy over *A Million Little Pieces,* only 1,729 people sought reimbursement for their purchase of Frey's memoir—a total of $27,348 out of the $2.35 million fund created to cover costs related to a class-action lawsuit.

THE (MIS)EDUCATION OF LITTLE TREE

• Forest "Little Tree" Carter's *The Education of Little Tree* (1976) is the inspiring story of a slice of the author's childhood: raised by his Cherokee grandparents, taught a variety of simple lessons about the world and Indian culture, forced into an orphanage where he confronts racism against his people, and eventually rescued. The book sold millions of copies and won the first American Booksellers Association Book of the Year (ABBY) award in 1991—and soon thereafter was proved to be a disturbing fraud. Not only was "Little Tree" Carter a fictional creation, but the true author, Asa Earl Carter, was a former Ku Klux Klan member who had penned Alabama governor George Wallace's hateful speech calling for "Segregation today! Segregation tomorrow! Segregation forever!"

• Some eight years after the truth about *Little Tree* was revealed, another breakout Native American author, known as Nasdijj, appeared in the pages of *Esquire* with the heartrending story of his adopted son, who suffered from fetal alcohol syndrome. The story was a finalist for a National Magazine Award and catapulted Nasdijj to instant literary fame: He wrote three critically acclaimed memoirs over the next five years—but then critics started to notice cultural anachronisms and hints that Nasdijj had cribbed portions of his books from other writers. The writer was eventually unmasked by *LA Weekly* as Lansing, Michigan, native Tim Barrus, previously an author of gay sadomasochistic fiction and coiner of the term leather lit.

- Margaret B. Jones, a half-Native American foster child, claimed to have grown up on the streets of L.A.'s South Central neighborhood and run with the Bloods. Her memoir, *Love and Consequences* (2008) scored a favorable *New York Times* review and a profile in the paper's Home & Garden section—which prompted her sister to call her publisher less than a week later, revealing the truth: Jones was really Margaret Seltzer, a thoroughly white girl who had grown up in upper-class Sherman Oaks, California.

CLOSE ENCOUNTERS OF THE FALSE KIND

Did you know that much modern computer and telecommunications equipment was made possible by alien technology recovered from a 1947 UFO crash near Roswell, New Mexico? Well, then, you must have read retired Army Col. Philip J. Corso's *The Day After Roswell* (1998), which purported to expose long-hidden government secrets about just such an incident. None of it was true, of course, but Corso's military credentials were enough to elicit a complimentary book blurb and foreword from Sen. Strom Thurmond—who thought the book was a straightforward memoir but promptly retracted his foreword when he discovered it was a preposterous story about little green men.

IS IT A "LITERARY" HOAX IF THEY NEVER WROTE THE BOOK?

In 1970, novelist Clifford Irving decided to pitch a biography of reclusive billionaire (and milk-bottle enthusiast) Howard Hughes—despite the fact that Irving had never met the man and had no prospect of doing so. But Irving hooked up with fellow writer Richard Suskind to forge interviews and documents with Hughes's signature and won a $750,000 advance for the project. The book failed to appear, and even Hughes emerged from hiding to condemn the writers, who served jail time.

HOLOCAUST HOAXES

To Thine Own Self Be True: In 1995, *Fragments: Memories of a Wartime Childhood* was published to near-universal acclaim. Binjamin Wilkomirski spilled out a heartrending tale: He was a Latvian Jew whose parents were killed in World War II, leaving him to serve out the rest of the war enduring the horrors of Polish concentration camps— followed by the added indignity of a postwar adoptive family that tried to suppress his memories and change his identity. Published in 12 languages, the book won a 1996 National Jewish Book Award, among others, and Wilkomirski established himself as a respected expert on the Holocaust. By 2000, however, Wilkomirski's story had been thoroughly debunked: He wasn't Jewish *or* Latvian . . . and had never been in a Nazi death camp; he was born Bruno Grosjean to an unwed mother in 1941, placed in an orphanage, and in 1945 adopted by a well-to-do Swiss family—who left him a substantial inheritance in 1986. Yet Wilkomirski refused to ever admit the fraud, first claiming he had been switched with the "real" Bruno Grosjean, then saying it had been the readers' "choice" to read his book as literature or as a true memoir.

Lying with the Wolves: Wilkomirski's story was fiction, but it was at least plausible. It's less easy to understand how people fell for Misha Defonseca's *Misha: A Mémoire of the Holocaust Years* (1997)—in which the author claimed that while she wandered Europe alone, searching for her Nazi-abducted Jewish parents, she was sheltered by a pack of wolves and stabbed a Nazi soldier. Her parents were really arrested, but that was virtually the only point of truth in the book: Her family was actually Catholic, and Misha spent the entirety of the war in the care of her other relatives.

The (Bad) Apple of His Eye: We're not sure why Oprah seems to attract (or fall for) so many dishonest authors, but she dubbed the tale of Herman Rosenblat "the single greatest love story…we've ever told on the air." Rosenblat claimed that a 9-year-old girl threw apples to him over a concentration camp fence, and decades later they met again on a blind date, fell in love, and were married. Unlike his fellow frauds, Rosenblat did spend time in the Buchenwald concentration camp. But the "hook" of his story, the apples and the "angel at the fence," were revealed as inventions—but not before the story had been made into a children's book, and filming was about to begin on a feature film.

LIVE FAST, DIE YOUNG...

Thomas Chatterton (1752–70), the son of a church sexton, was a creative boy whose writing failed to win any recognition—but when he "discovered" a sheaf of poems written by one Thomas Rowley, a hitherto unknown 15th century priest, he received all the attention he ever wanted and then some. Naturally, Rowley was a complete fiction and the poems were written by Chatterton; he continued to "find" Rowley poems, for which he was paid handsomely, but still yearned to be recognized on his own merits. That day never came, and at age 17, Chatterton wrote one final poem and poisoned himself with arsenic. In a cruel twist, his untimely end brought his own work to the attention of some of the greatest poets of the time: John Keats's *Endymion* is even dedicated to Chatterton.

LIKE FATHER, LIKE SON

William Henry Ireland (1777–1835) inherited an appreciation for old books from his father but also saw that enthusiasts could be easily taken advantage of—as when his gullible, Shakespeare-obsessed father was conned into buying counterfeit artifacts of the Bard. Inspired by earlier literary forgers, including Thomas Chatterton, Ireland embarked at age 17 on an ambitious and startlingly successful scam. William, who worked as a lawyer's apprentice, began collecting blank sheets of parchment from old mortgages and other files, on which he forged a variety of documents—including some with William Shakespeare's signature. After convincing his father that the "found" documents were genuine, young Ireland began churning out and selling a steady stream of forged Shakespearean artifacts: letters (to Anne Hathaway and Queen Elizabeth I), manuscript pages (from

Hamlet and *King Lear*), and even an entirely new play entitled *Vortigern and Rowena,* which opened in 1796 to great fanfare but closed after a single performance. The play was roundly panned in the press, and scholars and critics had already begun to debunk the claim of Shakespearean origin, with many accusing the elder Ireland of staging the hoax. William published a complete confession, but the scandal drove father and son apart, and their family reputation never recovered.

ANGRY PENGUINS AND NOSE-PICKING URCHINS

In 1944, a woman named Ethel Malley sent the manuscript of a long poem sequence entitled *The Darkening Ecliptic*—written by her brother, who had recently died of Graves' disease—to the editor of the Australian avant-garde literary magazine *Angry Penguins.* The editor not only published the poems, he rushed a special edition of the magazine to press, complete with a specially commissioned cover painting and a 3,000-word analysis of Malley's poems. But within a few months, he found himself subject to ridicule when it was revealed that the true authors of "Malley's" poems were James McAuley and Harold Stewart, who had thrown together the entire cycle in a single afternoon, copying random phrases from reference books and Shakespeare's plays, and intentionally choosing "awkward rhymes from a *Ripman's Rhyming Dictionary.*" Their target was the entirety of late-Modern poetry, which they felt had degenerated into incoherence.

Angry Penguins folded (not entirely for reasons related to the Malley scandal) but curiously, "Ern Malley" and his poems have had a lasting, serious impact on the arts in Australia—inspiring novels (Peter Carey's *My Life As a Fake*), an Ern Malley Jazz Suite (by musician and former *Angry Penguins* contributor Dave Dallwitz), and a play about Malley, *The Black Swan of Trespass.*

···

"Princess, you lived in Princess St.,
  Where the urchins pick their nose in the sun
  With the left hand."

—from "Perspective Lovesong" by Ern Malley

···

WAR OF THE WORDS

In the wee hours of one night/morning in 1956, New York DJ Jean Shepherd concocted a wild scheme to shake up the faith of "Day People" (in Shep's lingo, anyone who wasn't one of the "Night People" who listened to his 1–5:30 A.M. show) in the nation's supposedly authoritative best-seller lists. Shepherd solicited suggestions for elements of a fictional book from listeners, finally settling on *I, Libertine* by Frederick R. Ewing, a retired Commander in the Royal Navy and a scholar of 18th-century erotica (who, naturally, had never existed).

Armed with these details, Shepherd's listeners began requesting *I, Libertine* from every bookseller and library they knew—driving the nonexistent novel onto the best-seller lists and befuddling booksellers around the world. Yet one editor, Ian Ballantine, familiar with the source of the hoax, convinced Shepherd to team up with a real novelist to produce an actual book. The author they chose, curiously enough, was the sci-fi writer Theodore Sturgeon—a friend of Kurt Vonnegut and the inspiration for the fictional character Kilgore Trout (see pages 220 and 303–304) for *his* tangled tale). But Sturgeon was a notorious procrastinator and was eventually forced to bang out the complete manuscript in one marathon setting at Ballantine's home…only to fall asleep near the end, leaving Ballantine's wife to write the final chapter.

A TRUTH UNIVERSALLY REJECTED

David Lassman, the director of the Jane Austen Festival in Bath, England, was frustrated: He had spent three and a half years writing a novel but couldn't find a single publisher willing to buy it. Convinced that present-day publishers wouldn't recognize a great book if it bit them on the nose, he made slight changes to names and places in Austen's *Northanger Abbey* (substituting Austen's original title, *Susan*) and shipped sample chapters to 18 publishing houses in 2007. Some publishers returned the manuscript unread, refusing to read any work that didn't come from an agent; but those who did read his submission didn't detect the ruse, usually writing back to say the book was "not suitable for their lists." Acknowledging that *Northanger* wasn't one of Austen's best-known works, Lassman tried again with *Persuasion*, with nearly identical results. Finally, he shipped out the opening chapters of *Pride and Prejudice* (renamed *First Impressions*), complete with its instantly recognizable opening lines. "We don't feel that strongly about your work," responded one literary agent; another publisher said the book seemed "like a really original and interesting read," but didn't request additional chapters. Only one editor correctly identified the hoax, writing back that his own "first impressions" were "disbelief and mild annoyance—along, of course, with a moment's laughter."

....

" 'Gadzooks!' quoth I, 'but here's a saucy bawd!' "

—FREDERICK R. EWING, *I, LIBERTINE*

....

IF YOU DON'T KNOW ME BY NOW…

These writers found fame by compulsively chronicling the truth of their own sordid, hilarious, or shocking lives.

ME TALK TRUTHFULLY ONE DAY

One of America's funniest contemporary memoirists, David Sedaris has written about such events as disparate as taking guitar lessons (at age 12) from a midget named Mr. Mancini; being mistaken for a French pickpocket on the Paris Metro; and testing a kind of external catheter called a "Stadium Pal." A supposed "takedown" of Sedaris in 2007 compared his recollections with those of some of the real people mentioned in them and concluded that many facts had been highly exaggerated, if not completely made up. But Sedaris responded mainly with a shrug, noting that one *Esquire* assignment gave him "a whole new appreciation for people who can honestly tell the truth, because people didn't always say what I wanted them to." Still, in the wake of James Frey and other scandals, Sedaris bowed (slightly) to prevailing trends and added an author's note to his most recent book, describing its contents as "realish."

....

"When I am writing, I am there. I'm there … It's like a movie. It's extremely vivid. I'm a monkey at a typewriter, writing about the time it got M&Ms and the time a blue M&M came out instead of a red one."

—AUGUSTEN BURROUGHS

....

THE GREAT DEPRESSION

There seems to be an unwritten rule that the titles of raw, honest memoirs of depression must allude to classical works of art or literature—a rule that certainly holds true for these three authors.

Title	Origin of Title
William Styron, *Darkness Visible: A Memoir of Madness,* a chronicle of the *Sophie's Choice* author's bout with near-suicidal depression at age 60	Description of Hell, from Milton's *Paradise Lost:* *A dungeon horrible, on all sides round,* *As one great furnace flamed;* *yet from those flames* *No light, but rather darkness visible* *Served only to discover sights of woe*
Susanna Kaysen, *Girl, Interrupted,* a memoir of Kaysen's two-year stint in a mental hospital for treatment of borderline personality disorder	From the title of Jan Vermeer's painting *Girl Interrupted at her Music*–a figure she related to because her own life had been "interrupted in the music of being seventeen…one moment made to stand still and to stand for all the other moments, whatever they would be or might have been."
Rick Moody, *The Black Veil,* a meditation on Moody's struggles with addiction, paranoia, and psychiatric treatment	Nathaniel Hawthorne's story "The Minister's Black Veil," inspired by one Joseph Moody, who veiled himself after accidentally killing a childhood friend, and who was said to be an ancestor of Rick's (a family tale that turned out to be false).

THOSE MCCOURT BOYS

Though the McCourt brothers, Frank (*Angela's Ashes*) and Malachy (*A Monk Swimming*) have more or less established a monopoly on memoirs of hard-knock, Irish-American childhoods, there are still stories left to tell—especially for younger brother Malachy. Some of the stranger pursuits of his adult life include a recurring Christmas role on *All My Children* as "Father Clarence"; a rather bleaker turn as the incarcerated Father Meehan on the HBO series *Oz*; and a run as Green Party candidate for governor of New York in 2006—a race he lost to Democrat Eliot Spitzer, who turned out to have a few sins of his own to confess.

AN HONEST MISTAKE

You would be forgiven for wondering if there are any Oprah-endorsed memoirists whose works *haven't* been debunked. Fortunately, there are people like Mitch Albom, whose best-selling *Tuesdays with Morrie*—a record of his conversations with a former professor who fought and died of Lou Gehrig's disease—has been inspiring readers for more than a decade. Yet Albom isn't entirely scandal free: In 2005 he was suspended, along with four other editors of the *Detroit Free Press*, over an Albom-penned column that incorrectly placed two NBA players in attendance at an NCAA game. Scrutiny of his complete publishing record failed to turn up evidence of a pattern of wrongdoing, and Albom's excuse turned out to be little more than an excess of trust: The players said they would attend, and he took them at their word.

WHAT IS THE WHAT'S FOR SALE?

Dave Eggers, author of the best-selling, Pulitzer Prize–nominated memoir *A Heartbreaking Work of Staggering Genius* (as well as *What Is the What,* a "fictionalized autobiography" of Sudanese refugee Valentino Achak Deng), is also the founder of 826 Valencia, a nonprofit group that operates writing and tutoring centers for students aged 8 to 18 in several major cities. The twist is that each center is "fronted" by a uniquely outlandish business that sells real—though not always functional—products that help to fund each location:

The Pirate Supply Store (826 Valencia, San Francisco, CA): "Scurvy Begone," sea sickness tablets, mermaid bait (and repellent)

Brooklyn Superhero Supply Co. (826NYC, Brooklyn, NY): Grappling hooks, superhero tights, antimatter

Echo Park Time Travel Mart (826LA, Echo Park, CA): Line of fragrances, including "Caveman," "Gold Rush," and "2012"

Greenwood Space Travel Supply Co. (826 Seattle, Seattle, WA): Space vehicle repair supplies, "Zero-Gravity Spaghetti Containment Device"

The Boring Store (826CHI, Chicago, IL): Secret-camera glasses, mustache disguise kits, heated stakeout gloves

Liberty Street Robot Supply & Repair (826michigan, Ann Arbor, MI): Positronic brains, robot first-aid kits, Robodentures

Greater Boston Bigfoot Research Institute (826 Boston, Roxbury, MA): Cryptozoology career kits, unicorn tears

DEAR DIARY

A survey of notable (and notorious) diaries from famous novelists, scientists, celebrities, and other famous scribblers.

....

"My former boyfriend read [my diary] once, and he was mainly mad because he wasn't in it. I said, 'Yes, you are.' Then I looked, and he wasn't mentioned. It was as if he didn't exist. If you read somebody's diary, you get what you deserve."

—DAVID SEDARIS

....

Lewis Carroll The *Alice in Wonderland* author's diaries filled at least 13 volumes, from 1855 through 1897, but only 9 volumes survive, and some are missing pages—including one page that apparently described the mysterious event that caused a rift between Carroll and the Liddell family, whose daughter Alice was the inspiration for Carroll's best-known book.

John Cheever Left behind a massive collection of journals— roughly 4,300 pages, most of them typed and single-spaced.

....

"I am one of those old men; I am like a voyager who cannot remember the streams he has travelled."

—JOHN CHEEVER

....

Anne Frank Received her first diary on her 13th birthday (June 12, 1942) and addressed it about its place among her gifts, "The first to greet me was you, possibly the nicest of all." She kept writing for more than two years, pausing in May 1944 to recopy earlier entries. Her complete diary totaled 324 handwritten pages—which have been translated into at least 67 languages.

....

"I keep my ideals, because in spite of everything I still believe that people are really good at heart."

—ANNE FRANK

....

Kurt Cobain The Nirvana frontman filled 23 notebooks, amounting to some 800 pages, with everything from early drafts of hits like "Smells Like Teen Spirit" to his favorite CDs, unsent letters, and lists of rules for the band.

....

"There are a lot of bands who claim to be alternative and theyre [sic] nothing but stripped down, ex sunset strip hair farming bands of a few years ago. I would love to be erased from our association with Pearl Jam or the Nymphs and other first time offenders."

—KURT COBAIN

....

Charles Darwin The origin of the great naturalist's own *On the Origin of Species* lay within the diaries he kept on board the HMS *Beagle* as it traveled around the world. His total output included: at least 18 volumes of rough field notes; a four-volume zoological diary; a three-volume geological diary; an extensive catalogue of specimens; and an 800-page personal diary of the five-year journey.

Anna Dostoyevsky The second wife of the great novelist—they met when she was hired to transcribe his dictated text of *The Gambler*—read her famous husband's mail but kept her own diary secret from him by using a private shorthand, the code for which wasn't fully cracked until years after her death.

Buckminster Fuller The renowned author, architect, and inventor is responsible for one of the most impressive diaries in human history. Known as the "Dymaxion Chronofile," the diary contains a complete chronicle of his life from 1915 to 1983, including daily activities, newspaper clippings, receipts, and correspondence ... adding up to roughly 270 linear feet of paper.

....

"I could not be judge of what was valid to put in or not. I must put everything in, so I started a very rigorous record."

—BUCKMINSTER FULLER

....

Johanna Fantova Don't recognize the name? Fantova was Albert Einstein's last girlfriend, and her 62-page diary is the only known journal kept by a personal friend of Einstein at the end of his life. It includes poems he wrote to her and a wealth of surprising facts: For example, after deciding that a parrot received on his 75th birthday was "depressed," Einstein tried to cheer it up by telling bad jokes.

....

> *"[Einstein] tried all day to compose a radio message on behalf of Israel and did not succeed in finishing it. He claims he is totally stupid—that he has always thought so, and that only once in a while was he able to accomplish something."*
>
> —JOHANNA FANTOVA

....

THE AMERICAN WAY

Although an official "Presidential Daily Diary" exists for most presidents since Washington, it's only a rough chronicle of daily movements, meetings, and conversations, jotted down by secretaries. Through the end of the 19th century, only four presidents had kept personal diaries for large portions of their adult lives: George Washington, John Quincy Adams, James K. Polk, and Rutherford B. Hayes. And of those, only Adams's extraordinarily detailed journals (covering some 68 years) offer much entertainment or candid insight into the man. A gap of

100 years stands between Hayes and the next dutiful presidential diarist: Ronald Reagan. The Gipper, who self-censored curse words, wrote in his diary every day except while hospitalized after an assassination attempt. Upon resuming his diary, he noted: "Getting shot hurts."

....

"Wrote nothing."

—FRANZ KAFKA, JUNE 1, 1912, DIARY ENTRY

....

BLOGGING THE BLACK PLAGUE

Samuel Pepys (1633–1703) was born the son of a London tailor, attended Cambridge University's Magdalene College, and for most of his adult life rose steadily through the ranks of government service: He later served as Secretary to the Admiralty, a member of Parliament, and President of the Royal Society, and he helped lay the groundwork for England's first professional naval service. But his greatest legacy is the diary he kept from 1660–69—from age 27 to age 36, when he quit from fear of going blind—which is now regarded as one of England's national treasures and one of the most important diaries in history. As luck (of sorts) would have it, Pepys lived through two of the greatest disasters in English history: the Plague (1665–66) and the Great Fire of London (1666), both of which he chronicled in great and humanizing detail, along with scenes from his public life, commentary on cultural happenings (such as attending *The Woman's Prize, or the Tamer Tamed*, John Fletcher's sequel to *The Taming of the Shrew*), and his not-infrequent attempts to seduce random women around town.

PEN PALS

Romantic or grouchy, supportive or snarky, these well-known authors were also legendary letter writers.

Jane Austen is said to have been a prolific letter writer, though only about 160 letters (of an estimated 3,000) have survived: Most of the others were destroyed by recipients, many of whom were family members looking to protect Jane's privacy. A large number of the remaining letters were addressed to Austen's niece, Fanny Knight, advising the girl on her love life and conveying characteristic wit. Commenting about one of Fanny's acquaintances, who disapproved of Austen's writing, Jane wrote that "he deserves better treatment than to be obliged to read any more of my works."

Mark Twain, oddly enough, took the time in at least two personal letters to vent his loathing for Austen's prose. In 1898, he commented: "Every time I read 'Pride and Prejudice' I want to dig her up and beat her over the skull with her own shin-bone." And in a 1909 letter, criticizing another author's work, he wrote: "To me his prose is unreadable—like Jane Austin's [sic]. No there is a difference. I could read his prose on salary, but not Jane's. Jane is entirely impossible. It seems a great pity that they allowed her to die a natural death."

Ezra Pound and James Joyce carried on a decades-long personal correspondence, much of it revolving around Pound's efforts to place Joyce's stories in various magazines and to champion his longer works against harsh criticism (even *Finnegan's Wake,* which Pound once described as "toilet humor"). When one batch of stories was turned down by the magazine *The Smart Set,* Pound passed along the rejection note with a cover letter that began, "Dear Joyce: I enclose a prize sample of bull shit."

H. P. Lovecraft spent the latter years of his life living in Providence, Rhode Island, keeping in touch with friends and business acquaintances primarily through the mail. The already-prolific Lovecraft is said to have written an estimated 100,000 letters in his lifetime, of which 20,000 survive. For years, he wrote an estimated 40,000 words annually to fellow horror writer Clark Ashton Smith—often commenting on the petty frustrations of the writer's existence. Smoldering from one recent rejection by the Knopf publishing house, he wrote to Smith that "Knopf should remove the Borzoi from his imprint, and substitute either the Golden Calf or a jackass with brazen posteriors."

Elizabeth Barrett and Robert Browning: In 1845 the eminent poets began one of the most famous correspondences of all time, exchanging 574 letters over 20 months as their love for each other blossomed. Barrett's father forbade her from pursuing a relationship with Browning, so the star-crossed lovers eloped to Italy. Barrett sought reconciliation after her father disinherited her—only to discover years later that her father never even opened the many letters she had sent.

BOOKS THAT CHANGED THE WORLD

PLATO,
THE REPUBLIC (380 B.C.)

Why it's important: *The Republic* has had an enormous influence on philosophical and political thought, from ancient times to today. The Socratic dialogue is chiefly concerned with the concept of justice—specifically, whether the just man is happier than the unjust—but also touches on poetry, philosophy, and the immortality of the soul. The famous "Allegory of the Cave"—which attempts to illustrate that ideas, and not the things we perceive, are the "true" reality—comes from this work.

What you don't know: If you don't like poetry, you might find a kindred spirit in Plato: He (or rather, Socrates) proclaims near the end of the book that all poets will be banished from his ideal society because they produce "phantoms, not realities." *The Republic* also introduces the allegory of the Ring of Gyges, in which a shepherd discovers a magic ring that grants invisibility. The story—an acknowledged source for the "One Ring" of Tolkien's *The Lord of the Rings*—is part of an argument over whether all people would be unjust . . . if they could only get away with it.

THOMAS PAINE,
COMMON SENSE (1776)

Why it's important: Paine's pamphlet (originally titled "Plain Truth") was the first published work to call for the independence of the American colonies.

What you don't know: Paine was a rabble-rouser before he ever came to America—a tendency that was noted by Benjamin Franklin, who sponsored Paine's emigration. But like Franklin, Paine's talents extended into many other spheres: When he wasn't publishing incendiary political tracts, he even worked as an inventor, creating a new kind of iron bridge and a smokeless candle. His work was a strong influence on and inspiration to a young Thomas Edison, who later wrote that Paine "had a sort of universal genius."

....

> *"Society in every state is a blessing, but government*
> *even in its best state is but a necessary evil;*
> *in its worst state an intolerable one; for when we*
> *suffer, or are exposed to the same miseries BY*
> *A GOVERNMENT, which we might expect in*
> *a country WITHOUT GOVERNMENT, our*
> *calamity is heightened by reflecting that we*
> *furnish the means by which we suffer."*

—THOMAS PAINE, COMMON SENSE

....

ADAM SMITH, *THE WEALTH OF NATIONS* (1776)

Why it's important: Smith's tome provides a rationale for a global transformation from mercantilism—the primary economic theory from the 16th through the 18th centuries—to capitalism. Whenever you hear about a "laissez-faire" economic doctrine (Smith didn't introduce the doctrine, but this volume was its biggest proponent) or the "invisible hand" of the market, you're hearing the words of Adam Smith.

What you don't know: Book V contains a critique of English universities, which Smith believed to be inferior to their Scottish counterparts. Fortunately, it took the English only a couple of centuries to get over this slander: In March 2007, Smith became the first Scotsman to be featured on an English banknote.

MARY WOLLSTONECRAFT, *A VINDICATION OF THE RIGHTS OF WOMAN* (1792)

Why it's important: Wollstonecraft argued that women were as capable of rational thought as men, lacking only the benefit of formal education to develop their natural abilities. Many of her ideas wouldn't quite qualify as modern feminist thought, but they were certainly ahead of her time.

What you don't know: If anything, her personal life was actually more modern than her writing: Wollstonecraft had a long (and long-distance) romantic relationship with author William Godwin, but both were opposed to marriage as an institution that promoted inequality of the sexes. When Wollstonecraft became pregnant—with a daughter, also named Mary, who would go on to write *Frankenstein*—the two married for the sake of the child, but Wollstonecraft died in childbirth.

ALEXIS DE TOCQUEVILLE,
DEMOCRACY IN AMERICA (1835)

Why it's important: Tocqueville's book attempted to show why the American system of government had succeeded, when similar systems had failed in so many other places. It remains an insightful, readable, and oft-quoted analysis of contemporary politics and of dangers that could (and did) arise to challenge democracy in the United States.

What you don't know: This is *not* the book Tocqueville (age 25) and his partner, Gustave de Beaumont (28), were commissioned to write. France's King Louis-Phillipe had sent them to America to write an analysis of the nation's prison system. Incredibly, they managed to deliver on that promise, too: *The U.S. Penitentiary System and Its Application in France,* which drew on interviews with prison officials and prisoners across the country, contributed to the reform of the prison system in France.

KARL MARX AND FRIEDRICH ENGELS,
THE COMMUNIST MANIFESTO (1848)

Why it's important: This brief (only 23 pages, in its first appearance) declaration of principles inspired the major communist political systems of the 20th century—and thus was partially responsible for the cold war.

What you don't know: Though Karl Marx (and his magnificent beard) loom large in any modern discussion of communism, the *Manifesto* was first published without authorial attribution. Marx was a 30-year-old historian and political philosopher who was well known in radical socialist circles but was far from a household name. Soon after moving to London in 1847, he began meeting with a coalition of working-class parties who dubbed themselves "The Communist League" and who commissioned Marx to write down a statement of their principles. The manifesto was published anonymously in 1848; the first edition bearing Marx's name didn't appear until 1850, in an English-language printing.

THE BEARD TO BEAT

In 2008 the London *Times* dubbed Karl Marx's facial hair the #1 beard of all time—beating out even Charles Dickens (#5), Soviet leader Vladimir Lenin (#6), and ZZ Top's Billy Gibbons and Dusty Hill (#10).

HARRIET BEECHER STOWE, *UNCLE TOM'S CABIN* (1852)

Why it's important: Stowe's novel, first serialized in 40 installments in the antislavery periodical *The National Era* (for a fee of $300), put a human face on the issue of slavery. Her book won thousands of new converts to the abolitionist cause, allegedly inspiring President Abraham Lincoln to remark, upon meeting Stowe in 1862, "So you're the little woman who wrote the book that made this great war!" *Uncle Tom's Cabin* stands as perhaps the first "muckraking novel" in America (though that term wasn't coined until 1906, in a speech by President Roosevelt), and it directly inspired later activist writers, including Upton Sinclair and Rachel Carson.

What you don't know: Stowe's novel wasn't only an influential book, it was a bona fide blockbuster best seller. *Uncle Tom's Cabin* reportedly sold 3,000 copies in its first day, 10,000 in one week, and 300,000 in its first year—at a time when the total U.S. population was just over 23 million. In 1853, *Putnam's Monthly* magazine said that "all other successes in literature were failures when compared with the success of *Uncle Tom*."

A NOT-SO-CIVIL BUSINESS

In an ironic twist of fate, J. P. Jewett, Stowe's first publisher, was driven out of business by the Civil War. Jewett moved on to less history-making pursuits, including selling "Peruvian Syrup" (a medicinal "iron tonic") and working as a patent agent.

CHARLES DARWIN,
ON THE ORIGIN OF SPECIES (1859)

Why it's important: Darwin's revolutionary work (published 23 years after his five-year voyage on the HMS *Beagle*) introduced the concept of natural selection as the driving force in the development and diversification of species, upending centuries of erroneous thought about how and why various species came into being. Although it would be nearly 100 years before the discovery of DNA's double helix, his theories still form the foundation of virtually all modern biological science.

What you don't know: For some people, Darwin's name has come to symbolize a coldly scientific (if not atheistic) view of existence. But he was by all accounts a funny, kind, and gentle family man, who was profoundly awed by nature and felt a deep compassion for his fellow man. In fact, though he lived in a time when slavery was common, Darwin himself was a staunch abolitionist: he once said that "It makes one's blood boil, yet heart tremble, to think that we Englishmen and our American descendants, with their boastful cry of liberty, have been and are so guilty."

A TANGLED FAMILY TREE

Darwin's expert understanding of the inheritance of traits within species made him extra-anxious about his own breeding—or rather, inbreeding: he married his first cousin. But despite his concerns, all of his children who survived childhood were perfectly healthy, if not outright exceptional: among his five sons were a banker, an army officer, an astronomer, a botanist, and an engineer. (There is some speculation, however, that his sixth son, who died at 18 months old, was born with Down syndrome.)

UPTON SINCLAIR, *THE JUNGLE* (1906)

Why it's important: Sinclair's novel was filled with graphic detail about American slaughterhouses: poisoned rats ground up in sausage machines, diseased and spoiled beef sold to consumers, and workers using factory floors as toilets. The book sparked immediate worldwide outrage—purchases of American meat dropped by 50 percent at home and abroad—and led Congress to pass both the Meat Inspection Act and the Pure Food and Drug Act within only six months.

What you don't know: Sinclair, a fervent supporter of the Socialist party, wasn't primarily concerned with the health of the American consumer: He wrote the book hoping to win support for the factory workers who toiled under intolerable conditions. Slaughterhouse workers labored 12-hour days, were often ripped off by their employers, and were regularly maimed, burned, and blinded in the line of work—but the public was more shocked by the handful of pages describing dead rats and rotting meat. As Sinclair cleverly put it, "I aimed at the public's heart, and by accident I hit it in the stomach."

Although *The Jungle* failed to spark a Socialist revolution on its own, Sinclair used his profits from the book to build a utopian colony named "Helicon Hall" on the site of a boys' school (complete with swimming pool and bowling alley) near Englewood, New Jersey. But even this stab at promoting Socialist ideals fell short: Helicon Hall burned down after 4 months.

STARTING AT THE BOTTOM

Sinclair Lewis, 1930 Nobel Prize winner, worked as a janitor for 2 months at Helicon Hall.

JANE JACOBS,
THE DEATH AND LIFE OF GREAT AMERICAN CITIES (1961)

Why it's important: Jacobs contradicted the contemporary wisdom of modernist urban planners such as Robert Moses and Le Corbusier, who advocated efficient, segmented use of limited urban space, rather than Jacobs's ideal of neighborhoods of mixed-use blocks.

What you don't know: Jane Jacobs's theories were far from theoretical: she is well-remembered in New York's Greenwich Village for leading the fight against a Robert Moses–envisioned superhighway that threatened to cut a bisecting swath through lower Manhattan. She achieved similar success in Toronto, Ontario, where she joined the successful fight against the Spadina Expressway. Known as somewhat eccentric, Jacobs admitted to making many of her arguments in imaginary conversations with Thomas Jefferson—who, when she ran out of things to tell him, she replaced with Benjamin Franklin: "Like Jefferson, he was interested in lofty things, but also in nitty-gritty, down-to-earth details, such as why the alley we were walking through wasn't paved, and who would pave it if it were paved. He was interested in everything, so he was a very satisfying companion."

RACHEL CARSON,
SILENT SPRING (1962)

Why it's important: With its vivid description of a typical American town "silenced" from the devastating effects of the pesticide DDT boomeranging throughout the food chain, *Silent Spring* directly led to a ban on DDT, increased government oversight of pesticide and other chemical manufacturing industries, and heightened public aware-ness of mankind's ability to damage the environment.

What you don't know: This now-classic book was a harder sell than many people realize. DDT was invented in 1939 and was used heavily in World War II to purge South Pacific islands of malaria-carrying insects. In 1945, the pesticide passed into widespread civilian use; Carson tried to inter-est U.S. magazines (including *Reader's Digest*) in a story about the unexplored long-term effects of DDT but was shot down. Thirteen years later, a friend alerted Carson to large-scale bird deaths resulting from DDT use, but again Carson failed to secure interest from magazine publish-ers—even though she had become a best-selling author with a trilogy of books about ocean life: *The Sea Around Us* (1951), *The Edge of the Sea* (1955), and *Under the Sea Wind* (1941). It took another four years for Carson to write the book—and eight more years before the Environmen-tal Protection Agency came into being, under President Richard Nixon (1970).

RALPH NADER,
UNSAFE AT ANY SPEED (1965)

Why it's important: Nader's groundbreaking exposé of unsafe American automotive products led directly to the 1966 National Traffic and Motor Vehicle Safety Act, ensuring that all vehicles sold in the United States meet certain basic safety standards.

What you don't know: Nader first formulated the central argument of the book as a Harvard Law student, in an article entitled "American Cars: Designed for Death." When the book was finally published, General Motors hired a private detective to follow Nader and dig up information to discredit him, but Nader sued GM for invasion of privacy and eventually won $280,000 from the chastened automaker. Nader funneled much of that settlement into efforts to overhaul other industries, including meat processing and insecticide regulation; no doubt, Sinclair and Carson would have approved.

SIMPLY THE WORST

Unsafe at Any Speed singled out GM's Corvair for particular scorn (the car also made *Time* magazine's list of the 50 Worst Cars of All Time). The rear-engine layout made it hard to handle; fumes from the heating system seeped into the cabin; some models had a gasoline-burning heater in the front trunk; and in the event of a head-on collision, the driver risked impalement on the single-piece steering column. The impalement-averse American public stopped buying the Corvair in droves, sending sales plummeting from 220,000 in 1965 to 14,800 in 1968.

OFF THE PAGE

Sometimes, the most intriguing stories can't be found under the covers *or* between the sheets. How did famous authors choose their pseudonyms ... and why did some of them have no choice? Which big-time best-selling authors have been known to rock out almost as much as they write down? And how many writers experienced family and relationship drama that rivaled anything they set down on the page?

IMAGINARY FRIENDS

What happens when fictional characters suddenly start publishing books of their own—or when real people transform into cartoons? Here are a handful of mind-bending instances where the lines between fiction and reality were more than blurred.

SOMETHING'S FISHY

One of Kurt Vonnegut's most-loved characters (or at least most-used, appearing in person in three novels and named in three others), ever-struggling sci-fi writer Kilgore Trout, boasts one of the stranger biographies of any fictional creation. Trout was based on the real-life science-fiction writer Theodore Sturgeon, a friend of Vonnegut's who—like Trout—had failed to attract an audience beyond die-hard genre fans. Fans of Vonnegut's *Breakfast of Champions* will recall that Trout and Vonnegut actually meet near the end of the book—but even Vonnegut couldn't have imagined that his fictional character would break into the real world at a later date.

Yet another sometime sci-fi author, Philip José Farmer, while suffering from writer's block, decided to try his hand at writing a Kilgore Trout novel—and ultimately published *Venus on the Half-Shell* (1975) under Trout's name, with no hint of its true authorship. Farmer appears in an author photo virtually buried in a fake beard. The book went through dozens of printings, mostly because of the Vonnegut connection, but Vonnegut was not amused and refused to allow any more Trout books to be published. Farmer claimed that the book was meant to be nothing more than a tribute to one of his favorite writers and characters. And perhaps fittingly, he also maintained that he had profited less from this title than from many of his own titles, citing rumors that his publisher had siphoned off most of his royalties—a situation that would have been familiar to the fictional Trout.

KILGORE'S BELIEVE IT OR NOT

Though "Theodore Sturgeon" seems as if it couldn't be anything other than a pseudonym, and Sturgeon was born "Edward Hamilton Waldo," the former really was his legal name. After his father walked out, his mother married a man named William Sturgeon; young Edward adopted his new father's last name and changed his first from Edward (his birth father's name) to Theodore to better match his childhood nickname, "Teddy." Simple, right?

AN ANIMATED EXISTENCE

The real-life antics of legendary "gonzo" journalist Hunter S. Thompson seem almost cartoonishly bizarre at times; maybe that's why the man has been such a rich source of inspiration for cartoon and comic book characters:

Uncle Duke: a recurring character in Garry Trudeau's *Doonesbury* strip, whose omnipresent cigarette holder and fondness for recreational drug use (see pages 188–193) mark him as an obvious homage to Thompson—who once said, "I've never met Garry Trudeau, but if I ever do, I'll set him on fire."

Spider Jerusalem: the crusading gonzo journalist of the future from Warren Ellis's *Transmetropolitan* comic book series. The real Thompson was an aficionado of large firearms; Jerusalem shares this affinity, though his weapon of choice is the "bowel disruptor." Need we say more?

Hunter Gathers: a military officer on the Cartoon Network's animated television show *Venture Bros.* Given his response to Trudeau's Uncle Duke (and his fondness for big guns), one shudders to think what the late Thompson would have threatened to do to the creators of the transsexual Gathers.

HARRY POTTER AND THE MAGICAL MYSTERY BIDDER

Though Harry Potter's epic saga has come to an end, several "real" books from his fictional world have magically appeared in our own: Newt Scamander's *Fantastic Beasts and Where to Find Them,* Kennilworthy Whisp's *Quidditch Through the Ages,* and *The Tales of Beedle the Bard.* They were really written, of course, by *Harry Potter* author J. K. Rowling, who created them to raise money for charity. An original, handwritten copy of *Beedle* even made history in 2007 when it was purchased at an auction by a mystery bidder, later revealed to be online retailer Amazon, for nearly 2 million British pounds ($3.97 million)—the highest price ever paid at auction for a modern literary manuscript.

DON'T ASK, DO TELL

Of all the untold stories in the Harry Potter universe, it's doubtful that any will cause as much commotion as J. K. Rowling's 2007 revelation, in front of a packed house at Carnegie Hall, that in her mind Hogwarts headmaster Albus Dumbledore was gay. When the audience erupted in several minutes of sustained applause, a stunned Rowling added, "I would have told you earlier if I knew it would make you so happy."

A.K.A.

Here's the straight story behind a few authors who changed their identities—some out of necessity, some just for fun, and some practically by accident.

BIG NAMES

Lewis Carroll (Charles Lutwidge Dodgson): Chosen, in typically brain-teasing style, by translating his first two names into Latin (Carolus Lodovicus) and then anglicizing them.

George Orwell (Eric Blair): Would we still be studying *1984*'s Newspeak if it had been written by H. Lewis Allways? That was one of four pseudonyms a 29-year-old Eric Blair suggested to his editor, along with Kenneth Miles, P. S. Burton, and the eventual winner—borrowed from the River Orwell in Suffolk, England.

Dav Pilkey (Dave Pilkey): OK, so it's not much of a pseudonym; when a teenaged Dave worked at Pizza Hut, a broken label-maker spat out "Dav" instead of "Dave" for his nametag, and Pilkey stuck with it.

Lemony Snicket (Daniel Handler): Handler used the name Lemony Snicket as a joke when he was researching right-wing organizations for his first (non-Lemony) novel *The Basic Eight*; when he started writing children's books, he kept it and also gave his narrator the well-worn pseudonym.

Henry David Thoreau (David Henry Thoreau): What can be said about this, except that it may be the least interesting pseudonym of all time?

ALTER EGOS

Ray Bradbury: At times, this remarkably prolific writer was even more prolific than many people knew, thanks to his frequent use of pseudonyms. At age 19, he began publishing a short fanzine with a group of friends. The first issue contained an editorial and poem by Bradbury and a story by Ron Reynolds—a Bradbury pseudonym, created to give the illusion that more people had contributed to the magazine. The second issue contained no less than three Bradbury pseudonyms—a short story by Anthony Corvais, an article by Guy Amory, and a poem by Doug Rogers (a combination of Bradbury's middle name and Buck Rogers). Even Bradbury's breakthrough into "quality" fiction occurred under a pseudonym: In 1945 he had three stories accepted almost simultaneously by prestigious publications (*Mademoiselle, Charm,* and *Collier's*) under the name William Elliott—which prompted some quick phone calls to editors to prevent uncashable checks from being sent out to the nonexistent authors.

Anne, Charlotte, and Emily Brontë: The Brontë sisters lived in a time when female authors would commonly publish their works under a male pseudonym to avoid prejudice against works by women, and the Brontës were no exception.

A ROSE BY ANY OTHER NAME

The prejudice against women writers, sad to say, hasn't been entirely erased: Even J. K. Rowling is a pen name—chosen because Joanne Rowling's publisher believed that young boys were less likely to buy books that were obviously written by women.

They assumed the identities of three rather androgynously named brothers rather than take distinct pseudonymous surnames; thus, the world was introduced to Acton, Currer, and Ellis Bell. But even false identities weren't a guarantee of success: The now-renowned writers' first book, a self-published collection of poems by all three sisters, sold a none-too-promising two copies—though one reviewer noted some promise in "Ellis's" work.

Stephen King: Early in his career, the prolific King was told by his publishers that the public "wouldn't accept" more than one new book a year from a writer, so he began mixing in books written under a pseudonym with his regular publications. The first book to appear under a pseudonym was *Rage* (1977); King originally planned to publish it under his maternal grandfather's name (Gus Pillsbury), but because word had gotten out about the fake name, he had to make a last-minute change. When the publisher called to ask for a final pseudonym, King looked around his desk: He saw a novel by Richard Stark and heard Bachman Turner Overdrive playing on the stereo...thus, "Richard Bachman" was born. (The song, if you must know, was "You Ain't Seen Nothin' Yet.")

Gore Vidal: Though he eventually became one of the most respected figures in contemporary thought and literature, some of his early works—especially *The City and the Pillar* (1948)—outraged critics (and prompted some to boycott his novels) because of Vidal's frank and open treatment of homosexuality. Facing a blacklist, Vidal turned to genre fiction and produced three murder mysteries under the name Edgar Box: *Death in the Fifth Position, Death Before Bedtime,* and *Death Likes it Hot.* But these weren't Vidal's only forays into the world of pen names: He also wrote a book in the "international intrigue" genre, *Thieves Fall Out* (1953) by "Cameron Kay," and a Hollywood melodrama entitled *A Star's Progress* (1950) by "Katherine Everard"— whose last name was borrowed from a gay bathhouse in New York City.

Michael Chabon: When authors create literary alter egos for themselves, they usually don't go further than dreaming up a phony name. But for Michael Chabon, that wasn't far enough: August Van Zorn, "the greatest unknown horror writer of the twentieth century," was first mentioned in Chabon's *Wonder Boys* (1995), and was later credited as the author of a story called *The Black Mill* in Chabon's *Werewolves in Their Youth* (1999). But far from being a mere pseudonym, Chabon's alter ego boasted not only a detailed biography (his "real" name was Albert Vetch), but also a bibliography of more than 60 published works (including "Cock Robin," "The Pig God," and "The Rage of Elvira Ogletree"), and a short-story competition sponsored by *McSweeney's* magazine: The August Van Zorn Prize for the Weird Short Story. Chabon even invented a literary scholar—the anagrammatic "Leon Chaim Bach"—devoted solely to Van Zorn's works.

TIME TO MAKE THE DOUGHNUTS

A writer's life is legendarily difficult, and all but the most successful authors have had to find other ways to pay the bills in between royalty checks. Sometimes those money-making schemes have been their downfall (Mark Twain, we're looking at you!); for others, the moonlighting has been almost as noteworthy as their books. And even the biggest best-selling authors sometimes dip their toes into other careers. Who knew that the super-successful, hyper-educated Amy Tan was secretly dying to become a whip-cracking rock and roll dominatrix?

DOWN AND OUT

It's the oldest story in the book, so to speak: promising young writer toils away in obscurity, living hand-to-mouth in a string of dingy, degrading, and sometimes bizarre jobs, just waiting for the royalty checks to start rolling in. Sometimes those lousy jobs form the basis of great works of fiction . . . and sometimes they're better left forgotten.

Maya Angelou: It's hard to imagine Bill Clinton's dignified inaugural poet in such a position, but Maya Angelou worked at various times as a fry cook, a nightclub "shake dancer," and even a prostitute manager—all during a period in her late teens after she had given birth to her first son. But it wasn't all grit and grime for the young Angelou; she became the first black streetcar conductor in San Francisco before graduating from high school, and later went on to dance with Alvin Ailey and to work closely with both

Martin Luther King Jr. and Malcolm X in the civil rights movement.

Jeffrey Eugenides: *Middlesex* author Jeffrey Eugenides volunteered briefly at Mother Teresa's hospice in Calcutta during a college break, but it seems the sainted nun's ethics didn't completely rub off on Eugenides. He later lost a job at the Academy of American Poets after being caught working on his first novel, *The Virgin Suicides,* during business hours.

David Mamet: It probably comes as little surprise to fans of David Mamet's tough, trash-talking drama that the author spent time working for the hard-core pornographic magazine *Oui*...not as an editor but as a caption writer. Oddly, Mamet recalls the job as being "too hard," because it took an activity he enjoyed (looking at pictures of naked women) and turned it into "homework."

Arthur Miller: Though he would later gain distinction as one of America's greatest dramatists, win the Pulitzer Prize, and marry Marilyn Monroe, Arthur Miller paid his dues in a variety of menial jobs—including a $15-per-month stint in a "mouse house," feeding mice used in medical experiments.

John Steinbeck: The classic chronicler of America's working class spent well-known stints working as a fruit picker (which provided material for *Of Mice and Men*) and as a reporter in San Francisco (generating articles that provided the foundation of *The Grapes of Wrath*). But Steinbeck also pulled a less fruitful stint in New York City in 1925, where he worked on the construction of Madison Square Garden.

John Kennedy Toole: Unlike his memorable antihero Ignatius Reilly (*A Confederacy of Dunces,* 1980), who claimed he had never gone farther from New Orleans than Baton Rouge, John Kennedy Toole saw a great deal of the outside world: He received a master's degree from Columbia University and spent two years teaching English to Army recruits in Puerto Rico. Back at home, Toole spent time working in a men's clothing factory and helped a friend sell food from a street cart—both episodes that showed up in his novel—and like the gruff Reilly, Toole lived out the latter part of his tragically short life with his domineering mother in New Orleans.

ROCK BOTTOM OR TOP OF THE HEAP?

In publishing lingo, a "remainder" is an author's worst nightmare: It's a book that a publisher has sold off at a deep discount (usually too deep to generate royalties for the author) to make room for new titles. But that isn't a big concern for the members of the Rock Bottom Remainders, an occasional rock and roll supergroup whose revolving member list has boasted some of the biggest names on contemporary best-seller lists, including Stephen King, Dave Barry, Mitch Albom, Scott Turow, and Amy Tan.

The Remainders were founded in 1992 by Kathi Kamen Goldmark, a musician who worked part-time driving authors on book tours. She found that many of them were more interested in talking about music than writing, and she eventually put together an ad hoc group of author-musicians to perform a benefit concert at a Los Angeles book fair. Founding member Dave Barry is fond of saying that the group "plays music as well as Metallica writes novels," though some members, including Albom and Ridley

Pearson, worked as professional musicians before their writing careers took off.

Despite the occasional presence of superstar guests like Warren Zevon and Bruce Springsteen, none of the regular members take things too seriously: Über-best-seller Scott Turow tends to take the stage wearing a huge curly blond wig, and *Joy Luck Club* author Amy Tan dons skin-tight leather and carries a whip to sing her signature tune, "These Boots Are Made for Walking."

....

"The book of my enemy has been remaindered
And I am pleased."

—CLIVE JAMES

....

THE ROCK AND ROLLER'S GUIDE TO THE GALAXY

English author Douglas Adams (1951–2001) is best remembered as the man who dreamed up the *Hitchhiker's Guide to the Galaxy,* the wisecracking and seemingly infinite "standard repository for all knowledge and wisdom" in the humorous sci-fi book series of the same name. Fans may also remember numerous rock and roll references throughout the books, with a particular predilection for British bands like Dire Straits and The Beatles. But Adams was more than a mere fan; he was an accomplished amateur musician—and an occasional member of the Rock Bottom Remainders—who was friends with a number of bona fide rock stars, including Pink Floyd guitarist David Gilmour. The fictional rock band Disaster Area, whose apocalyptic stage show plays a pivotal role in Adams's *The Restaurant at the End of the Universe,* was inspired by Pink Floyd—and Gilmour returned the favor by inviting Adams to name the 1994 Pink Floyd album *The Division Bell* (a name that Adams simply chose from the album's lyrics).

MUSIC TO HIS EARS

Daniel Handler, aka Lemony Snicket, has had a rather fitting (and semi-thriving) side career as a musician: he plays accordion on several albums, including The Magnetic Fields's album *69 Love Songs,* and wrote the lyrics for One Ring Zero's song "Radio." But he hasn't let his musical success go to his head: "If you play the accordion," he has said, "you're usually the best accordion player anyone knows."

THE MOTHER (AND FATHERS) OF INVENTION

For some who live "the life of the mind," the drive to invent carries over into other creative areas. Writers of sci-fi or speculative fiction may be more susceptible than most, but the bug can strike virtually anyone.

> **Margaret Atwood:** Margaret Atwood made her reputation with speculative fiction like *The Handmaid's Tale* but also had a hand—so to speak—in the development of a gizmo that could have come straight out of science fiction. Weary of long author tours, Atwood dreamed up the LongPen, a "remote signing device" that allows authors to sit comfortably at home, communicating with fans at book signing events via webcam and signing books with an Internet-linked mechanical arm. Unotchit Inc., makers of the device, claim

that it has prevented 76 tons of carbon dioxide emissions; no word yet on how they'll tackle robot writer's cramp.

Roald Dahl: In real life, Roald Dahl didn't quite match the inventive output of his manic chocolate-wizard Willy Wonka—but he did play a role in the creation of a device arguably more important than the Everlasting Gobstopper. Dahl's son was struck by a car in 1960 and suffered from excess fluid buildup in his brain. The best available shunt (a valve to drain excess fluid) was prone to blockage, so Dahl, a model aircraft enthusiast, worked with fellow flyer Stanley Wade—who specialized in tiny hydraulics— and neurosurgeon Kenneth Till to develop an improved model. The Wade-Dahl-Till (WDT) valve spared Dahl's son and thousands of other patients from complications of hydrocephaly, and the Roald Dahl Foundation continues to provide funds for young people suffering from neurological conditions.

Neal Stephenson: Notoriously erudite and verbose (his *Baroque Trilogy* runs to some 2,600 pages), Neal Stephenson's fascination with advanced technology has led him to pursue some impressively complex schemes in service of his books—from programming software to generate maps for his book *Cryptomonicon* to inventing a new language in *Anathem.* He also spent several years working for Blue Origin, the private aerospace company that was started by Amazon.com founder Jeff Bezos, studying different kinds of space launch technologies. Stephenson even lent a hand in the construction of *Blue Origin Goddard,* a prototype space vehicle test flown in November 2006.

THE STEPFATHER OF INVENTION?

Samuel Langhorne Clemens reinvented himself as Mark Twain and created dozens of unforgettable characters like Tom Sawyer and Huck Finn. He was also friends with Nikola Tesla and fancied himself something of an inventor in other fields—but his track record off the page wasn't so stellar. Twain created just one profitable product, a scrapbook with preglued pages that made him some $12,000 in profits over a short period. Other personal projects, including a clamp designed to keep infants from kicking off their bedsheets, were disappointing failures, and Twain proved even less astute at evaluating other people's inventions. Among his notable investment failures were:

Invention	Twain Invested	The Result
Kaolatype (method of printing illustrations)	$50,000	Never took off; supplanted by other printing technology
Paige Compositor (an automated typesetting machine)	$300,000	Drained Twain's fortune and most of his wife's inheritance
Method of carrying human voice by electric wire	$0	In a rare moment of restraint, Twain refused to invest in the one product that could have made him ridiculously wealthy: Alexander Graham Bell's telephone

WUNDERKIND

Most authors pay the bills during their early attempts at writing with not-so-desirable jobs—but not James Patterson, who was conspicuously successful long before he launched into true literary superstardom. For years, Patterson had flirted on and off with writing, even winning an Edgar Award for best first novel in 1977. But while serving as youngest-ever CEO of the J. Walter Thompson ad agency—where he created the memorable "Toys R Us Kid" campaign—Patterson wrote *Along Came a Spider* (1992), the first of his Alex Cross murder mysteries. Small wonder that this advertising whiz kid went on to claim the record for the most #1 *New York Times* best sellers (39 of them, so far).

MOONLIGHTING

Some authors are so free-ranging in their interests, no new publication is surprising. But others are so closely identified with a single series or genre that it's virtually impossible to conceive of their doing anything else. Here are some notable side projects or different paths that famous authors have gone down.

H. A. Rey: Forever identified with *Curious George* and *The Man With the Yellow Hat*, Rey was also a keen astronomer in his private life. Frustrated by the quality of existing star guides, he wrote *The Stars: A New Way to See Them* (1952), which remains one of the most popular and easy-to-use books in the field.

Dan Brown: The *Da Vinci Code* author has built an empire out of a fascination with secret codes and ancient mysteries. But it's hard to imagine any cryptographer finding the keys to success in his early musical efforts, which included a self-produced children's cassette *SynthAnimals,* and a self-titled pop music album featuring gems like "976-Love." Sample lyric: "I take you to bed / I push the phone to my head / You make me feel like a man." Yikes.

Haruki Murakami: This award-winning Japanese writer has produced a string of challenging postmodern novels, including 1995's *The Wind-Up Bird Chronicle*—but they're nothing compared with the challenges he faces as a marathon runner and triathlete, a pursuit he chronicled in *What I Talk About When I Talk About Running.* Murakami even competed in a 100-kilometer ultramarathon in 1996.

On the Mound: It's no secret that Beat Generation auteur Jack Kerouac was a talented athlete in high school and during his brief time in college—but until 2009, virtually nobody knew that he also spent most of his life developing and playing a spectacularly complex fantasy baseball game. Chronicled in Isaac Gerwirtz's slim book *Kerouac at Bat: Fantasy Sports and the King of the Beats,* Kerouac's imaginary baseball league featured teams like the Boston Fords and Cincinnati Grays, and players with such colorful names as "Wino Love." Most of Kerouac's work on the game was concentrated in his teenage years, but he wrote imaginary press reports into his 30s and continued to fine-tune the game's formulas for another decade or so beyond that.

HAPPY FAMILIES ARE ALL ALIKE...

The old adage "Write what you know" never sparks as much controversy as when the writer's eye turns back on his or her own family.

AMIS & AMIS

Kingsley Amis and his son Martin made their names with superficially similar comic novels, set in or around the British university system—Kingsley's *Lucky Jim* (1954) and Martin's *The Rachel Papers* (1973). Though father and son remained close, their opinions of what made for good writing couldn't have diverged more: Kingsley recoiled from Martin's complicated postmodern style, allegedly throwing *Money* (widely viewed as his son's best work) across the room when a character named "Martin Amis" showed up. Likewise, Martin viewed his father's traditional narrative style as a relic: "He was always saying, 'I think you need more sentences like "He put down his drink, got up and left the room,"' and I thought you needed rather fewer of them."

Yet father and son were notorious, apart and together, for their various vices and scandals: Kingsley acknowledged that he was widely viewed as "one of the great drinkers, if not one of the great drunks, of our time," and both were legendary for their love of women—whether they were married to them or not. One of Kingsley's wives took revenge in 1962, scrawling "1 Fat Englishman I F**k Anything" on his back in lipstick as he slept on a Yugoslavian beach, and capturing the moment in a photograph.

MAN OF MANY VICES

Kingsley Amis is remembered as many things, but "model parent" isn't one of them: He allowed his boys, Martin and Philip (the latter named for writer Philip Larkin, a close friend), to smoke one cigarette each on Christmas—starting at age 5. At age 9, he upped the ante to one pack apiece.

BETTER HALF

In the early 1970's, Stephen King's wife, Tabitha, saved him from what could have been the most *horrifying* mistake of his life. King had achieved some meager success, publishing a number of short stories (most of them in men's magazines) and toiling on several novels while he taught at a Maine high school. Discouraged by constant rejection, he tossed the first few pages of another new novel into the trash—but Tabitha fished them out and encouraged him to continue the tale. The book? *Carrie* (1973), which sold more than 1 million copies in paperback and enabled King to devote himself full-time to writing.

THE ICEMAN COMETH

The dark clouds hovering above the works of misanthropic dramatist Eugene O'Neill plagued his family in real life, as well. O'Neill himself was a clinically depressed alcoholic; his mostly estranged sons, Eugene Jr. and Shane, both suffered from addictions of their own and ultimately each took his own life. Daughter Oona seemed to be the one exception to the rule: Her beauty was great enough to elicit daily letters from a smitten J. D. Salinger and a marriage to Charlie Chaplin. But O'Neill disowned Oona over her relationship with Chaplin (who was 36 years her senior).

THE BROTHERS SIMON

Two of Neil Simon's most enduring and recognizable creations, Felix Unger and Oscar Madison of *The Odd Couple,* are partly based on Simon's older brother Danny—himself a radio and TV comedy writer—and Hollywood agent Roy Gerber. The two men shared a home as both went through painful divorces, and their collective foibles inspired Danny, not Neil, to start writing a play about two mismatched male roommates. But Danny couldn't get past page 15 of the script and eventually turned it over to Neil, who awarded his brother one-sixth of the royalties from the hit play in perpetuity. Even though he lived the part, Danny always found it hard to connect with the play: When Neil brought an all-female *Odd Couple* to Broadway in 1985, Danny was brought on to direct . . . but was fired during the tryout tour.

....

> *"Everything, unequivocally, that I learned about comedy writing I learned from Danny Simon. Also, he was very nice."*
>
> —WOODY ALLEN

....

THE BITCHES ARE BACK

Novelist Jackie Collins and her actress big sister, Joan Collins—otherwise known as *Dynasty's* Alexis Carrington—have both built thriving careers from creating and portraying the rich, beautiful, and deviously decadent. And each has at least dipped a toe into the other's waters: Jackie started out as an actress in the 1950s and '60s, before turning full-time to writing books like *The Stud*

(1960) and its sequel, *The Bitch* (1979), both of which became films starring her older sister. Joan has been known to put pen to paper, too: In addition to the requisite beauty and lifestyle books, she has written six best-selling novels of her own (starting with 1988's *Prime Time*).

HARD TO BELIEVE

Though she's known for creating scheming, beautiful, fashion-obsessed female characters, Jackie Collins claims to have never had a facial or a professional manicure—but admits to being a "makeup-aholic."

BIG BROTHER, CIRCA 1940

Had network television been in business in 1940, it might have produced an early installment of the reality show *Big Brother* by training its cameras on the fascinating artistic and social experiment known as February House. Dreamed up (literally) by headstrong, idiosyncratic George Davis, the fiction editor of *Harper's Bazaar,* February House was an experiment in communal living by some of the most notable names of the time, many of whom pooled their funds to live in a huge four-story walkup in Brooklyn Heights. This ad hoc family included:

W. H. Auden: Davis enticed him with a promise of low rent and a view of the Brooklyn Bridge; Auden brought British composer Benjamin Britten (and his partner, Peter Pears) with him and wrote the libretto for Britten's *Paul Bunyan* while living there. For a time, the mostly straight-laced Auden acted like the father of the group, setting rules for everything from chores to dining-table conversation—but was also tormented by his unfaithful 20-year-old male lover and ultimately was driven away by the increasingly rowdy antics of later arrivals.

Carson McCullers: One of the original tenants, McCullers moved in, partially to expand her circle of friends outside of her troubled marriage. She became known in the house for cooking her signature dish "Spuds Carson," made from potatoes and any other leftover food she could find. Her creativity at February House wasn't limited to the kitchen—it was there that she laid the groundwork for *The Member of the Wedding* and *The Ballad of the Sad Café.*

Gypsy Rose Lee: The legendary stripper took up residence in part to burnish her serious-artist credentials, picking Davis's brain for assistance in finishing *The G-String Murders,* a mystery novel starring herself as the sleuth uncovering a series of strip-club killings.

Jane and Paul Bowles: The promiscuously bisexual couple brought a new element of wildness to February House, roping in temporary guests like Salvador Dali and his wife, Gala, and sparking feuds with other residents. Paul and Britten quarreled over where each would place his piano, with Auden siding with Britten, forever damaging his friendship with Bowles. The Bowleses famously chased each other around their bedroom one night, with Jane screaming "I'll get you for this; you've ruined my uterus!" Yet during their stay, Jane began *Two Sophisticated Ladies* and Paul shifted his focus from music to fiction.

ALL IN THE FAMILY

The grandfather of civil disobedience, advocate Henry David Thoreau led the first recorded student protest in the United States ... against the quality of food at Harvard University. His group's slogan? "Behold, our Butter stinketh!"

GOSSIP: GIRLS

Philosophers Jean-Paul Sartre and Simone de Beauvoir (intriguingly nicknamed *le Castor,* or "the Beaver," by an early boyfriend) were in their 20s when they first met in Paris in 1929; and against all odds, the beautiful Beauvoir and short, half-blind Sartre formed a lifelong relationship as unconventional as their philosophies. Though the two were physical with each other at the start of their "romance," their love affair later consisted primarily of sharing stories of sexual exploits with other people— or even assisting each other in the seduction of young women. On one occasion, when one of these girls fell into an affair with Beauvoir but refused Sartre's advances, he duly moved on to the girl's sister ... and when the seduction was finally consummated, he ran to Beauvoir to share the details.

....

"The word love has by no means the same sense for both sexes, and this is one cause of the serious misunderstandings that divide them."

—SIMONE DE BEAUVOIR

....

FANTASTIC FRIENDS

It was probably inevitable that C. S. Lewis and J. R. R. Tolkien would become friends (and at times, rivals): Both were World War I veterans, scholars of medieval and early modern literature, and lovers of ancient Icelandic myths. At Oxford University Tolkien welcomed Lewis into a group called the Coalbiters, a *Dead Poets Society*–type club for men who enjoyed sitting around reading old Icelandic tales (in the original Norse, naturally) with each other. Tolkien was also instrumental in Lewis's conversion to Christianity—without which Lewis would probably never have written the *Chronicles of Narnia*. Lewis praised "the inexhaustible fertility" of Tolkien's imagination, while Tolkien spoke of the "unpayable debt" he owed Lewis for his support and encouragement.

But like many longtime friends, the two could be catty: Tolkien disapproved of the overt Christian symbolism of the *Narnia* books, calling them "about as bad as can be." Lewis struck back by creating John Ransom, the hero of his "Space Trilogy," as a not-entirely-flattering version of Tolkien; Tolkien put some of Lewis's mannerisms into the character Treebeard, the loquacious but slow-talking leader of the *Lord of the Rings'* Ents. But the two could always rally together in their dislike of Modernist literature, as in Lewis's poetic takedown of T. S. Eliot:

> *For twenty years I've stared my level best*
> *To see if evening—any evening—would suggest*
> *A patient etherised upon a table;*
> *In vain. I simply wasn't able.*

UNTIMELY DEMISES

Far too many talented writers have ended their own lives. In memoriam, a look at a few:

- The poet Hart Crane (1899–1932) was just 33 years old when he died in 1932. The author of the epic poem "The Bridge" (1930), Crane had made little progress on newer works in later years as his drinking problem escalated. On a ship returning to New York from Mexico, Crane was involved in a fight in the sailors' quarters, then threw himself into the Gulf of Mexico.

- *Mrs. Dalloway* author Virginia Woolf (1882–1941) and her husband, author and critic Leonard Woolf, had made preparations to commit suicide together in the event of a Nazi invasion of Britain. But Virginia, a longtime sufferer of depression, instead drowned herself alone in a river near the Woolf's country house. The note she left for her husband read, in part, "I have a feeling I shall go mad. I cannot go on longer in these terrible times. I hear voices and cannot concentrate on my work. I have fought against it but cannot fight any longer."

- Always a heavy drinker but especially so in later years, Ernest Hemingway (1899–1961) was given electroconvulsive therapy to treat depression. Some critics theorized that he was so disturbed by the resulting memory loss that he shot himself with his favorite shotgun. Obituaries at the time noted his wife's statement that the gun had accidentally gone off while Hemingway was cleaning it, but "Papa" was a known firearms expert, unlikely to make such a novice mistake. Hemingway's father had also committed suicide.

- The first poet to posthumously win a Pulitzer prize, Sylvia Plath (1932–63) left a note for a neighbor to call a doctor, sealed off the rooms between her kitchen and her children with wet cloths, and turned on the oven. Several years later, the longtime mistress of Plath's husband, Ted Hughes (a renowned poet), killed herself in a similar fashion, with even more-tragic results: The couple's 4-year-old daughter died as well.

- John Kennedy Toole (1933–69) ran away from home following a fight with his mother in January 1969. He was found asphyxiated in his car several months later, after a road trip that took him to the Georgia home of fellow Southern writer Flannery O'Connor. *A Confederacy of Dunces* lay in Toole's desk drawer for more than a decade after his death, until his mother finally persuaded Walker Percy to read it.

- The exact date of *Trout Fishing in America* (1967) author Richard Brautigan's (1935–84) death has never been determined; he had clearly been dead from a self-inflicted gunshot wound for several weeks when his body was found. Strangely, it was only after his death that Brautigan's father found out about the existence of a famous son: Brautigan's mother and father had separated before he was born.

- Perhaps fittingly for a man who, as a young writer, investigated why Ernest Hemingway had committed suicide (and made off with the elk horns that hung over the entrance to Hemingway's Idaho home), Hunter S. Thompson (1937–2005) shot himself in February 2005. He left a note, entitled "Football Season Is Over" that read:

  "No More Games. No More Bombs. No More Walking. No More Fun. No More Swimming. 67.

That is 17 years past 50. 17 more than I needed or wanted. Boring. I am always bitchy. No Fun— for anybody. 67. You are getting Greedy. Act your old age. Relax—This won't hurt."

- After suffering depression for most of his adult life, David Foster Wallace (1962–2008) hanged himself in September 2008. He had stopped taking Nardil, an anti-depressant, more than a year before his death. Wallace had taken extreme measures—including electroconvulsive therapy—trying to alleviate his mental illness.

BEDTIME FOR GONZO

Hunter S. Thompson's 2005 memorial celebration was as irreverent as Thompson himself. According to Thompson's wishes, a 15-story cannon modeled on Thompson's "gonzo fist" (a double-thumbed fist clutching a peyote button, a symbol first used in his 1970 campaign for sheriff of Aspen), shot fireworks filled with Thompson's ashes into the air. The actor Johnny Depp, who portrayed Thompson in a movie version of *Fear and Loathing in Las Vegas* (1998), covered most of the cost of construction. As the fireworks erupted and ashes fell on some 250 guests in attendance, actor Harry Dean Stanton said, "I have never seen an event like this. And I'm old. Very old."

DEATH BY MISADVENTURE

These writers were legends in their own times, but their lives didn't have the most glorious of endings.

Li Po (701–762): The Chinese poet is said to have drowned after falling out of a boat, trying to embrace the moon's reflection in the water.

Christopher Marlowe (1564–93): The infamously hot-tempered playwright (who also is believed to have served as a spy for Queen Elizabeth I) was stabbed in the head, allegedly over payment of a bar tab—though some believe it was a politically motivated murder.

Edgar Allan Poe (1809–49): For almost 150 years, Poe's death was believed to have resulted from complications of alcoholism: He was found unconscious outside a Baltimore saloon and died four days later, after slipping in and out of a coma. But in 1996 Dr. R. Michael Benitez reviewed Poe's case and concluded that the writer had more likely died from rabies, possibly contracted from one of his own pets.

Leo Tolstoy (1828–1910): At age 82, the renowned author of *War and Peace* left his estate in the hands of his secretary, Vladimir Chertkov, and embarked on a new life as a wandering ascetic—but soon after died of pneumonia at a remote railway station.

Sherwood Anderson (1876–1941): After accidentally swallowing part of a toothpick embedded in an hors d'oeuvre at a cocktail party, Anderson contracted peritonitis and died a few days later.

Tennessee Williams (1911–83): Under the influence of drugs and alcohol in a New York hotel room, the playwright choked to death on the cap from a bottle of eyedrops.

....

"Life does not cease to be funny when people die any more than it ceases to be serious when people laugh."

—GEORGE BERNARD SHAW

....

Index

Note: Page references in **boldface** indicate boxed text.

A

Absolutely True Diary of a Part-Time Indian, The, 260
Adams, Douglas, **217,** 313–14
Adams, Harriet Stratemeyer (Carolyn Keene), 267, 268
"Address to a Haggis," **208**
"Adventure of the Missing Three-Quarter, The," 237
Adventures of Huckleberry Finn, The, 261–62
Adventures of Pinocchio, The, 248
Aeneid, 185
Albert, Laura (J. T. LeRoy), 271
Albom, Mitch, 282, 312–13
Alcott, Louisa May, 256
Alexie, Sherman, 260
"Allegory of the Cave," 291
All the King's Men, 198
"American Cars: Designed for Death," 301
Amerika, 186–87
Amis, Kingsley, 319, **320**
Amis, Martin, 319
Anathem, 315
Andersen, Han Christian, 249

Anderson, Sherwood, 329
Andrzejewski, Jerzy, 200
And to Think That I Saw It on Mulberry Street, 213
Angelou, Maya, 310–11
Angels & Demons, 196
Animal Farm, 204, 213
Answered Prayers, 183–84
Armory, Guy (Ray Bradbury), **217,** 307
Asimov, Isaac, 207
Atwood, Margaret, 314
Auden, W. H., **26,** 322–23, 324
Austen, Jane ("A Lady"), 232, 279, 289
Auster, Paul, **223**

B

Bach, Leon Chaim (Michael Chabon), 309
Bachman, Richard. *See* King, Stephen
Baldwin, James, 212
Barrett, Elizabeth. *See* Browning, Elizabeth Barrett
Barrus, Tim (Nasdijj), 272–73
Barry, Dave, 312–13
Bell, Acton, Currer, and Ellis (the Brontë sisters), 308
Bellamy, Edward, **217**
Bennett, Gertrude Barrows (Frances Stevens), **219**

Benson, Mildred Wirt (Carolyn Keene), 267

Binder, Jack, 207

Biographical Stories for Children, 249

Black Veil, The, **281**

Blair, Eric (George Orwell), 204, 213, 306

"Blind Bard" (Homer), 197

Block, Lawrence, 240–41

Blume, Judy, 263

Bond, James, 229, 230

Borges, Jorge Luis, 197, 212

Bowdler, Thomas, 203

Bowdlerize, 203

Bowles, Jane and Paul, 323

Box, Edgar (Gore Vidal), 308–9

Bradbury, Ray (Ron Reynolds, Anthony Corvais, Guy Armory, Doug Rogers, William Elliott), 194, **217,** 307

Bramy Raju (Gates of Paradise), 200

Brautigan, Richard, 327

Brave New World, **217, 264**

Breakfast of Champions, 303

Bridget Jones's Diary, **235**

Bridwell, Norman, **254**

Britten, Benjamin, 323, 324

Brod, Max, 186

Brontë, Anne, Charlotte, and Emily, 307–8

Brooks, Max, 226–27

Brown, Dan, 196, 317–18

Brown, Margaret Wise, **263**

Brown, Solyman, **245**

Browning, Elizabeth Barrett, **189,** 290

Browning, Robert, 290

Buck, Pearl, 212

Bukowski, Charles, 191

Bunnicula, 254

Burgess, Anthony, 194

Burnford, Sheila, **254**

"Burning Chrome," 209

Burns, Robert, **208**

Burns Night, 208

Burroughs, William, 191–92

Butler, Octavia, **219**

Byron, Lord, 218, 224

C

Call for the Dead, 229

Capek, Karel, 207

Capote, Truman, 183–84, 195

Carmilla, 225

Carrie, 320

Carroll, Lewis (Charles Lutwidge Dodgson), 284, 306

Carson, Rachel, 299–300

Carter, Forest "Little Tree" (Asa Earl Carter), 272

Catch 186, **206**

Catcher in the Rye, The, 262

Cat in the Hat, The, **254**

Caulfield, Holden, 262

Chabon, Michael (August Van Zorn), 309

Chandler, Raymond, 182–83, 215, 239, **241**

Charlotte's Web, 251

Chatterton, Thomas (Thomas Rowley), 276

Cheever, John, 284

Chinaski, Henry (Hank), 191

Christie, Agatha, 238

Christmas Carol, A, 205

Chronicles of Narnia, 325

Cinderella, 248

City and the Pillar, The, 308–9

Clancy, Tom, **230**

Clarke, Sir Arthur C., 208, 216

Clemens, Samuel Langhorne. *See* Twain, Mark (Samuel Langhorne Clemens)

Clifford the Big Red Dog, **254**

Coalbiters, 325

Cobain, Kurt, 285

Coleridge, Samuel Taylor, 193

Collins, Jackie and Joan, 321–22, **322**

Collodi, Carlo, 248

Common Sense, 291–92

Communist Manifesto, The, 294–95

Confederacy of Dunces, A, 312, 327

Cook, Robin, 228
Cool, Bertha, 239
Copeland, Douglas, 207
Cornwell, David John Moore (John le
    Carré), 229
Corso, Col. Philip J., 273–74
Corvais, Anthony (Ray Bradbury), 307
Crane, Hart, 326
"Crooked Man, The," **237**
Cryptomonicon, 315
Curious George, 252, 317

D

Dahl, Roald, 258, **258,** 315
Dailey, Janet, 234
Dali, Salvador and Gala, 323
Danielewski, Mark Z., 200–1
Dansel, Michel (Michel Thaler), 200
Darkening Ecliptic, The, 277
Darkness Visible: A Memoir of Madness,
    281
Darwin, Charles, 286, 296–97, **297**
Da Vinci Code, The, 196, 317–18
Day After Roswell, The, 273–74
Death and Life of Great American Cities,
    The, 299
"Death of a Pig," 251
de Balzac, Honore, 192–93
de Beaumont, Gustave, 294
de Beauvoir, Simone, 189–90, 324
Defonseca, Misha, 275
Democracy in America, 294
dc Tocqueville, Alexis, 294
Dick, Philip K., 190
Dickens, Charles, 181–82, 195, **204,** 205
Dickinson, Emily and Lavinia, 186
Dixon, Franklin W. (Leslie McFarlane),
    267
Doctor De Soto, 252
Dodgson, Charles Lutwidge (Lewis
    Carroll), 284, 306
Dostoyevsky, Anna, 286
Doyle, Sir Arthur Conan, 237, **237,** 238

Dracula, 225
Dracula, Count, 225–26
Duke, Uncle (from Doonesbury), 304
Dumbledore, Albus, **305**
Dupin, C. August, 236, 237, **237**
"Dymaxion Chronofile," 286

E

Eclogues, 185
Education of Little Tree, The, 272
Eggers, Dave, 283
Einstein, Albert, 287
Elliott, William (Ray Bradbury), 307
Ellison, Harlan, 221
Engcls, Friedrich, 294–95
Equalizer, The, 209
Eugenides, Jeffrey, 311
Everard, Katherine (Gore Vidal), 309
Ewing, Frederick R., 278

F

Fahrenheit 451, 194, **217**
Fair, A. A. (Erle Stanley Gardner), 239
Family Shakespeare, 203
Fantova, Johanna, 287
Farmer, Philip José, 303
Faulkner, William, 212
Faust, 193
February House, 322–24
Fielding, Helen, **235**
Finnegan's Wake, 198–99, 289–90
Fireman, The, 194
Fitzgerald, F. Scott, 182
Fleming, Ian, 229
Fragments: Memories of a Wartime
    Childhood, 274
Frank, Anne, 212, 285
Frankenstein, 218
Frey, James, 271, **272**
From the Earth to the Moon, **217, 218**
Fuller, Buckminster, 286

G

Gaddis, William, 200
Gadsby: Champion of Youth, 199
Gardner, Erle Stanley (A. A. Fair), 239
Garman, Steven, 243
Gathers, Hunter, 305
Geisel, Theodor (Dr. Seuss), **213, 254, 257,** 266
Generation X: Tales of an Accelerated Culture, 207
Gernsback, Hugo, **217**
Gerritsen, Tess, 228
Gerrold, David, **209**
Gerwirtz, Isaac, 318
Gibson, William, 209, 221
Giovanni's Room, 212
Girl, Interrupted, **281**
Gogol, Nicolai, 185–86
Golden Compass, The, **265**
Golding, William, **264**
Goldmark, Kathi Kamen, 312
Good Earth, The, 212
Goodnight Moon, 263, 263
Grahame, Kenneth and Alastair, 253
Grahame-Smith, Seth, 225
Grapes of Wrath, The, 311
Great Gatsby, The, 182
Grimm, The Brothers, 247–48
Grisham, John, **230,** 231
Grosjean, Bruno (Binjamin Wilkomirski), 274

H

Hamlet *(Hamlet),* 202, **203**
Hammer, Mike, 239–40
Hammett, Dashiell, 215, 239, **241**
Handler, Daniel (Lemony Snicket), 306, 314
Handmaiden's Tale, The, 314
Hansel and Gretel, 247
Hardy Boys series, 267, 268
Harlequin, 232, **232**
Harris, Thomas, **231**

Harry Potter, 253, 263, 265, 305
Harvest, 228
Hawthorne, Nathaniel, 210, 249
Heller, Joseph, **206**
Hemingway, Ernest, 195, 210, 261, 326, 327
Hillerman, Tony, 212
Hitchhiker's Guide to the Galaxy, **217,** 313–14
Holmes, Sherlock, 205, 236, 237, **237**
Homer (the "Blind Bard"), 197
House of Leaves, 200–1
Howe, Debbie and James, 254
Hugo, Victor, 196
Huxley, Aldous, **193, 217, 264**

I

I, Libertine, 278
I, the Jury, 239–40
Incredible Journey, The, **254**
Innocence Project, The, 231
Innocent Man, The, 230
In Search of Lost Time (Remembrance of Things Past), 213
In the Night Kitchen, **264**
"Invisible Prince, The" (Joseph Sheridan le Fanu), 225
Ireland, William Henry, 276–77
Irving, Clifford, 274
Irving, John, **196**
Irving, Sir Henry, 225–26, **225**
Islands in the Sky, 208

J

Jacobs, Jane, 299
Jasper, John, 181
Jenkins, Jerry B., **223**
Jerusalem, Spider, 304
Jones, Margaret B. (Margaret Seltzer), 273
Joyce, James, 198–99, 289–90
JR, 200
Jungle, The, 297–98

K

Kafka, Franz, 186–87, 204

Kafkaesque, 204

Kay, Cameron (Gore Vidal), 309

Kaysen, Susanna, **281**

Keeler, Harry Stephen, 242–43

Keene, Carolyn (Mildred Wirt Benson, Harriet Stratemeyer Adams), 267

Kerouac, Jack, **201,** 212, 318

Kerouac at Bat: Fantasy Sports and the King of the Beats, 318

Kesey, Ken, **264**

King, Stephen (Richard Bachman) and Tabitha, 192, 221, **223, 230,** 308, 312–13, 320

Koontz, Dean, **230**

Kubla Khan, 193

L

La Disparition (A Void), 199

"Lady, A." *See* Austen, Jane

LaHaye, Tim, **223**

"Lamb to the Slaughter," 258

Lassman, David, 279

Lawrence, D. H., 196

le Carré, John (David John Moore Cornwell), 212, 229

Lee, Gypsy Rose, 323

Lee, Harper, **264**

le Fanu, Joseph Sheridan ("The Invisible Prince"), 225

Left Behind, **223**

Left Hand of Darkness, The, 213

Le Guin, Ursula K., 213, **219**

Leonard, Elmore, 241

LeRoy, J. T. (Laura Albert), 271

Lessing, Doris, **219**

Lethem, Jonathan, 220

Lewis, C. S., 242, 325

Lindgren, Astrid, 259

Li Po, 328

Listen, Little Man!, 257

Live and Let Die, 229

Lolita, 187, 206, 213

Long Goodbye, The, 182

Longstocking, Pippi, 259

"Long Thing, The," 184

Lorax, The, 266

Lord of the Flies, **264**

Lord of the Rings, The, 291, 325

Loring, Linda, 182–83

Love and Consequences, 273

Lovecraft, H. P., 215, **219,** 290

Luntiala, Hannu, 201

M

Maddox, Tom, 221

Maggots: Poems on Several Subjects, Never Before Addressed, 245

Malaprop, Mrs., 205

Malapropism, 205

"Malley, Ern" (James McAuley and Harold Stewart), 277

Mamet, David, 311

"Man Who Disappeared, The" (Amerika), 186–87

Man With the Yellow Hat, The, 317

Marx, Karl, 294–95

Marlowe, Christopher, 329

Marlowe, Philip, 182–83, 236, 239

Martin, John, 191

Matheson, Richard, **223**

McAuley, James ("Ern Malley"), 277

McCarthy, Cormac, **223**

McCourt, Frank and Malachy, 282

McCullers, Carson, 323

McFarlane, Leslie (Franklin W. Dixon), 267

"McJob," 207

Melville, Herman, 210

Mermaid, The Little, 249

Metalious, Grace, 233–34

Miller, Arthur, 311

Million Little Pieces, A, 271, **272**

Milne, A. A. and Christopher Robin, 253

Milton, John, 197–98

Misha: A Mémoire of the Holocaust Years, 275

Moody, Rick, **281**

Mother Goose's Melodies, 250

Munro, Alice, 211

Murakami, Haruki, 318

"Murders in the Rue Morgue, The," 236

Mystery of Edwin Drood, The, 181–82

N

Nabokov, Vladimir, Vera, and Dmitri, 187, 200, 206, 213

Nader, Ralph, 300–1

Nancy Drew series, 267, 268

Nasdijj (Tim Barrus), 272–73

Neuromancer, 209

Nin, Anaïs, 213

1984, 204

Norton, Andre (Alice Mary Norton), **219**

O

Odd Couple, The, 321

Odyssey, The, 197

Of Mice and Men, **264,** 311

One Flew Over the Cuckoo's Nest, **264**

O'Neill, Eugene, 320

Onion, The, 265

On the Origin of Species (Origin of Species), 286, 296–97

On the Road, **201**

Original of Laura, The, 187

Origin of Species (On the Origin of Species), 286, 296–97

Orwell, George (Eric Blair), 204, 213, 306

Orwellian, 204

P

Paine, Thomas, 291–92

Pale Fire, 200

Pale King, The, 184

Paradise Lost, 198

Parker, Dorothy, 189

Parker, Robert B., 183, **241**

Patterson, James, **230,** 317

Pearson, Ridley, 312–13

Perchance to Dream, 240

Perec, Georges, 199

Perrotta, Tom, **269**

Persuasion, 279

Peyton Place, 233–34

Pilkey, Dav (Dave), 306

Pinocchio, 248

Places I Never Meant to Be, 263

"Plain Truth," 291–92

Plath, Sylvia, 213, 327

Plato, 291

Poe, Edgar Allan, 236, 329

Poky Little Puppy, The, **254**

Polidori, John, 226

Pollyanna, 206

"Pomperipossa in the World of Money," **259**

Poodle Springs, 240

Poodle Springs Mystery, 182–83

Porter, Eleanor, 206

Potter, Harry, 305

Pound, Ezra, 289–90

Pride and Prejudice and Zombies, 225

Proust, Marcel, 195, 213

Pullman, Philip, **265**

Q

Queer, 191–92

R

Ransom, John, 325

Reich, Wilhelm, 257

Reilly, Ignatius, 312

Remembrance of Things Past (In Search of Lost Time), 213

Republic, The, 291

Rey, H. A. (Hans Augusto) and Margret, 252, 317

Reynolds, Ron (Ray Bradbury), 307

Riddle of the Traveling Skull, The, 242–43

Rivals, The, 205
Road, The, **223**
Roberts, Nora (J. D. Robb), 234
Rock Bottom Remainders, 312–13
Rogers, Doug (Ray Bradbury), 307
Ros, Amanda McKittrick, 242
Rosenblat, Herman, 275
Rostand, Edmond, 196
Roth, Philip, 195
Rowley, Thomas, (Thomas Chatterton), 276
Rowling, J. K. (Joanne, Newt Scamander, Kennilworthy Whips), **230, 253,** 263, 305, 307
Rumpelstiltskin, 248
R.U.R. (Rossum's Universal Robots), 207
Rymer, James Malcom, 225

S

Saint Genet, 189–90
Salinger, J. D., 262
Sanctuary, 212
Sarah, 271
Sartre, Jean-Paul, 189–90, 324
Scamander, Newt (J. K. Rowling), 305
Scrooge, Ebenezer, 205
Scudder, Matthew, 240–41
Sedaris, David, 280
Seltzer, Margaret (Margaret B. Jones), 273
Sendak, Maurice, 253, **264**
Seuss, Dr. (Theodor Geisel), **213, 254, 257,** 266
Shakespeare, 202, 203
Shaw, George Bernard, 181, 329
Sheldon, Alice Bradley (James Tiptree, Jr.), **219**
Shelley, Mary, 218, 223, 293
Shepherd, Jean, 278–79
Sheridan, Richard, 205
Silent Spring, 299–300
Silverstein, Shel, 257–58, 260
Simon, Neil and Danny, 321

Sinclair, Upton, 297–98, **298**
Slaughterhouse-Five, **264**
Smiley, George, 229
Smith, Adam, 292–93
Smith, E. E., 208
Smith, Liz, 183
Snicket, Lemony (Daniel Handler), 306, 314
Snow White, 247–48
"Space Trilogy," 325
Spade, Sam, 239
Spillane, Mickey, 239–40
Spock, Dr. (*Star Trek*), 220
Stars: A New Way to See Them, 317
Star Trek, **209,** 220–21
Steel, Danielle, **230,** 233
Steig, William, **252,** 256–57
Steinbeck, John, **264,** 311
Stephenson, Neal, 315
Stevens, Frances (Gertrude Barrows Bennett), **219**
Stewart, Harold ("Ern Malley"), 277
Stoker, Bram, 225–26, **225**
Stowe, Harriet Beecher, 295–96
Stratemeyer, Edward, 267
Stratemeyer Syndicate, 267–68
Stross, Charles, 222
Sturgeon, Theodore (Edward Hamilton Waldo), 220–21, 278, 303, **304**
Styron, William, **281**
Suskind, Richard, 274
Sweet Valley High series, 269
Sylvester and the Magic Pebble, **252**

T

Tales of Beedle the Bard, The, 305
Tan, Amy, 310, 312–13
Tenggren, Gustaf, **254**
Tenth Good Thing about Barney, The, 260
Thaler, Michael (Michael Dansel), 200
Thomas, Dylan, 188
Thompson, Hunter S., 190, 304, 327–28, **328**

Thoreau, Henry David, 306, **324**

Tiptree, James, Jr. (Alice Bradley Sheldon), 219

Toad of Toad Hall, 253

To Kill a Mockingbird, **264**

Tolkien, J. R. R., 242, 291, 325

Tolstoy, Leo, 329

Toole, John Kennedy, 312, 327

Le Train de Nulle Part (The Train from Nowhere), 200

Treebeard, 325

"Trouble with Tribbles, The," **209**

Trout, Kilgore, 220, 278, 303–4

Tuesdays with Morrie, 282

Turow, Scott, 231, 312–13

Twain, Mark (Samuel Langhorne Clemens), 195, **225,** 242, 261–62, 289, 316

2001: A Space Odyssey, 216

Tycoon, The Last, 182

U

Uncle Tom's Cabin, 295–96

Unsafe at Any Speed, 300–1, **301**

U.S. Penitentiary System and Its Application in France, The, 294

V

826 Valencia, 283

Vampyre, The, 224

Van Zorn, August (Michael Chabon), 309

Varius, 185

Varney the Vampire, 225

Venus on the Half-Shell, 303

Verne, Jules, **217, 218**

Vetch, Albert (Michael Chabon), 309

Vidal, Gore (Edgar Box, Cameron Kay, Katherine Everard), 308–9

Viimeiset Viestit (The Last Message), 201

Vindication of the Rights of Woman, The, 293

Vinge, Joan, **219**

Viorst, Judith, 259–60

Virgil, 185

Vollmer, Joan, 191

Vonnegut, Kurt, 215, 220, 264, 303–4

Vortigern and Rowena, 277

W

Waldo, Edward Hamilton (Theodore Sturgeon), 220–21, 278, 303, **304**

Walker, Alice, 198

Wallace, David Foster, 184, 328

Warren, Robert Penn, 198

Watson, Dr., 237

Wealth of Nations, The, 292–93

Wells, H. G., **217**

Wesley, Samuel, 245

When HARLIE Was Won, **209**

Whips, Kennilworthy (J. K. Rowling), 305

White, E. B., 251

Wilkomirski, Binjamin (Bruno Grosjean), 274

Willamson, Jack, 209

Williams, Tennessee, 215, 329

Winnie the Pooh, 252–53

Wollstonecraft, Mary, 293

Woolf, Virginia and Leonard, 326

Wright, Ernest Vincent, 199

X

X-Files, The, 221

Z

Zombie Survival Guide, The, 226–27

spring forward • Vonnegut • red sky

bona fide • Animal Farm • c

• bête noir • cause célèbre • c'est la vie

coup d'état • déjà vu • objet d'art

pluribus unum • auto da fé • faux SP

Woolf pli gratia (e.g.) • ménage à tr

• pro bono • post scriptum (P.S.) • tê

ad infinitum • o domini (A.D.) • afici

nado • bona fide • caveat emptor co

poco • bête noir • cause célèbre • c'

a vie • coup d'état • déjà vu • objet d'a

e plchloe rhodes • auto da fé • fa

pas • exempli gratia (e.g.) • ménage à tr

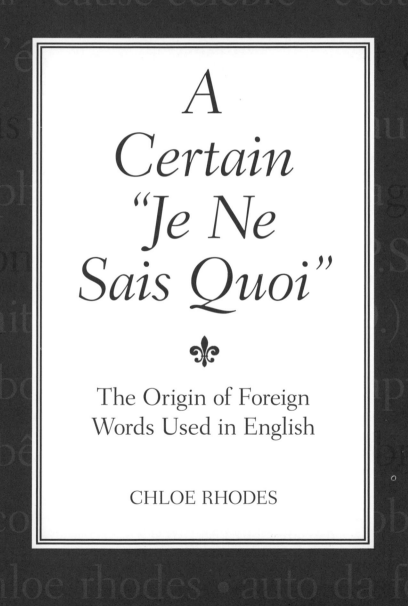

A
Certain
"Je Ne
Sais Quoi"

✤

The Origin of Foreign
Words Used in English

CHLOE RHODES

Introduction

———————⊶⟨⟩⟜——————

The wonderful thing about words is that once we've learned their meanings, we rarely have to give them a second thought. Whether we're arguing a point, expressing our passion, or simply ordering a pizza, the words are there; generally we have no need to pause to consider their precise meanings or ponder over their provenance.

However, for all the benefits such fluency brings, it does mean that we're often oblivious to the fascinating origins of the words and phrases we use every day, which is why this book came to be. The list of words and phrases within it is by no means exhaustive, and it doesn't offer an academic look at etymology, but it does attempt to tell the stories of some of the thousands of foreign words and phrases that have come to be commonly used in English.

That there are so many should come as no surprise; English speakers have been linguistic magpies since at least the fifth century, when the dialects of Anglo-Saxon settlers, Celts, and Norse invaders were cobbled together to create Old English. When the Normans arrived in 1066, it must have seemed only natural to appropriate some of their vocabulary, too; by the end of the thirteenth century, more than 10,000 French words had been absorbed into English, 75 percent of which we continue to use today. The Norman conquerors also shared with us a fondness for Latin, both ancient Gaul and Britain having been invaded by the Romans in 58 BC and AD 43 respectively, and a few centuries later the European Renaissance brought Latin and ancient Greek to the fore once more.

As the British Empire grew from the late sixteenth to the early twentieth centuries, marauding seafarers filled their boats not only with strange Asian spices and exotic fabrics but also with words for all the new foods, animals, and items of clothing they had seen. In North America, meanwhile, English was to receive its most vigorous boost yet. Words from Italy, Spain (via Mexico), Poland, Germany, and eastern Europe were soon spilling from the immigrant ships to be mopped up by the giant lexical sponge of American English.

Very often the new terms had no practical purpose—English speakers didn't go around gobbling up foreign words because they were short of their own—they did it because, where self-expression is concerned, you can never have too many options. Very often there is just something about throwing in a foreign word or phrase that lends whatever we have to say, well—how best to put it?— a certain *je ne sais quoi*.

A Note from the Publisher

The convention in written English is to place unfamiliar foreign terms, or relatively newly acquired ones, in italics. Opinions differ as to when a word has been so fully absorbed into English that it no longer needs italics, but our vade mecums (see page 500) have been the eminently reliable *New Oxford Dictionary for Writers and Editors* and *New Oxford Spelling Dictionary*.

A

---~⚬⚬⚬~---

A cappella

in the manner of the chapel or choir
(Italian, from the Latin "*a cappella*")

This phrase comes to us via the Late Latin "*cappa*," meaning "cap"
or "cloak"—the chapel that housed the cloak of Saint Martin, kept
as a relic, was thus the "*capella*." The meaning of the term has now
expanded to include any unaccompanied vocal performance, from
the doo-wop bands of 1950s America to barbershop quartets to
modern TV talent shows.

*The neighborhood dogs all howled along when Jeremy began his
a cappella serenade.*

---~⚬⚬⚬~---

A la carte

according to the menu (French)

An "à la carte" menu features individually priced items as
opposed to a set-price menu. The concept was introduced by
celebrated French chef Georges Auguste Escoffier during his
tenure at the Carlton Hotel in London at the turn of the last
century. Escoffier's 1903 cookbook *Le Guide Culinaire* is still
revered as a culinary bible, though his greatest claim to fame is
that one of his pupils was Ho Chi Minh, who presumably

thought he'd better get a bit of pastry practice under his belt before leading Vietnam to independence.

't'll have to be the à la carte menu for me; I've got a terrible craving for truffles.

A la mode

fashionable (French)

The link between France and fashion was established by King Louis XIV, whose court became such an epicenter of good taste that the British aristocracy didn't simply want to dress in French fashion, they wanted their phrase for it, too. In the seventeenth century the term was anglicized to become "alamode"—a light silk used to make scarves. In the United States the phrase has also come to mean "with ice cream"; there must have been a time in small-town America when the combined flavors of cooked apple, sweet pastry, and vanilla represented the very latest in fashionable, cutting-edge gastronomy.

Can I suggest these divine little ankle boots, madam? Python-skin platforms are so à la mode.

———❧☙❧———

A priori

from what precedes (Latin)

In philosophical debate, "a priori" knowledge is a form of knowledge that comes from what we know rationally to be true, without having to test or research it. Its opposite is "a posteriori" knowledge, which is gleaned through experimentation or experience. The great eighteenth-century German philosopher Immanuel Kant initiated the modern use of the term and believed that a priori knowledge was transcendental, stemming from an individual's cognitive faculties. In more general terms it is used literally or ironically for any argument or idea that is based on inherent knowledge rather than observation.

We know a priori that Tom won't say no to some kind of dinner; it doesn't matter what we get, that boy will eat anything.

———❧☙❧———

Ad hoc

for this (Latin)

This is one of many politically, administratively, and commercially useful terms to have retained its Latin form. It means something that is designed for one set purpose. "Ad hoc" committees are established by the government to help solve a specific problem; they're usually created in response to an urgent need and last only for the duration of the task in hand. This has led the phrase to have a broader meaning of improvised or provisional. For example, if plans are said to be "ad hoc," they might be seen as last minute and haphazard.

Jeffrey preferred to plan his plane-spotting trips for himself; the itineraries of his fellow enthusiasts seemed alarmingly ad hoc.

———

Ad lib

according to one's pleasure (Latin, from "*ad libitum*")

This was originally used to mark out the points within a piece of sheet music or theatrical script where performers could add their own personal flourish. In modern times the phrase is most often used to describe the unscripted, off-the-cuff comments that comedians, actors, or presenters add to their scripted material, either to get an extra laugh or to conceal the fact that they have forgotten their lines.

Oh, darlings, that was awful! The words just went right out of my head; I had to ad lib my way through the death scene.

———

Ad nauseam

to sickness (Latin)

An "*argumentum ad nauseam*" is an argument that is repeated until everyone is sick of hearing it. Much of the language of debate comes from the adversarial conventions established by Roman orator Cicero in the first century BC. "Ad nauseam" has been used in English since the early 1600s and is still employed to pour scorn on a well-rehearsed political argument. It's also used in reference to other annoyingly repetitive things, like people who recite lines from their favorite TV comedy until you want to tear your ears off.

Late again, Brian. Don't try to explain. I've heard your excuses ad nauseam.

Aficionado

ardent fan or devotee (Spanish)

In Spain "aficionado" is used most frequently to describe fans of bullfighting. Ernest Hemingway was a famous one; "*Aficion* means passion," says his narrator, Jake Barnes, in *The Sun Also Rises*. In English the term indicates a devoted fan of a sport or art form that evokes strong, primal feelings. There are jazz, opera, rugby, and ballet aficionados, but you're unlikely to hear the term applied to badminton fans, no matter how potent their ardor for the perfect drop-volley.

Sid "The Savage" Simmons lived in fear of being outed as a figure-skating aficionado; he'd been smitten since he saw Torville and Dean dance to Ravel's Boléro.

---⚬⊙⚬---

Agent provocateur

inciting agent (French)

A secret agent employed by the police or government to encourage criminals or dissidents to break the law so that they can be arrested. The phrase is still used in this way; in the United States the FBI has used agents provocateurs to infiltrate radical political groups like the Black Panthers and the Ku Klux Klan, and in the UK it's the name of a risqué lingerie firm that hopes to incite bad behavior of a different kind—*ooh la la!*

> *Agent Peters, we need you in there as an agent provocateur. Your undercover name will be "The Strangler."*

---⚬⊙⚬---

Agitprop

agitation and propaganda
(Russian, from "*agitatsii i propagandy*")

The Agitation and Propaganda section of the Communist Party's Central Committee was responsible for the education of the people after the 1917 Revolution. It used speeches, radio broadcasts, posters, film, and visual art to influence public opinion, though in Soviet Russia at that time there was no negative connotation to the word "propaganda." In modern Western usage it usually refers to political propaganda, especially of dissident or protesting groups, but also works of art and literature whose aim is to indoctrinate its audience with extreme leftist ideology.

Frederick feigned illness on the night of the Socialist Amateur Dramatic Society's monthly wine and poetry evening. He'd had his fill of agitprop at the last one.

Aide-mémoire

memory aid (French)

Early use of the phrase, which means a "note" or "memorandum," was limited to military and diplomatic fields. G. Lewis's 1846 book *Aide-Mémoire to the Military Sciences* was one of the first written references to it. In more recent times it has also come to refer to a memory-jogging symbol, like a knot tied in a handkerchief, or a mnemonic device, like the rhyme "i before e except after c."

Mr. Green's scowl was putting off the voters, so his political advisers drew smiley faces on each page of his speech as an aide-mémoire to look more cheerful.

Al dente

to the tooth (Italian)

This is the term Italians use to describe the way pasta should be served—cooked through but still firm, retaining some bite. The enormous popularity of Italian food in the UK and the United States has led the phrase to be widely used in English. It has also been adopted to describe vegetables like green beans and zucchini, which have been cooked briefly so they retain a bit of crunch.

The craze for al dente vegetables hadn't really caught on at Mrs. Higginson's guesthouse: her greens were so well cooked you had to eat them with a spoon.

———⟋ⵟⵟ⟍———

Al fresco

in the fresh (Italian)

In English we use the phrase to mean "in the fresh air," but to Italians it's a slang term for "in prison," like the English phrase "in the cooler." To avoid confusion when visiting Italy, ask for a table "*all'aperto*," meaning "in the open," if you want to dine, um, al fresco. The phrase has been used in English since at least the eighteenth century—the picnic at Box Hill in Jane Austen's *Emma* is described as an "al-fresco party."

I'd rather not eat al fresco again; last night I lost half my spaghetti to a seagull.

Algebra

reunion, restoration (Latin, from Arabic al-jabr)

Ninth-century Persian mathematician Muhammad bin Musa al-Khawarizmi first used the term to describe the methods by which letters and other symbols are used to represent numbers and quantities in equations and formulas. In fact, the romanized version was first used in English in reference to reuniting broken bones. In the twelfth century a Latin translation of al-Khawarizmi's work was published, and we have used "algebra" as a mathematical term ever since.

Sarah had found a pleasing way to practice the balancing principles of algebra—every time she ate one of her own sweets, she ate one of her brother's, too.

Alma mater

nourishing mother (Latin)

Your "alma mater" is your university or school. The phrase was originally used by the Romans as a title for goddesses and by early Christians to describe the Virgin Mary. "*Alma mater studorum,*" which translates as "nourishing mother of studies" was the motto of the University of Bologna in Italy—the oldest university in the world—and it may have been through this association that the term came to refer to places of education. Its meaning has extended in the United States to mean the school song or anthem.

Boris could barely contain his excitement on the way to the reunion at his alma mater. Ten years had passed since his failed attempt to woo Tiffany Plumbings, and he felt ready to give it another go.

Alter ego

other self (Latin)

The phrase, in the sense of a second self or alternative persona, was first used in reference to schizophrenia in the early nineteenth century. It is now also used to refer to a number of more benign double identities, from cross-dressers to authors whose characters are fictionalized versions of themselves. An alter ego has even become a fashionable accessory in the music business. David Bowie started it with Ziggy Stardust: Britney Spears, Mariah Carey and Beyoncé Knowles each have one, and Prince has two.

Barry in accounts seemed like such a mild-mannered and steady man, and yet the rumor was that he had an alter ego—Rosalita Lamé—and performed at the local cabaret club every other Friday.

Amok/amuck, to run

furious attack (Malay)

The word comes from the Malay description of a psychiatric disturbance, in which the sufferer is first subdued or even depressed before suddenly becoming wild, maniacal, and usually violent toward others. It is still used to describe the condition of people who commit a sudden, unprovoked attack, but it has also developed a colloquial meaning. When people are said to be "running amok"—like rioters, for example—they are acting wildly and without rational self-control.

Police had to be called to a major department store sale today after shoppers ran amok in the toy department.

Amuse-bouche

mouth amuser (French)

Something to tickle the taste buds before the arrival of a starter, an "*amuse-bouche*" will never appear on a menu, as it is complimentary and chosen by the chef. The concept of a bite-size taster of the chef's signature style was introduced as part of the nouvelle cuisine movement, which specializes in offering small, beautifully presented and intensely flavored courses. In France the colloquial phrase "*amuse-gueule*" ("*gueule*" being slang for "mouth") is more often used.

Tonight, mademoiselle, we have a speciality of roasted sea bass in a tarragon jus and to begin, an amuse-bouche of green pea and mint sorbet in a crisp Parmesan tuile.

Angst

fear (German)

Angst is generally translated simply as "fear," but it is often used to describe a profound horror, or existential dread, as coined by German philosophers in the mid-1800s. English novelist George Eliot wrote of "*Die Angst*," which brought on a pain in the heart, and the word became more widespread in English after the translation of Austrian psychologist Sigmund Freud's work. The 1980s saw the birth of teen angst—based on the sense of injustice and futility that comes with raging hormones, and you can now regularly find sports fans and businesspeople "angsting" over match results and corporate deals.

> *I've never known anything to cause as much angst as this week's unemployment numbers.*

Annus horribilis

horrible year (Latin)

A pun on "*annus mirabilis*," which described a year of British victories in the eighteenth century, this phrase was first used in Queen Elizabeth's speech at the end of 2002. Her year had been marred by the breakdown of three royal marriages and a devastating fire at Windsor Castle. Two years later Kofi Annan, then the UN secretary-general, repeated the phrase to describe a year in which the UN's Iraq "Oil for Food" program had been tainted by charges of corruption. It is now used widely to describe a bad year.

> *With the highest rainfall on record this really has been an annus horribilis for fans of beach volleyball.*

Anorak

heavy hooded jacket (Greenland Inuit)

The cozy, hooded "*anoraq*" is the garment worn by the Inuit people of the Arctic to protect them against the very harshest weather conditions. In the 1960s the "anorak" became popular in Britain as a style of jacket with a fur-trimmed hood beloved of Mods. The European version was a prototype for the technical clothing that evolved later for mountaineers, sailors, cavers, and other adventurers. At the time, it was innocent of negative associations. Today the word is used pejoratively for an enthusiast interested in information regarded as boring or unfathomable by the rest of us, probably because it's long been favored by trainspotters.

Rodney, an unashamed enthusiast for technical detail, was wearing a high-quality Gore-Tex anorak on the day he rescued three barely dressed fashionistas caught in a blizzard.

―⦿―

Appellation contrôlée

officially certified origin (French)

This refers to "*appellation d'origine contrôlée,*" the French system of guaranteeing the specific origin of their wines. Established in 1935, this method of classification controls seven aspects of the wine-producing process: the land vines are grown on, grape varieties used, viticultural methods (pruning and fertilization), yield, alcohol content, historical practices employed, and the taste, which are all tested before certification is given. In the UK and the United States our familiarity with the term is generally restricted to reading it on a wine label with a sigh of satisfied anticipation.

Ah-ha, an Appellation Bordeaux Contrôlée—perfect with roast beef!

―⦿―

Après-ski

after skiing (French)

"Après-ski" is used in English to describe the activities, primarily the nightlife, indulged in at ski resorts once the sun goes down. In the Alps the first après-ski drink is usually enjoyed in a bar near to the slopes while you're still sporting your ski wear. In France the term actually refers simply to the snow boots that you change into once you've taken your skis off, but most people would agree that the anglicized version has wider appeal. In the United States its meaning is broader still and extends to the general ambience of a resort.

Susan loved her winter breaks, though she never actually hit the slopes; she preferred to save her energy for the après-ski.

Apropos

on the subject of (French, from "*à propos de*")

There are several interlinked definitions for this phrase; the first is used, as in French, for "on the subject of," but more broadly it has come to mean "pertinent to," or "apt." For example, "an excellent point and very apropos." But it can also be used for "by the way," or "incidentally," when you're saying something that isn't to the point at all but seems worth saying anyway.

I should probably point out, apropos, that there are many foreign phrases that we use very liberally in English without ever having the faintest idea what they actually mean.

Arriviste

a person who has arrived (French)

An "arriviste" is someone who has risen to a higher rank in society but hasn't yet earned the respect of those he or she is joining. It was first used widely during the dramatic class changes that took place during the Industrial Revolution in the UK, when working-class families were able to ascend the social ladder with money made through enterprise rather than inheritance. In English the phrase is synonymous with "social climber," and in a modern context, it might be used to describe someone who is rather obnoxious or pushy.

Lady Budley-Hoebottom was determined not to make eye contact with Miss Carter. She was an arriviste if ever there was one—fake tan and acrylic nails always gave the game away.

Ars longa, vita brevis

the art is long, life is short (Latin)

This aphorism was coined by ancient Greek physician Hippocrates and comes from a longer quotation, which translates as, "Life is short, the art [in the sense of craft or skill] long, opportunity fleeting, experiment dangerous, judgment difficult." Hippocrates had surmised that none of us should be too hard on ourselves if we make mistakes, given that life is generally a very tricky business. In modern use the "life is short" bit has assumed a greater significance and is often quoted to remind someone to make the most of every minute (see *Carpe diem* page 372).

Don't beat yourself up about it, Dave, you'll pass next time— ars longa, vita brevis and all that.

Art nouveau

new art (French)

This was the international style of art and architecture that developed in the late 1800s and took its name from a Parisian gallery called the Maison de l'Art Nouveau, though, ironically, the French themselves often used the English term "modern style" to describe it. In the UK the architect Charles Rennie Mackintosh

(1868–1928) was the movement's leading practitioner. The popularity of the style gave rise to many copies, and now we also use the term to describe designs that imitate the art nouveau style.

Veronica's collection of coffee cups was her pride and joy—her favorite was a little pink one that she thought was rather art nouveau.

Assassin

hashish-eater (Arabic, from "*Hashshashin*")

The Assassins, also known as the Hashshashin, were a militant Islamic sect founded in the ninth century when Yemeni Shiite Hasan-I Sabbah led them in their mission to overthrow the Suni Muslims by killing off their leaders. The name Hashshashin, meaning "hashish-eaters," was given to them by their enemies. The word "assassin" was first recorded in English in 1603 and is now used to describe a hired killer, usually with a political target.

As a boy, Lance had dreamed of becoming a spy or a highly trained assassin. He still couldn't work out how he'd ended up in telemarketing.

———◦⌒◦———

Au fait

informed (French)

In French this expression can mean "by the way," but if it is embedded within the line "*être au fait de*," it means "to be informed about" or "up to a respectable level in." There are, of course, many synonymous phrases in English, such as "conversant in," "up-to-date with," and "abreast of," but somehow announcing that you're "au fait" with all the latest developments sounds infinitely more impressive.

Deborah would have liked a promotion, but there seemed to be only one route to the top, and she'd never been au fait with golfing terminology.

———◦⌒◦———

Auto-da-fé

act of faith (Portuguese)

The phrase comes from the Spanish Inquisition and describes a public ceremony, which included a procession, Mass, and sermon, before the sentences of condemned heretics were read out by the grand inquisitor. In English the term is used primarily in art to describe an image of a heretic being burned at the stake, although in fact, the executions didn't take place until the following day. It can also mean suicide by fire.

Painting number three is an oil painting depicting an auto-da-fé in Plaza Mayor in Madrid, circa 1683.

Avalanche

snow slide (Romansch)

Romansch, closely related to French, is the least commonly spoken of Switzerland's four native languages and is thought to have come from the vulgar Latin spoken by the Roman settlers in that area. In the high Swiss Alps, sudden movements of ice and snow are common, and sixteenth-century English-speaking visitors to the region brought the Romansch word for them home. We now use the word figuratively for any overwhelming deluge.

> *I'd love to join you for lunch, sweetie, you know I would, but I'm trapped under an avalanche of fan mail—it seems my award-winning juggling act went down rather well.*

B

Baksheesh

gift (Persian)

The most direct English equivalent is "tip," but "baksheesh" has a much more intricate meaning depending on the context in which it is used. In the Middle East and South Asia, the word originally meant a charitable donation—alms paid to a beggar or an offering to the gods. It is still used imploringly by Arab beggars: "*Baksheesh, effendi?*" In modern usage it refers more often to an extra payment to taxi drivers, hoteliers, waiters, and doormen. In the West it has developed somewhat shady undertones and occupies the territory somewhere between a tip and a bribe.

Why don't you give him a little something to oil the wheels? I've heard a bit of baksheesh goes a long way around here.

———⁓⊙⊙⊙⁓———

Bandanna

to tie (Hindi, via Sanskrit)

The tie-dying technique used to decorate scarves and handker-chiefs in India is called "*bandhana.*" The anglicized "bandanna" was incorporated into the English language during the days of the British Raj, when these tie-dyed scarves were worn around the necks and waists of English masters. Bandanna has since come to mean any triangular scarf worn round the neck or head, tie-dyed or not, though they're now more popular with wrestlers and cowboys than the English aristocracy.

It was rodeo day, and Hoyt wasn't taking any chances—he'd been up all night sewing his initials onto his lucky bandanna.

———⁓⊙⊙⊙⁓———

Bazaar

marketplace (Persian)

The first bazaars were established in the Middle East around the fourth century, and the word is thought to come from "*baha-char,*" which means "the place of prices" in the Middle Persian writing system Pahlavi. Crusaders from Italy got their first intro-duction to the Middle East in the tenth century and borrowed the word as "*bazzara,*" and it is probably through this European route that it came to be used in English.

Oh, Marni, I just love your gem-encrusted sandals! I must have a pair—please don't tell me you found them in some untraceable bazaar in the depths of Morocco.

Berserk
bear shirt (Old Norse)

He'll just have to wait like everyone else.

In the ninth century the Vikings used the word to describe their ferocious warriors, who wore bearskins instead of armor. "Berserkers" worked themselves into a frenzy before battle—some historians have suggested that they ate hallucinogenic mushrooms to heighten their rage—thus taking on the bear's bloodthirsty fury. It wasn't until a thousand years after the Viking invasions that the word appeared in English; Sir Walter Scott was one of the first to put it in print in his 1822 novel *The Pirate*. We still use it to mean "dangerously violent," but it can also indicate a much milder angry outburst or any kind of wild, unrestrained behavior.

Don't let your father catch you going out like that—he'll go berserk if he sees the length of your skirt.

Bête noire

black beast (French)

Think of the person or thing that you most loathe and detest—he, she, or it is your very own "bête noire." The term was originally reserved for mortal enemies or the stuff of your most terrifying nightmares—the sorts of things you might find in Room 101 in George Orwell's *1984*. But in recent times it has been diluted to mean any person or thing that you find personally troublesome or irritating, like a more universally applicable version of "pet hate." It's also a common way of referring to a sports team's biggest rival.

For two and a half hours Melissa kept her eyes firmly glued to her magazine, she liked to relax while she had her highlights done—chatty hairdressers were her bête noire.

Bijou

jewel (French)

The French term comes from the Breton word "*bizou,*" which means "ring for the finger." By the mid-sixteenth century, the French had replaced the "z" with a "j" and adopted it for any small gem or jewel, and by the late seventeenth century it had hopped across the Channel. In English its meaning has expanded still further to cover any exquisite and stylish little thing; today we use it to describe everything from jewels and restaurants to boutiques, hotels, and even cars.

Now, this flat is simply fantastic; less discerning buyers might say it's on the shabby side, but personally I think it's wonderfully bijou.

Bimbo

baby boy (Italian, from "*bambino*")

A bimbo is a clueless young woman who has plenty of sex appeal but not much in the brains department. Interestingly, the word is actually a contraction of the Italian for baby boy, "*bambino*," rather than the feminine version, "*bambina*"; early English usage was reserved for brainless men, but it quickly became more common as a description of a vacuous but pretty female. In the United States, the UK, and Canada, the term can also infer a rampant sexual appetite. A jealous wife might use it to refer to a woman who she thinks is trying to seduce her husband.

I'm sorry, Simon, we'll have to leave. I can't sit here with that bimbo batting her eyelashes at you.

Blasé

indifferent (French)

This word invokes a world-weary disinterest or nonchalance that comes about through overexposure or over-indulgence. "*Blaser*" means to "satiate" and may have come to French via the Middle

Dutch word "*blasen*"—to "blow up" or "swell." So someone who is "blasé" about something has had such a fill of it that he or she feels bloated and loses interest in it completely.

> *By the time she reached the eighth gallery, Matilda was feeling blasé about the Old Masters and was much more interested in finding the coffee shop.*

Blitz

lightning war (German, from "*Blitzkrieg*")

A "*Blitzkrieg*" is a lightning-fast attack (from "*Blitz*" lightning, and "*Krieg*" war), the tactical opposite to "*Stellungskrieg*" ("*Stellung*" meaning "position"), which is warfare from prepared positions, such as trenches or fortifications. In a 1938 German military journal it is defined as a "strategic attack" employing tanks, aircraft, and airborne troops, but official use of the term by the German forces during the war was rare. The sustained aerial bombardment of Britain by the Nazis from September 1940 to May 1941 became known as the Blitz. Modern usage is less specific and can refer to anything done with vigor and speed.

> *For the perfect winter soup just chop the leftovers from your Christmas dinner, blitz them together with some stock in the food processor, and there you have it!*

Bon mot

right word (French)

In English a "bon mot" is a quip or witty remark. The phrase crossed over from France around 1730 and became a fashionable way to describe the clever and amusing asides that entertained eighteenth-century high society. Oscar Wilde was later famous for peppering his plays with them. Sadly, many genuinely funny bons mots have been turned into clichés through overuse. The worst examples of these tend to be alcohol-related and can be found adorning the walls and menus of cheap bars and restaurants.

If you spent as much time studying as you dedicate to delivering bons mots to your classmates, Stevens, you might one day be able to graduate.

Bona fide

in good faith (Latin)

The original definition still stands in legal terminology, where an agreement or contract signed in good faith is said to be "bona fide," but in everyday use the phrase has become interchangeable with the word "genuine" and is usually used to describe a person or thing whose authenticity can be trusted. The plural also refers to the documentation that proves legitimacy, so an employer might ask to see an applicant's bona fides before offering him a job.

Ladies and gentlemen, boys and girls, prepare to be amazed— may I proudly present Bernice, our bona fide bearded lady.

Bonhomie

simple good-heartedness (French)

"Bonhomie" is the quality of good-natured friendliness—the term might be applied to someone who enjoys amiable conversation and has an affable disposition. The phrase first appeared in English literature in the mid-1800s and is still used in reference to warm, outgoing people, often men. Its absence in a person is also often noted as a subtle way of conveying when someone is somewhat cold and unfriendly.

Ted and Mary were dreading their dinner with the Joneses; Mr. Jones wasn't exactly known for his bonhomie, and Mrs. Jones usually loitered in the kitchen quietly quaffing the cooking wine.

———◦❧◦———

Bordello

brothel (Italian)

Though English speakers have borrowed this word from Italy, its true origins are Germanic—"*borde*" meant hut, which became the Old French word "*bordel*." In modern use "bordello" is an alternative word for brothel. The word is thought to date back to the late-sixteenth century. Despite its link to the oldest profession, it wasn't used in the modern sense until around 1850. In recent years its meaning has mellowed still further, and it is now sometimes used to describe a type of opulent interior design. There are even a few Italian restaurants called Il Bordello.

I thought we'd go for a bordello feel in this room, Deirdre—lots of velvet drapes and candelabra.

———◦❧◦———

Bourgeois

middle or merchant class (French)

This word comes from the old French "*burgeis*," which meant a "townsperson." It has evolved as a label for the powerful strata of society whose status comes from self-made wealth rather than aristocratic lineage. Originally there was nothing negative about the label. Even Karl Marx, who criticized the bourgeoisie for hypocrisy in *The Communist Manifesto*, used the term descriptively rather than pejoratively. Since then, though, it has taken on negative connotations, and in English we tend to use it to mean boringly middle-of-the-road, materialistic, or uncultured.

> *We'll have to turn the invitation down, Nova. I wouldn't sit through another of those bourgeois dinner parties if my Anarchist Club membership depended on it.*

---⌘---

Brio

vigor, vivacity (Italian/Spanish)

This is an Italian and Spanish word with Celtic origins; "*brigos,*" from which it is derived, meant "power," "strength," or "force." It is thought to have entered the English language around the eighteenth century through the Italian musical instruction *con brio*, which means perform "with vigor." We now use it to describe the kind of verve and liveliness that we imagine we would feel at a Spanish fiesta after a jug or two of sangria.

> *Did I tell you that Madeleine has started ballet lessons? Oh yes, she's only three, but her performance of the "Teddy Bears' Picnic" was full of brio.*

Bungalow

a small house or cottage with a single story (Hindi)

The Indian words "*bangala*" (Hindi), "*bungalow*" (Bengali), "*bangalo*" (Gujarati) all refer to a thatched or tiled one-story house surrounded by a wide veranda, sometimes with an additional attic story. The English suburban fondness for such houses, especially near the coast, changed the landscape in the twentieth century. However, the 1968 Beatles song "The Continuing Story of Bungalow Bill" was inspired by the real thing when John Lennon mocked a rich American at the Maharishi's meditation camp who proudly shot a tiger. (In fairness, the young man's action may have been necessary, and he never hunted again.)

With the elevator broken and a ten-story climb ahead, Arthur and Enid first conceived their dream—a bungalow by the sea.

C

Camaraderie

comradeship (French)

This word conveys a spirit of fellowship and trust between friends or colleagues. It has been used in English since the 1800s, when it described the strong bonds that developed between those who suffered alongside one another in wartime. We still use the word to describe the good relationship fostered in the military between troops and within any team or group of like-minded people united by a common cause.

Ever since the photocopying incident at the office Christmas party, the accounting department team had been bound by a real sense of camaraderie.

Carpe diem

seize the day (Latin)

The Roman poet Horace coined this phrase in his poem "Tu ne quaesieris" from Book 1 of *The Odes*, published in 23 BC. The poem was directed at a woman worrying about her future; its final line reads: "*Carpe diem, quam minimum credula postero*," which translates as, "Seize the day, trusting tomorrow as little as possible." The popularity of the phrase was renewed by the 1989 film *Dead Poets Society*, in which a teacher, played by Robin Williams, uses it to encourage his pupils to make their lives extraordinary.

At the airplane's hatch Brian was frozen with fear, what if the parachute failed, what if he landed in the middle of the ocean? "Carpe diem," he managed to whisper, and then he jumped.

Carte blanche

white or blank card (French)

This is a military term meaning "surrender," dating from the early 1700s, when a blank piece of paper was given to the victorious army on which they could write their terms. A "carte blanche" gave complete power to whomever it was given, and we still make use of this sense of the phrase today. If someone is given carte blanche, it means she has a free hand to do whatever she chooses.

Sarah stared at the orange wallpaper in horror—she knew she should never have given Francisco carte blanche with the choice of decor.

Cause célèbre

famous case (French)

This phrase comes from the *Nouvelles Causes Célèbres*, a collection of famous French court verdicts published in 1763. The term became common in English after the false conviction of Alfred Dreyfuss, a Jewish officer of the French army, for espionage in 1894. Still applied to court cases that incite public protest, the phrase can also be used to refer to any publicly controversial issue. Confusingly, many modern causes célèbres have supporters who are themselves famous, which has led the term to be mistakenly used for causes with celebrity backing.

From his cell Ernie Roberts thought he could hear the clamoring of an angry mob. For a heady moment he let himself believe it was for him, but he knew deep down that a financial fraud case would never become a cause célèbre.

Caveat emptor

let the buyer beware (Latin)

This phrase has stayed in the English language as a legal term; in property law it is used as a warning to potential buyers that the responsibility for checking the condition of a building lies with them. It has become an important phrase in the wider consumer market, too, particularly in the purchase of secondhand goods. The word "caveat" is also often used alone (without italics) as a noun to describe a warning, condition, or restriction.

Having got her special-offer impulse purchase home, and finding not only that did it not fit but that beige and shocking pink stripes weren't really "her," Susan was unable to prevent the phrase "caveat emptor" from entering her mind.

Cenotaph

empty tomb (French)

This word entered the French language from the Latin "*cenotaphium,*" which in turn took it from the Greek words "*kenos,*" meaning "empty," and "*taphos,*" meaning "tomb." A "cenotaph" is a monument to the dead whose bodies are either lost or buried elsewhere. The large numbers of unmarked graves and enormous numbers of soldiers and sailors with no known grave after the First World War led to the construction of cenotaphs across the world to honor the dead. The Tomb of the Unknown Soldiers in the

United States and France, and the UK's national war memorial, which is simply called the Cenotaph, are the best-known examples.

Crowds gather at the Tomb of the Unknown Soldier on Memorial Day to remember the US fallen heroes of both world wars and other conflicts of the twentieth and twenty-first centuries.

C'est la vie

that's life (French)

This phrase originated in France, where it was said with a sigh after something difficult or disappointing had happened to mean "that's just the way life goes." It is still used in France in this context, though these days it is considered old-fashioned. In English the phrase has stuck, but it does have to compete with such modern variations as "that's the way the cookie crumbles" and the somewhat more prosaic "shit happens."

Come on, Tony, you've got to put that French girl out of your mind and move on.

I know, Dave, but everywhere I turn there's something French that reminds me of her.

C'est la vie, I'm afraid.

Chagrin

distress (French)

The origins of this word, which is used to convey a sense of aggravation, sheepishness, or displeasure, are widely disputed. Some etymologists believe that it comes from a rough leather of the same name (English "shagreen"), while others say it comes from a French translation of the German word for hangover—*Katzenjammer*. Most likely, though, it comes from the Germanic word "*grami*," meaning "sorrow" or "trouble," as the earliest English usage was

375

for "anxiety" and "sadness." Nowadays the word is used in English to signify slight disappointment, tinged with irritation.

Malcolm had planned to pass the store-bought salmon terrine off as his own creation, but much to his chagrin, Stephanie sauntered into the kitchen just as he was taking it out of the package.

Cherchez la femme
look for the woman (French)

This phrase was taken from the 1854 book *Les Mohicans de Paris* by French author Alexandre Dumas *père* (not to be confused with his son, also named Alexandre Dumas). He was best known for his historical adventure fiction, and this phrase conveys the view that a woman was almost always behind the misadventures of men. It retains this meaning in modern use, though sometimes with sardonic overtones, and it can also be used more generally to encourage someone to look for the underlying cause of a problem.

Charles let out a gasp as he opened his credit card bill. "Cherchez la femme," he muttered under his breath as he dialed the number of his accountant.

Chic
elegant (French)

In English "chic" is synonymous with "fashionable" and "stylish." It is thought to originate from a German word "*Schick*," which means "fitness" and "elegance," though the French monopoly on all things related to fashion ensured that English speakers took the francophone version. It is used today to denote an outfit, object, or place that exudes sophistication and style.

I felt very out of place in my socks and comfortable sandals, I can tell you; we just weren't expecting it to be so chic.

Chop-chop

hurry (Chinese, from "*k'wâi-k'wâi*")

The phrase originated in the South China Sea, as a Pidgin English version of the Chinese term "*k'wâi-k'wâi*." The adoption of the "chop-chop" pronunciation was in harmony with the long-standing use of "chop" and "chop-up" by British seamen, with the meaning "quick" or "hurried." The seafaring usage of "chop up" referred specifically to a sudden change in the wind and the waves (hence "choppy"). The British say "chop-chop" when they want someone, usually a child but originally a foreign servant, to hurry up. They may also clap their hands to underscore the urgency.

Miss Brindle flared her nostrils. "Chop-chop, girls!" she said briskly as her charges reluctantly tidied the nursery.

Chop suey

bits and pieces (Chinese, from "*tsap sui*")

Chop suey is widely believed to have been invented in America by Chinese immigrants but seems to originate in Taishan, a district of Guangdong Province. A popular story has the dish invented during Premier Li Hongzhang's visit to the United States in 1896.

His chef tried to create a dish suitable for both Chinese and American palates. When asked what food the premier was eating, the cook found it difficult to explain and replied "mixed pieces."

Unfamiliar with Chinese food, Jeff said, "I'll have whatever, bits and pieces."
"Chop suey, excellent choice!" his host replied.

Chutney

to taste (Hindi)

The name for this sweet and spicy condiment comes from the East Indian word "*chatni*." Traditionally reserved for special occasions because they required an intensive preparation process, chutneys began to be imported by Western countries in the late 1600s, and by the nineteenth century more subtly spiced versions were being produced, especially for export. We now use the word for a huge variety of preserved condiments and pickles.

The most popular stall at the town fair was always Mrs. Hubbard's. People flocked from far and wide for a taste of her green tomato chutney.

Chutzpah

audacity (Yiddish)

This comes from the Hebrew word "*hutspah*" (which is how "chutzpah" is pronounced), meaning "insolence." It originally referred to someone who had brazenly broken the rules of respectable behavior and was used only in a disapproving sense. In Yiddish and subsequently English, however, it can convey a quality worthy of a sort of reluctant admiration—a daring effrontery that we might describe as "gutsy." It might also be used today to describe the performance of a precocious musician or dancer who has delivered a challenging interpretation of a particularly difficult piece.

The president smiled as the pro-vegan protester was escorted away. Leading a live cow into Congress was a crazy idea, but he couldn't help but admire the man's chutzpah.

———✂❧✂———

Cogito, ergo sum

I think, therefore I am (Latin)

This famous philosophical quotation is from René Descartes's 1673 *Discourse on Method,* in which he asserted the fact that the power of thought was proof of the existence of the self. He originally wrote it in French rather than Latin ("*Je pense, donc je suis*") so that it was accessible to a broader range of readers, but he switched to Latin in his later work *Principles of Philosophy.* Modern philosophers refer to the phrase as "the cogito."

I thought I deserved a far better grade than a D for that, sir.
   Well, that's something, Toby. Cogito, ergo sum—take comfort from that.

———✂❧✂———

Cognoscenti

those who know (Italian)

This word arrived in Italian from the Latin "*conoscere,*" which means to "know." The spelling we have taken on is now in fact obsolete in Italy, where "*conoscenti*" has taken its place. In English the word is usually used to describe people who are experts in the fields of art, literature, or fashion, indicating a certain refinement in taste and judgment. It is also used more colloquially to describe those who are "in the know" on any subject; a member of the cocktail cognoscenti could guide one to the perfect Manhattan, while the techno cognoscenti would lead you to the best computer.

You couldn't find leopard-print leggings that year for love or money. The fashion cognoscenti had bought up every last pair.

———— ❧❧❧ ————

Compos mentis

a composed mind (Latin)

This Latin phrase has survived through both medical and legal use. In neurological terms it means "sane" or "mentally healthy," and in law it indicates that someone is of sound enough mind to stand trial. The term's opposite—"non compos mentis," meaning "not of sound mind," is just as frequently used in modern English to argue that a person should not be held legally responsible for his actions. This has extended in everyday use to mean anyone who through tiredness or heavy drinking isn't quite "with it."

You'd better get Gavin a cab home, Lou. I don't think he's fully compos mentis.

———— ❧❧❧ ————

Confetti

sweets (Italian)

The term is the plural of "*confetto*" meaning "candy," but the term is exclusively used in Italy for sugared almonds, which are eaten at weddings, baptisms, and first communions. The British and American tradition of throwing confetti at weddings is related to the very old tradition of throwing rice, dates, or nuts that may reach back beyond ancient Rome or Egypt. It brings good luck and represents fertility and abundance. In Italy the earliest form of confetti may have consisted of sugar-coated nuts and similar confections. In modern-day, eco-sensitive times, flower petals are often preferred by licensed wedding venues, but the sentiment and significance remain unchanged.

It wasn't nerves or emotions that made Stanley feel choked up; he'd just inhaled three mouthfuls of confetti.

Connoisseur

expert (French)

Most members of the cognoscenti (see page 379) could be referred to as connoisseurs. The word comes from "*connaître*," which means "to be acquainted with," and is used to describe a person who has a specialized knowledge of a subject or thing. True connoisseurs are found mainly in the art world—collectors, curators, or art critics. In the eighteenth century the word was used to describe any person of taste, and nowadays it also applies to knowledgeable devotees of everything from real ale to contemporary Dutch sculpture.

The waiter left Mr. McNair to pore over the menu of single malts at his leisure—the gentleman's florid complexion marked him out as something of a whisky connoisseur.

———◦◦◦◦———

Contretemps

against the time (French)

In the seventeenth century a "contretemps" was a mistimed or inopportune thrust in a fencing bout. This meaning extended in English use by around 1770 to cover any jarring mishap that was out of pace with social mores. We still use the term to describe an unexpected interruption in normal proceedings, but since the mid-twentieth century, it has been used more widely to mean an embarrassing set-to or minor skirmish.

Hugh felt edgy as he arrived at the restaurant. The parking ticket was stuffed uncomfortably into his back pocket, and he couldn't get his contretemps with the traffic cop out of his head.

———◦◦◦◦———

Cordon bleu

blue ribbon (French)

The blue ribbon was awarded by the sixteenth-century Bourbon kings to knights of the highest order. The term was incorporated into English in the 1720s for noblemen, and the phrase has since become an accolade for top-quality cooking. An 1827 cookbook called *Le Cordon bleu ou nouvelle cuisinière bourgeoise* was the first to use the phrase in this context, and when a branch of Le Cordon Bleu school was founded in London in 1933, the phrase became part of the English culinary dictionary, synonymous with high-class cuisine.

Peter stood back and admired his creation. It wasn't exactly cordon bleu, but it didn't look too bad now that he had sliced off the burned pieces.

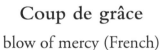

Coup de grâce

blow of mercy (French)

This is a final death blow that ends the suffering of someone who is wounded. On the battlefield it referred specifically to a bullet shot to the heart or head. These days we also use it to describe the final stroke of misfortune that results in the demise of a business or relationship, but in our attempt at an authentic French accent, we often mispronounce it. By leaving out the final "s" sound, it sounds as if we're saying "*cou de gras*" or "neck of fat," which doesn't have quite the same pathos.

The relationship had been on the rocks for a while, but Leo's decision to watch football on Valentine's Day was the coup de grâce.

Crime passionnel

crime of passion (French)

Until the 1970s French juries were allowed to take into account the circumstances surrounding a murder. If someone had killed for love or out of jealousy, rather than as part of a premeditated plan, jurors often found reason to acquit them. A case like this was known as a *crime passionnel,* and the term became common in English in 1955 during the trial of Ruth Ellis, who in a jealous rage shot her unfaithful lover five times outside a London pub. She became the last woman in Britain to receive the death penalty.

Sharon wondered if she could get away with claiming it was a crime passionnel, but the chances of anyone believing she was in love with her neighbor's dog seemed slim.

Curriculum vitae

course of life (Latin)

This is a summary of everything we have achieved educationally and professionally in our lives up to the present day. Most of us have written one at some point, and many of us may have read through a selection of other people's when looking for a new employee. Though the full translation sounds rather poetic, most curricula vitae, CVs, or résumés, reduce the course of life to its barest shell, leaving room only for word-processing qualifications and spurious hobbies, such as relaxing and socializing with friends.

Caitlyn seems a lively girl, but I don't think we can possibly employ her. When I asked for her curriculum vitae, she said, "Five foot four, 34D."

Cushy

easy/pleasant (Urdu, from *"khushi"*)

The Urdu word *"khushi"* meaning "happy," "easy," or "soft," was adopted as "cushy" by members of the British army serving in India in the late-nineteenth century. It was considered slang then, as it is today, and used to describe a situation that is not only highly agreeable but also considered lucky; the sort of position that we might describe as "nice work if you can get it." In the United States the term is also employed to describe a pleasingly plump person.

And you get paid just to look after someone else's house while they're on holiday? That's a bit cushy, isn't it?

D

De rigueur

necessary (French)

Like so many English phrases that relate to etiquette and fashion, we borrowed this term from the French. If something is "de rigueur," it is necessary according to the strict codes of protocol despite not being enshrined by an official rule or law. The term was especially useful in the rigidly rule-bound Victorian era, but since then it has also come to mean anything that is in line with the latest trends.

Charlotte spent the last few moments before her guests arrived decanting her supermarket-brand coffee into an unmarked tin; along with organic vegetables, fair-trade coffee had become de rigueur at dinner parties these days.

De trop

in excess (French)

This phrase means "too much" and can be used in two ways. Its original meaning in English was simply "too many" or "a superfluous amount," and it is still used in this way to point out—in a delicate French way, of course—that something is over the top or beyond the bounds of good taste. It is also used when a person's presence isn't welcome, like when your boyfriend's best friend tags along on every date.

I thought wearing a cloak and sword with his dinner jacket was rather de trop.

Debacle

collapse (French)

This word comes from "*débâcler*," which means "to unbar" or "break loose," but in both French and English its true definition is a "catastrophic failure" or "collapse." It originally referred to the caving in of a physical structure, like a roof, or to flooding caused by the breakup of ice in a river, and also to a terrible defeat in battle. Over time it has become a useful way of describing less dramatic defeats as terrible muddles and failure, such as sports events in which one team was severely beaten or for sometimes ludicrous political or organizational failures.

Kevin once had his hopes pinned on the top job, but his career had never quite recovered from the "pay raise for politicians" debacle.

---◦⟨ɣ⟩◦---

Decree nisi

unless (Latin)

This phrase means simply "not final or absolute," but it has retained its place in English as a legal term. A "decree nisi" is a ruling by the court that won't come into effect until a certain condition has been met—usually that there are no further presentations of relevant material to the court. We use the term to refer to a conditional divorce, which will become absolute after the passing of a set amount of time, unless there is just cause to modify it.

Nicole gave a little skip of joy as she left the lawyer's office. The judge had issued a decree nisi, and in six weeks and a day she would be free.

---◦⟨ɣ⟩◦---

Déjà vu

already seen (French)

This term is used to describe the feeling of having already been through an experience you are actually having for the first time. Its earliest use was in a French translation of Sigmund Freud's *Psychopathology of Everyday Life*, published in 1901, in which he suggested that the feeling corresponded to the memory of a subconscious daydream. We still use it to describe this as-yet-unexplained phenomenon, but a sense of déjà vu is also now used when an event feels similar to something that has happened in the past.

Home owners watched interest rates rise with an unnerving sense of déjà vu.

Delicatessen

fine foods or delicacies (German)

This word has its origins in the Latin word "*delicatus*," which means "pleasure-giving," but arrived in English via the German "*Delikatessen*," which described ready-to-eat foods, such as cold meats, cheeses, and salads. In English the term is almost exclusively used to describe not the foodstuffs themselves but the shops that sell them. Colloquially known as "delis," these are often Italian, rather than German, and are characterized by the smell of freshly roasted coffee and vats of garlic-infused pickles.

There was only one person to blame for the failure of Jenna's diet— the proprietor of her local delicatessen, who, she felt sure, laced his chocolate brownies with some sort of highly addictive chemical.

Demimonde

half-world (French)

An 1855 play called *Le Demi-Monde* by Alexandre Dumas *fils* gave the French this word for "mistresses." It describes a half-world on the fringes of eighteenth-century society inhabited by courtesans. Mistresses were an accepted part of upper-class life in both France and the UK, and the term soon migrated across the Channel, though its use in this context faded in the twentieth century as the women's rights movement grew. It was subsequently used to describe a world of penniless bohemian artists and those on the edges of respectable society.

That's it, I'm going back to the day job. Ventriloquism is all I've ever wanted to do, but I can't live in this demimonde a moment longer.

Denouement

an untying (French)

Have you got to the bit where the policeman confesses?

After the climax of a story, there are usually a few loose ends to tie up—this is the "denouement." Confusing perhaps, since the French word means "untying," but whichever tying metaphor you feel most comfortable with, the final outcome is the same—a neatening-up of a plot's complexities. As with so many theatrical methods, Shakespeare is the master of the denouement, and most of his dramas conclude with false identities being uncovered, justice being done, and everyone getting married.

I just can't follow these murder mysteries; I usually just nap through until the denouement.

Derrière

behind (French)

The bottom is one of the few parts of the body for which we have a plethora of words. Many of these arrived in the English language in the seventeenth and eighteenth centuries, either as slang or as euphemisms, and "behind" was among them. Exactly how or why this was translated to "derrière" is unclear. It could have been because few people, especially servants and children, spoke French. Or perhaps it was felt that the Frenchness took the edge off its vulgarity and lent the term a certain continental dignity that "butt" and "backside" lack.

I don't know what I'm going to do with that little bird. I bent down to pick up some seeds that had dropped from its cage and it leaned through the bars and pecked me on the derrière.

Déshabillé (also dishabille)

undressed (French)

Dating back to the seventeenth century in English usage, this word is used to convey the state of being either very casually dressed or only partially clothed. In settings where propriety required a certain dress code, it would have referred to an inappropriately informal and careless way of dressing, which gave rise to the additional meaning of disordered thinking. These days it is still used to mean undressed and can also mean a garment that you wear when mostly undressed, like a nightgown or underwear.

Things had been strained in the Mortimer household since Mr. Mortimer had been caught in a state of déshabillé in the church hall with two members of the women's group.

———⁓ᴑᴑᴑ⁓———

Deus ex machina

god from the machinery (Latin)

This describes a plot device used in Greek tragedy in which seemingly impossible situations were resolved by actors playing gods being lowered onto the stage by a crane and whisking everyone off to a happy ending. The phrase was first used by Horace in his *Ars Poetica*, in which he warned his fellow Roman poets against resorting to such unimaginative methods in their craft. Over time its meaning evolved to encompass any sudden and unrealistically simple external solution to a complex problem in a narrative, and critics still use the phrase in this way today.

> *A sentimental novel with a deus ex machina so clunky that you could almost hear the ropes creaking.*

———— ⚬☙⚬ ————

Diaspora

scattering (Greek)

This comes from the Greek word *"diaspeirein,"* which means to "spread about" in the sense of sowing or scattering, but in references as far back as the Old Testament, it is used specifically to describe the body of Jews living outside Israel after their exile to Babylonia in the sixth century BC. Jewish communites around the world are still referred to in this way, though the word is also now applied to any dispersion of people or entities that originate in one fixed place.

Union Jacks and cafés serving egg and fries are the usual calling cards of the British diaspora in the Mediterranean.

———— ⚬☙⚬ ————

Diktat

something dictated (German)

A punitive decree issued to a defeated nation is called a "diktat," since its terms are dictated by the victor. The 1919 Treaty of Versailles was called "The Diktat" by the Germans because they had no option but to accept its damaging and humiliating terms. Its use became widespread in English from that point onward, and we now use it as a label for any harsh order or compulsory instruction issued by an individual or organization in authority.

A collective sigh of resignation echoed through the auditorium as the headmaster delivered his latest diktat.

—◦◦◦◦◦◦—

Dilettante

one who delights (Italian, from "*dilettare*")

This is an example of a word that starts out with a friendly, positive meaning but after three centuries of use has ended up with a negative one. In the early 1700s it meant someone who took delight in fine art, without becoming an expert in it—an enthusiastic dabbler, as we might say now. No harm in that, you might think, but the word began to turn; the lack of expertise it implied became a suggestion of unprofessionalism and superficiality, and by the twentieth century it defined someone lacking in skill and commitment and possibly even a bit useless.

At first he'd seemed like the perfect man for the job, but he was exposed as a dilettante when a dog-eared copy of The Bluffer's Guide to Antiques fell out of his briefcase.

—◦◦◦◦◦◦—

Diva

goddess (Italian)

The term now applies to any well-known female performer or prima donna and, more generally, to an acclaimed female in any sphere of endeavor. Pejoratively the word also means a person who considers herself (or by extension himself) more important than others and becomes angry or petulant when her standards or demands are not met. The literal meaning of the term is "goddess," the feminine of the Latin word "*divus*," "god." Diva even is used as a girl's name ("divine one" or "goddess"), which might be hard for a girl to live up to.

> *Margery considered herself a diva, so when her lotus-blossom throat syrup wasn't in the dressing room, you could hear her complaining right across the village hall.*

Dolce vita
sweet life (Italian)

A life of luxury and self-indulgence has been described in English as "*la dolce vita*" since the 1960 release of a film of that name by Federico Fellini. The film documented the opulence and material-ism of modern Rome at the start of Europe's most liberal decade and painted the city as a hub of romantic decadence. Originally the phrase was employed ironically to describe a morally flawed way of life, but in recent years its meaning has softened into something more literal, and "ah, *la dolce vita*" can now be heard in place of the English phrase "this is the life."

> *Mick and Lorraine arrived at the airport with three hours to spare. They wanted their two weeks of living la dolce vita to start as soon as they'd got through check-in, and they needed plenty of time to drink duty-free champagne.*

———◦◦◦◦———

Doolally

camp fever (Urdu, from *"Deolali"*)

In 1861 the British army established a military base at Deolali, about a hundred miles north of Mumbai, that was used as a transit camp for soldiers who'd completed their tour of duty and were waiting for a boat back home or were on their way up-country. The wait often lasted for months, and in the boredom and heat many men began to behave oddly. Troops would say, "He's got the Doolally tap," of anyone who seemed a bit mad; "tap" translates as "fever." We now use the phrase "gone doolally" to describe someone who is behaving strangely.

Sorry I'm late, Margaret! I've gone completely doolally; I thought I'd lost my car keys and finally found them in the fruit bowl when I went to pick up an apple!

———◦◦◦◦———

Doppelgänger

double goer (German)

In psychiatry a "doppelgänger" is a delusion of a human double, but the word long predates modern psychiatric analysis. It referred originally to a ghostly phantom double, the sight of which was considered a bad omen. Romantic poet Percy Bysshe Shelley saw his in Italy in 1822, pointing solemnly out to sea. Soon afterward Shelley drowned in a sailing accident. Now the word is used for someone who looks strangely similar to yourself or another person or for your avatar in alternative-reality online games, where you can create your very own virtual doppelgänger.

Are you sure we haven't met before? If not, I think I'm acquainted with your doppelgänger. She was on the same cruise as us last year in the Canary Islands.

—⁍⁘⁍—

Double entendre

double understanding (French)

This expression is now obsolete in France, where "*double sens*" or "*double entente*" are used in its place, but in English it retains its original definition as a phrase that has an innocent first meaning and a saucy or ironic secondary meaning. Such phrases have been a pillar of English wordplay since Shakespeare's time, when ribald humor was the order of the day, and are still widely used in comedy today.

> *I made the most embarrassing double entendre in the supermarket yesterday; the cashier handed me a grocery bag, and I asked him if he had a big one!*

—⁍⁘⁍—

Doyen/ne

senior member of a group (French)

This word came to French from the Latin "*decanus*," which means "commander of ten men" and from which we also get the word "clean." Though this usage has long been obsolete, the modern meaning of the most senior or eldest male member of a group is probably derived from this ancient definition. Nowadays we are more meritocratic in our use of the word, the feminine version "doyenne" is just as frequently used, and both words describe the most successful, most admired, or most influential figures in their field.

> *Ladies and gentlemen, would you please welcome to the stage our star speaker, Mr. Bruce Badgett, the doyen of health care.*

Du jour

of the day (French)

This is used in English in two ways—in the context of a dish on a menu to mean something freshly prepared and available on that day only, such as a soup *du jour*, or in more recent use, to signify something that is "very now" or of the moment, with the implication that its popularity will be short lived. An extended version of the phrase—*femme du jour*—might also be used to describe the latest girlfriend of a man with a commitment problem.

Monique had slept through her alarm on the morning of the Paris Fashion Show, but she thanked her lucky stars as she caught sight of the catwalk. Unbrushed bed hair was apparently the look du jour.

Dungarees

thick cotton cloth/overalls (Hindi)

During the days of British colonial rule in India, sails and tents were made from a thick, hard-wearing cotton cloth called "*dungri.*"

It was shipped from India to England in great quantities during the eighteenth century when it picked up an additional syllable and turned into "dungaree." The durability of the fabric made it ideal for work overalls and the trousers with a bib and shoulder straps that we know as dungarees were born.

I'm sorry, sweetie, but dungarees are not a good look for you; you need more of a hip-hop look to pull them off these days, and your style is more Bananarama.

E

Eau de toilette

toilet water (French)

Not that kind of toilet . . . in the seventeenth century a "*toilette*" was a cloth cover for a ladies' dressing table, having originally meant a cloth cover as a wrapper for clothes. By extension, "*toilette*" came to mean the process of dressing, and later of washing, thus "eau de toilette" is a scent. It differs from perfume only in that the percentage of aromatic compounds used to make it is slightly lower, making it lighter and less expensive. We use the French term not only because it sounds less unsanitary but because during the seventeenth and eighteenth centuries, when infrequent bathing made perfumes most popular, France was the center of a prospering perfume and cosmetic trade.

With the boiler still broken, Elspeth hadn't bathed in over a week, but it was amazing what a damp cloth and a spritz of eau de toilette could do to give the impression of cleanliness.

———❀❀❀———

Éclat

splinter, brilliance, burst (French)

The original meaning of this word in English was "notoriety" or "scandal." It comes from the Old French word "*esclater*"—"to burst out," like a skeleton from a closet, perhaps. Now, though, it is firmly lodged in our vocabulary as a description of a scintillating performance worthy of great acclaim. Women may also recognize it from the tube of Lancôme's "Touche Éclat" in their makeup bag, though brilliant might not be how most of us would describe even the best-concealed of under-eye shadows.

Leonard packed his karaoke machine away with pride. He could tell from the open mouths in the audience that he'd given a performance of great éclat.

———❀❀❀———

Élan

leap, fervor, burst (French)

One of the French meanings of this word is synonymous with "éclat" (above)—a "burst" or "surge" (of activity). In English, however, they are often used together to convey panache and flair. But next to "élan," éclat can seem brash and flashy, élan is éclat's sophisticated older brother, redolent of a refined, understated elegance. It comes from the Old French "*eslan*," which means "rush," and is most commonly used in English to describe a kind of ardent vigor and zeal.

The students seemed to be waving a different banner every day but fought every battle with equal élan. They were rebels with multiple causes.

———❦———

Embonpoint

in good condition, fleshy (French, from *"en bon point"*)

This word sums up the way our ideals about body shape have changed over the centuries. Its literal translation means pleasingly plump, like the voluptuous women Rubens was painting in the early seventeenth century, which was around the time the word was first used. In women this quality of desirable fleshiness is often accompanied by a heaving bosom, and the word is still used euphemistically to refer to this most peachy part of the female body.

The two leads were so ill-matched in physical stature that at one point the tenor nearly disappeared into the soprano's generous embonpoint.

———❦———

En masse

in mass (French)

This term is so similar in French to its English translation that it seems strange that we felt the need to adopt it, but around 1800, with protest marches from the cotton spinners, the Chartists and the Anti-Corn-Law League on the horizon, the British borrowed from the French, who had already established themselves as the leading authority on civil unrest. We still use it to indicate a group moving as one, but the context is often less worthy; these days we're more likely to head en masse to the bar after work.

There were a few pink cheeks in the capital yesterday as four thousand nudists marched through the city en masse.

Enfant terrible

terrible child (French)

Though not often used literally, this term can be applied to children who humiliate their parents by making loud, embarrassingly candid declarations in public. Usually though, it is reserved for radical, unorthodox adults, mostly in the art world, whose outrageous behavior shocks and unnerves mainstream society. The phrase was coined by Thomas Jefferson to describe the headstrong architect Pierre Charles L'Enfant, who was commissioned to build the U.S. Capitol in Washington, D.C., but was fired after eleven months for tearing down the home of the city's commissioner to build a boulevard.

Reuben had tried everything to get himself known as the new enfant terrible of the art world; he'd even pickled his own hand in formaldehyde, but so far no one seemed to have noticed.

Ennui

boredom (French)

We claimed this word from the French in the eighteenth century when cultivated society needed a term that distinguished the listless dissatisfaction felt by the elite from the bog standard boredom of the man on the street. In 1809 it became the title of a novel by preeminent writer Maria Edgeworth in which she critiqued the lethargy of the leisured upper classes. We still use the word to describe a profound sort of boredom today.

I don't think I can ever turn the television on again, Lucinda; the vacuous nonsense they show these days overcomes me with ennui.

Entre nous

between ourselves (French)

There is something about the French language that makes it seem just right for secrets. Perhaps it's the relaxed Gallic attitude toward illicit liaisons or the fact that using a smattering of French while revealing some hush-hush little morsel makes us seem so French. Whatever it is, "*entre nous*," which dates back to the 1680s in its homeland, has become an almost obligatory precursor to any juicy revelation. It means that what you're about to say must stay between you and the recipient of your information.

Marion? It's me—Barbara. Meet me in the coffee shop at three fifteen, usual table. And come alone; I've got something to tell you that's strictly entre nous.

Erratum

mistake (Latin)

This comes from the Latin verb "*errare*," which means to "stray" or "err," and is used specifically in printing and, more recently, in computer programming. It refers to an error that has been formally noted by editors after the completion of the production process when the text cannot be changed. Rather than incur the expense of reprinting a whole run of books, an erratum, or a list of errata, can be printed on a separate page and bound into the book.

It had taken Richard Pratt sixteen years to complete his memoir of Fluffy the Peruvian guinea pig, so it was with some frustration that the final page of his manuscript contained that dreaded word "erratum."

Ersatz

replacement (German)

This comes from *"ersetzen,"* which means to "replace," and in Germany the term is straightforward; in sports an *"Ersatzspieler"* is a "substitute player." But the word picked up some negativity on its route into English. During the First World War, when Allied blockades prevented the delivery of goods to Germany, substitutes had to be found for the basic essentials. Coffee, for instance, was made using roasted grains rather than coffee beans. The practice resumed in the Second World War, when Allied prisoners of war who were given this tasteless *"Ersatzkaffee"* took the word home with them for any inferior substitution or imitation.

Pass me that glass of champagne quickly, Gloria! I think that last canapé was some kind of dreadful ersatz caviar.

———— ⌁ ————

Esprit de corps

group spirit (French)

Used especially in reference to members of a military unit, this word conveys the pride and sense of unity that arises in teams of people who are working closely together. Camaraderie (see page 371) is a crucial ingredient in it, as is a shared sense of purpose and commitment to reaching a goal. Regrettably, in recent years the term has been appropriated by corporate team-building gurus who try to drum up this now elusive force with orienteering exercises and games of Twister.

Okay, everybody, the aim is to hold the balloon under your chin and pass it on to the person next to you without it popping. This is really going to generate some esprit de corps. I can just feel it!

———— ⌁ ————

Et cetera

and the rest (Latin)

This is a remarkably efficient phrase that is usually shortened to "etc." with a period at the end. It allows the user to give the gist of her meaning without having to list every example she can think of. Usually "etc." is used when the list of things that is too lengthy to write in full has some pattern or order, such as a group of ingredients or items you need to remember to pack for your holiday. It is also used informally in the titles of European monarchs to denote that the number of grand titles is simply too long to list.

There will be four days of camping, so everyone needs wet weather gear: raincoat, rubber boots, etc., etc.

Eureka

I have found it (Greek)

Archimedes' famous exclamation on discovering how to measure the volume of an irregular object has been in our vocabulary for centuries as an expression of discovery. The legendary Greek scholar reportedly realized while stepping into a bath that water displacement could be used to measure the volume of an irregular object. He was so excited by his discovery that he apparently jumped straight back out of the bath and ran naked onto the streets of Syracuse.

Eureka! That's the turn we need ahead on the left, Jennifer. I told you I knew where we were going!

Ex libris

from the books of (Latin)

This term has been used since Roman times to denote the ownership of a book. It refers to the label or mark within the cover of a book that details the library or individual that it belongs to. The earliest recorded *ex libris* dates from around 1400 BC and proclaims ownership by the Egyptian pharaoh Amenophis III. Paper labels or ink stamps are still used for this purpose today, though the phrase is mostly used by collectors and librarians.

This is a lovely present, James, but are you sure you bought it? It's just that the ex libris says it's the property of the public library.

⤐⟶⊷☙⊶⟵⤏

Exposé

exposed (French)

Originally used to describe a verbal or written explanation that "exposed" the reasons behind a decision, particularly in diplomatic circles, "exposé" is now used for a report that unveils the truth about an individual or organization. Modern-day exposés usually appear in tabloid newspapers; their subjects are celebrities, politicians, or public bodies, and what they expose is often a scandalous secret or discreditable fact.

Annabelle felt betrayed, heartbroken, and a bit strapped for cash, so she decided to sell her story to the press—a lurid exposé would be the perfect revenge.

F

Factotum

do everything (Latin)

This word originally described a servant employed to do a range of different kinds of work; usually someone employed by a family to run the household. By the sixteenth century the meaning had shifted to someone who gets everywhere and knows everything, and it had the same negative connotations as the modern equivalent "busybody." Now, though, some of the original sense of the word has returned, and we use it to describe someone who can turn his hand to anything, a jack-of-all-trades or general assistant.

I like to keep my options open workwise. When I filled in that careers assessment form, it came back with two options: fraudster or factotum. I kept my nose clean and chose the latter.

Fait accompli

accomplished fact (French)

Though French in origin, this phrase was introduced to our language by an Englishman, in a travel book about Spain. Richard Ford's *Handbook for Travellers in Spain* was published in 1845 to great literary acclaim. In it he describes a previously settled fact as a "fait accompli," and the phrase took its place in the English lexicon. It is still very commonly used to describe decisions that have been made before those affected can have any input or to situations that are irreversible.

If there was one role that Darius Donovan hoped he'd never play it was the back end of the cow, but by the time he arrived for casting, it was already a fait accompli.

Faux pas

wrong step (French)

It's heartening to know that cultural slipups occur even in sophisticated French society. Perhaps to comfort ourselves with a reminder of this fact, English speakers have adopted the French phrase for them. A "wrong step" is the perfect way to describe such mishaps, as they usually leave us metaphorically stumbling, cheeks flushed with embarrassment and confusion, until we find our feet again. A visit abroad is the primary setting for these incidents, since social mores differ so dramatically between cultures.

> *He asked me to pass the bread; I had my fork in my right hand, so I used my left, and the whole room went quiet—I still don't know why, but somehow I'd made a terrible faux pas.*

Femme fatale

deadly woman (French)

The dangerously seductive female has been a figure in the popular imagination since the days of ancient folklore. Salome, Cleopatra, and even Eve have all been retrospectively labeled as such, but this term didn't come into use in English until around 1912, when women were beginning to challenge Victorian notions of female propriety. It is now used mostly to describe sexually powerful female figures in film and literature, including spies or assassins, who use their charm and beauty to ensnare men or, more colloquially, for women who dress in an overtly seductive way.

By day Laura-Jane was a sweet, cardigan-wearing schoolteacher, but by night she was a leather-clad femme fatale.

Feng shui

wind and water (Mandarin Chinese)

"Feng shui" is the Chinese art of placing objects in patterns, such as yin and yang, compass points, and astrology, so that the flow of "chi" ("life force"), is healthy. In the English-speaking West the term most often refers to the repositioning of furniture within a house so that the environment is in line with the landscape and the movement of the earth. There are many authentic feng shui practitioners who can make these recommendations, though in recent years there has also been a proliferation of mediocre interior designers who use the word for a more generalized Chinese-style decor.

Have you seen what my neighbor Margery has done to her garden? It's all rock pools and bamboo shoots—very feng shui.

Fest

festival (German)

The German word for "festival," used to describe gatherings that celebrate a specific activity, has become a useful suffix in English. There are now fests of every description, from knit fests to truffle fests and chili fests. And if a music festival gets a bit slippery underfoot, we call it a mud fest. Its use became widespread in the 1970s, possibly inspired by the growing reputation of Munich's world-famous "Oktoberfest," a carnival of beer and bratwursts that has been running since 1810 and is attended by six million people each year.

The frying pans are sizzling, and the tasters are at the ready— it's time to declare the inaugural fish-stick fest officially open!

Fiasco

failure or bottle (Italian)

"Fiasco" is, in fact, an Italian word used to describe a type of bottle with rope wound around the bottom, but its dual meaning of failure comes via the French phrase "*faire fiasco.*" Because it is a slang term, its origins are hazy, but one possibility stems from the phrase's earliest (and very specific) use: to describe a linguistic mistake made by Italian actors working on the French stage in the eighteenth century. The now obsolete French expression "*faire une bouteille,*" which meant "make a mistake," was probably then Italianized to "*fare fiasco.*" We still use it to mean a humiliating failure.

Brian checked the elastic on every team member's shorts person-ally. He was determined there would be no repeat of last season's wardrobe-malfunction fiasco.

Fiesta

festival or celebration (Spanish)

The Spanish know how to throw a party, and with saints' days liberally scattered throughout the Spanish calendar, there are plenty of opportunities for processions, feasts, and dances. The word is used in English primarily to describe Spanish or Latino festivals, particularly when the speaker happens to have attended one on his holidays and wants to show his friends how relaxed and Latin-spirited he is about using the local terminology.

Graham put on his papier-mâché horse's head and looked in the mirror. He felt dressed more for a freak show than a fiesta, but the parade was about to begin and Juan had insisted.

Frisson

shiver (French)

This word evolved in French from the Late Latin "*frigere*" ("to be cold"), and the term applies to a sensation of fear or excitement as physically discernable as a shiver caused by a blast of cold air. Unlike a real icy shudder, though, there is always an element of pleasure in a frisson. The word arrived in English from the French in the late eighteenth century, and we still use it to describe the sort of pleasing terror elicited by a good horror story or a thrilling sexual tension.

Sally-Anne trembled as she wrote her number on the back of her shopping list. She'd felt a definite frisson with the man in the pet-food aisle and decided it was too good an opportunity to miss.

Froideur

coldness (French)

It seems somehow apt that English speakers have embraced a French word for cold superiority, given that we often view the French, or the Parisians at least, as those most likely to exhibit the trait. The word is used in both languages to describe a reserved manner or even a marked frostiness between two parties. It is particularly useful in international relations, when to say outright that there is distrust or active hatred between two countries might be diplomatically uncouth.

There had been a palpable froideur between the two women since they knocked each other unconscious while diving for the bouquet at a mutual friend's wedding.

Frottage

rubbing (French)

The word comes from the French verb "*frotter*," to "rub," and for a while it was a psychiatric name for a sexual disorder characterized by the desire to rub up against another person without his or her consent (now known as "frotterism"). It does have a more innocent meaning in the art world, where it refers to the technique for making brass rubbings, but these days it's generally reserved for the kind of consensual, through-the-clothes body rubbing that we might otherwise be forced to call "dry humping."

Sorry I was so long with the drinks; I got waylaid by a bit of dance-floor frottage.

Furvor

excitement/controversy (Italian)

In British English this word is spelled "furore." The British stick to the Italian spelling, but both versions have the same meaning: "a sudden excited outburst," usually by a large body of people, about something that has caused a stir. It originates from the Latin word "*furor*," meaning "a raging," but the modern usage doesn't always imply anger, just a dramatic and clamorous reaction to an event or a decision.

Geraldine left the school hall feeling rather ruffled; she couldn't believe that moving the date of the summer festival had caused such a fervor.

G

Gamine

impish girl or urchin (French)

First used in French to describe street urchins or playful, waiflike children, the word was incorporated into English with this meaning in the mid-eighteenth century, when Thackeray used the term in *The Paris Sketchbook*. By the twentieth century its meaning had shifted, and it now refers to a sexually alluring girl or woman with a slight frame, short hair, and sweetly boyish or impish looks: Audrey Hepburn is often considered a classic example

Jessica kept her hat firmly on despite the warmth of the room. She had told the hairdresser she wanted to go for a gamine look, but she hadn't been prepared for the short back and sides.

—◦◦◦◦◦—

Gauche

left or clumsy (French)

Anyone with even the most rudimentary grasp of French will be familiar with the word for "left," but "gauche" also has another meaning: "awkward" or "inelegant." English speakers have adopted the latter sense of the word but use it to describe not physical but social clumsiness. The link may be a reflection of old negative superstitions about left-handedness (we get the word "sinister" from the Latin for "left"), or it may have come about as a result of the difficulties right-handers face when performing tasks with their left hand.

Sonya fiddled with her napkin nervously; too much fancy cutlery always made her feel gauche.

Gesundheit

health (German/Yiddish)

It's a tradition across many cultures to bless people or wish them good health after they sneeze. Hebrew tradition has it that the soul of man was blown into Adam through his nostrils and might leave the same way after hearty sternutation. The term is thought to have emigrated to America with the first wave of German-speaking settlers in Pennsylvania and spread more widely from 1900 onward, when large numbers of Jewish immigrants moved to the United States.

James held his breath and pinched his nose, the sound of a sneeze alone was embarrassing enough in an almost silent theater, but far worse were the cries of "Gesundheit!" that would echo around the auditorium.

Gigolo

male escort or paid lover (French)

In the shady world of male prostitution, the gigolo is at the respectable end of the spectrum. The term is thought to come from the French "*gigolette*," which meant "dancing girl" or "female prostitute," but in the masculine form it refers to men who are hired as either social or sexual companions for older, wealthier women. These days it describes a range of male "service" providers, from those who receive financial support from a female lover to professional escorts who accompany women to social functions. It can also describe young men who prey upon older, wealthy women.

I can't face going to the gala ball on my own again, Mary. I've decided it's time to hire myself a gigolo.

Glasnost

public openness (Russian)

In 1985 Mikhail Gorbachev, leader of the former Soviet Union, introduced this word as a central tenet of his government's policy to create political transparency and allow greater freedom of speech. He hoped it would restore the Soviet Union's reputation in the world, but in fact, glasnost revealed the repression and corruption that had characterized the Soviet regime and eventually led to its disintegration. The word is now used to describe any drive for openness by a government or organization.

> *There was to be a green glasnost at Eco-Warrior House—week one was an amnesty for unrecycled coffee cups.*

Glitch

slip up (Yiddish and German)

So that's a glitch.

The exact etymology of this word is uncertain, but it is believed to stem from the Yiddish word *"glitshen"* and the German *"glitschen,"* both around 1962, meaning to slip or slide. It is thought to have been used for the first time in English around

1962 by American astronauts to describe a spike in voltage in an electrical current. They broadened its meaning to cover other minor technical mishaps, and the rest of us have extended it still further to mean any small mishap or malfunction.

Sorry, Simon, there's been a bit of a glitch in tonight's plans. I know it was meant to be a double date, but Katie just canceled on me. Still, three is the magic number!

———— ⋙⋘ ————

Gratis

free (Latin)

This word was incorporated into Middle English from the Latin "*gratis*," which came from "*gratiis*," meaning "for thanks," hence without recompense. We still use it as a slang term for anything that is complementary or free of charge. Since around 1985 it has also been used in the field of computing to differentiate software that is free in the sense of not costing anything from software that is free in the sense of having freedom from legal restrictions.

Come on, Ted, get a drink down you. We may as well make the most of it while they are gratis.

———— ⋙⋘ ————

Gravitas

heaviness, seriousness (Latin)

In ancient Rome "*gravitas*," along with "*pietas*" ("piety"), "*dignitas*" ("dignity") and "*iustitia*" ("justice") made up the four cardinal virtues. It meant, as it still does today, a respectable depth of judgment and seriousness that befits a person in high office or someone in a position of responsibility. It implies the kind of moral fiber and experience that are seen as essential traits in modern-day politicians (though sadly they often fall short of our expectations) or even in actors playing weighty roles.

Mr. Walton sighed as the auditions drew to a close. Choosing Shakespeare for the school play had seemed such a good idea, but it was proving tricky to find a twelve-year-old with the gravitas to play King Lear.

Gung ho

work in harmony (Mandarin Chinese)

In Chinese the word "*gung*" translates as work, while "*ho*" means "peace" or "harmony." It was an abbreviation of "*gongye hezhoushe*," the name given in the late 1930s to the industrial cooperatives springing up in rural China. It was adopted by English speakers to mean a "can do" attitude after Lieutenant Colonel Evans Carlson of the U.S. Marine Corps, inspired by the spirit of the cooperatives, used it as a motto for his battalion. Recently it has developed negative associations and can mean overenthusiastic or needlessly aggressive.

From his uncomfortable resting place in the ditch, George reflected that perhaps he'd been a little gung ho in his use of the whip for a first attempt at horse riding.

—∘⟨⟨⟩⟩∘—

Guru

teacher (Sanskrit)

Stemming from the Sanskrit root "*gru*," which means "heavy" or "weighty," this word for teacher has its origins in Hinduism. Its connection with spiritual wisdom ensured its passage into English through the journeys of self-discovery made on the 1960s hippie trail. In the more materialistic West, its meaning expanded to include authorities on anything from footwear to designer wallpaper, and thanks to large numbers of self-styled "gurus" with dubious qualifications, it now carries with it the faint whiff of fakery.

Sorry, darling, I can't do tonight. I've got an appointment with my waxing guru that we both know I can't afford to miss.

H

—∘⟨⟨⟩⟩∘—

Habeas corpus

you have the body (Latin)

A "habeas corpus" (short for "*habeas corpus ad subjciendum*"—"may you have the person subjected [to interrogation]") is a writ that commands a prison to bring an inmate to court so that a judge can ascertain whether he has been imprisoned lawfully or whether he should be released. Prisoners who believe they have been wrongfully detained file the writ, which must prove that the court that sentenced the prisoner made a legal or factual error if it is to be successful. The phrase stems from the medieval Latin used in the original writ, and the right of habeas corpus was later enshrined in the Habeas Corpus Act passed by Parliament in 1679—and in the U.S. Constitution.

They've sent me down for five years, mate—I know, it's scandalous. The lawyer says he might be able to get me off, though. Something to do with a habeas corpus.

———❦———

Hamburger

person from Hamburg (German)

In nineteenth-century Hamburg, Germany, pounded beef patties called Hamburg steak were popular. Emigrants took it to America, and "hamburger" appeared on menus as early as 1836. By 1902 a recipe for ground beef with onions and peppers had appeared, and the modern hamburger was born. The shortening to "burger" followed and paved the way for the cheeseburger and other variations. The freedom to enjoy a hamburger, although not formally written into the Constitution, stands side by side with the most solemn American rights of man. In Cold War Berlin, President Kennedy was said to have proclaimed himself a "Berliner"—a kind of doughnut. There's a joke in Germany that it's lucky he wasn't in Paris. ("Pariser" is old-fashioned German slang for "condom.")

I'll have the triple-decker supreme hamburger with extra onions, extra cheese, and extra bacon; a large portion of chili fries; onion rings—and a diet Coke. I'm watching my waistline.

———❦———

Hara-kiri

cutting the belly (Japanese)

In feudal Japan, Samurai warriors bound by a strict code of honor would commit suicide using "hara-kiri" if they had shamed themselves or their masters or if they were captured by enemies. The practice involves a ritual self-disembowelment during which the stomach is cut from side to side; the more formal term for it is "*seppuku*," though non-Samurai Japanese and Westerners have always referred to it as "hara-kiri." We now use the word more generically to denote figurative rather than literal acts of self-destruction.

I'm sorry, Jasmine, but that was terrible. You simply can't pick a song that's full of notes you can't reach on a show like this—it's hara-kiri.

———⁂———

Hasta la vista

see you later (Spanish)

Until 1991 this was a relatively common, though unremarkable, Spanish phrase. It made the transition into English as a kind of slang alternative to "see you later," but wasn't used widely. Then came *Terminator 2: Judgment Day*. Arnold Schwarzenegger, playing the Terminator, said, "Hasta la vista, baby," every time he was about to wipe somebody out, and for reasons that remain unclear, his delivery of the line was deemed to be so witty that it was taken up by vast swathes of the English-speaking population.

I'm sorry, Doreen. It's been lovely getting to know you, but I must be off to new pastures—hasta la vista, baby.

———⁂———

Haute cuisine

high cooking (French)

High-quality food prepared in hierarchically run kitchens by the best chefs is known as "haute cuisine." Originally the phrase referred to the highest standard of French cooking, but we now apply the term to the highest standard cuisine of any origin. Official ratings, such as the Michelin star system, have made it easier to identify haute cuisine restaurants, most of which place great emphasis on the presentation of their food, which has led those who prefer more basic cooking to regard the term with suspicion.

Is there nowhere around here that we can just get a steak and fries? I can't stand all this haute cuisine nonsense.

Hinterland

backcountry (German)

English usage carries a resonance not present in the German usage and signifies a remote or backwoods region. "Hinterland" also refers to the area from which products are delivered to a port for shipping elsewhere. Historically, the term was applied to areas surrounding former European colonies in Africa, which, although not part of the colony, were influenced by the settlement, often without the safety and order that prevailed in (or was imposed) the colony.

The intrepid twenty-first-century celebrities bravely essayed the hinterland with camera crew and assistants in close attendance.

Hoi polloi

the many (Greek)

In ancient Greece, this term for the common populace had none of the negative connotations we give it today. It is thought to have passed to English via Pericles's Funeral Oration, in which he praised the democratic system in Athens for giving a voice to the majority. In rather more snobbish nineteenth-century Britain, when class could be judged by whether you had been taught the classics, it gained its modern usage to describe the vulgar crowd, also known as the "great unwashed."

Oh, for goodness' sake, Jeremiah. Will you please get the hoi polloi out of the VIP area.

Honcho

squad leader (Japanese)

It sounds like Spanish, doesn't it? But in fact, it comes from the Japanese word "*hancho*," which has its origins in Middle Chinese. "*Han*" translates as "squad," and "*cho*" means "chief," which is a common suffix in Japanese for words that denote leadership—

"*kocho*," for example, means "school principal." The term was brought back to the United States and the UK in the 1940s and 1950s by soldiers serving in Japan and Korea. English speakers use it as slang for "boss," often preceded by the word "head," which, though extraneous, does make for a pleasingly alliterative whole.

Okay, team, this is the beginning of a brave new era. You may think you know how to market paper clips, but I'm the head honcho around here now and we'll sell them my way.

Hubris
insolence/pride (Greek)

In ancient Greek society "hubris" was considered to be the greatest of all sins. It meant a kind of terrible pride that led to violence and caused harm to others; it was seen as a direct insult to the gods. It arrived in English in the late 1800s, with its meaning only slightly watered down, to incorporate egotistical acts of vanity and exhibitions of immorality. We now use it to describe arrogance or a lack of humility, particularly when it's likely to result in disaster.

The hubris of the man astounds me. Doesn't he realize that at sixty-three he's well past his horse-racing prime?

I

───◦⟨∞⟩◦───

In camera

in the chamber (Latin)

This is a legal term that means "in private with a judge," rather than in an open court. In general, the principal that justice must be seen to be done for it to be done at all means that courtrooms are open to reporters and the public, but there are exceptions to this rule. In the UK, when a witness's privacy needs to be protected or when the disclosure of the case's details could threaten national security, the case can be heard in closed chambers. A photographic camera takes its name from the same source, since its body is essentially a sealed box with a shutter.

We've had some threats to the jury in this case, sir, so we'd like it to be in camera.

───◦⟨∞⟩◦───

In flagrante delicto

in the blazing offense (Latin)

This is a legal term that means that someone has been caught in the act of committing a crime. In modern English the phrase is often shortened to "in flagrante" and usually is preceded by the word "caught," so it is interchangeable with "red-handed." Outside the law, it is used widely to refer to the interruption of any illicit act, and through this usage it has also become a euphemism for being caught in a sexual act, even one where everything is aboveboard.

The Petersons had been rather less adventurous in their love-making since they were caught in the bushes in flagrante by the vicar and his cocker spaniel.

―✴―

In loco parentis

in place of a parent (Latin)

This is a legal term that relates to someone who takes responsibility for another person's child. Foster parents and legal guardians who have not adopted the child in their care are said to be "*in loco parentis.*" It is most commonly used in the school environment, where until the late-nineteenth century, teachers shared moral responsibility for their students with the parents. It is also used in a self-referential way by parents looking after someone else's child.

No, Daniel, you cannot have another chocolate cupcake. I'm in loco parentis today, and I know your mother wouldn't like it.

―✴―

In vino veritas

truth in wine (Latin)

The universally acknowledged fact that alcohol loosens the tongue had been observed as far back as ancient Rome. Pliny the Elder provided the first written reference to the phrase, describing it as a saying, so it must have been long proven even by his day. Similar sayings existed in ancient Greek and Hebrew. In modern-day

English it seems more useful than ever, and it can be heard in pubs and bars across the country whenever someone breaks into a drunken rant.

Billy woke up in a cold sweat with what felt like an angry woodpecker trapped inside his head. He was entirely naked except for a small Post-it note stuck to his chest that read ominously—in vino veritas.

———— ❧ ————

In vitro

in glass (Latin)

Often used in reference to laboratory experiments carried out in test tubes or other glass vessels, the term describes the artificial environment in which a test or technique is conducted outside of a living organism. (An experiment that uses the complete organism is described as "in vivo".) The term became instantly recognized the world over after scientists conducted the first birth of a human baby from an *in vitro*–fertilized human egg in 1978.

Britney never really understood in vitro fertilization—it seemed impossible to her that a baby could have enough space to grow inside one of those narrow test tubes.

———— ❧ ————

Incognito

in disguise (Italian)

This Italian term for having your identity concealed or going by an assumed name comes from the Latin "*incognitus*," meaning "unknown." The term was first used in the mid-seventeenth century and was widely used in wartime when spies had to assume different identities to evade discovery. It was especially used with reference to traveling without revealing your true identity, and in modern English it is often used when celebrities give false names to keep their whereabouts secret from the media.

I'd like to check in as Mr. X please—well, YOU may not recognize me, darling, but my fans are everywhere. I've simply no choice but to stay incognito.

———⋅⊙⋅———

Incommunicado

cut off from communication (Spanish)

Most commonly used in the military, this Spanish word comes from "*incomunicar*," which means to deny communication, and is used to describe a situation in which prisoners are held in seclusion with no way of contacting the outside world. In modern English use it can also refer to someone who is uncontactable due to work commitments or who is deliberately avoiding communication, either to protect her privacy or just to take a break.

Right, if you have any questions let me know now. In half an hour's time I'm officially on holiday, and I intend to be incommunicado for a full two weeks.

———⋅⊙⋅———

Ipso facto

by the fact itself (Latin)

Frequently applied in the realms of philosophy, law, and science, this term is used to assert that a particular effect is undeniably the result of the action being discussed. More commonly the term is applied to demonstrate the causal links between an action and its reaction or impact. For example, if you take out a fixed-rate mortgage, ipso facto you cannot benefit from changes in interest rates. The term can also be heard in settings ranging from offices to pubs by people wishing to add a flashy credence or intellectual weight to any given point.

Look, pal, it doesn't matter what formation the Giants play in. They've got O'Hara and Jacobs up front so, ipso facto, they'll beat the Eagles.

Je ne sais quoi

I know not what (French)

This French phrase is always prefixed in English with "a certain" and is used to recognize a quality or characteristic that is hard to describe, yet makes the subject in question instinctively appealing. Often used to acknowledge a woman's mystifying beauty or charisma, the phrase is also widely applied to appreciate that certain something that makes a superb plate of food so tasty or a vintage champagne so deliciously refreshing. However "a certain *je ne sais quoi*" is increasingly being overlooked in favor of the more mundane "X" or "wow factor."

The herbs and spices in that fillet just simply gave the whole dish a certain je ne sais quoi.

Jezebel

wicked, blasphemous woman (Hebrew)

According to Hebrew scriptures and the Old Testament, Jezebel was a queen of ancient Israel whose patronage of a pagan religion made her none too popular with the Israelites (or the prophet

Elijah). She was a scheming and manipulative woman and was eventually defenestrated by her eunuchs and eaten by dogs. Though there's no evidence of it in the Bible, she has developed a reputation for sexual promiscuity, and we now use Jezebel as a synonym for coquette or "tart."

Belinda smoothed down her skirt and hoisted her top up precisely two inches. She wanted to come across as a sophisticated seductress, not some sort of Jezebel.

Jodhpurs

wide-hipped trousers, fitting tightly from knee to ankle (Anglo-Indian)

In 1459 in the heart of Rajasthan in northern India, the ruler Rao Jodha founded the beautiful city of Jodhpur. Men of Rajasthan wore trousers that were ideal riding breeches, being made of a stout material with a comfortable arrangement of seams, and were thus adopted by the British during the Raj. The term "jodhpurs" then passed into English, and it is still the garment of choice for most horse-riding events and also in some military dress uniforms, although these days they are usually tight fitting.

Although Virginia has occasionally been seen in a dress, she's happiest in jodhpurs, enjoying rides on her pony, Tristram.

Joie de vivre

joy of living (French)

Often confused with "*joie de vie*" ("joy of life"), "*joie de vivre*" is the even more positive attitude of the "joy of living." Because of its catch-all nature, the phrase can be used to express the enjoyment of specific things, such as eating or drinking, or the more profound and comprehensive joy felt throughout one's whole being for the simple reality of being alive. The term is also used to describe someone who has a particularly carefree attitude.

> *I don't know if it was that beer I had at lunchtime, Barry, but I feel full of joie de vivre this afternoon.*

Juggernaut

lord of the universe (Sanskrit)

Juggernaut, or Jagannatha, is one of many forms of Krishna, the revered Hindu deity, and is often represented as a young boy playing a flute. The Jagannath Temple in Puri, India, is famous for its annual procession of chariots carrying statues of the deities, and British visitors who witnessed the parade in the colonial era marveled at the forty-five-foot-high statues, which are pushed along on sixteen wheels that are seven feet in diameter. The word "juggernaut" has been used ever since to describe an uncontrollable force that will crush whatever falls into its path.

> *The Juggernaut may seem a strange nickname for a man weighing only 112 pounds, but the new flyweight champion of the world is truly unstoppable in the ring.*

---⟊⟊⟊---

Junta

committee (Spanish)

Despite the term's origins in sixteenth-century Spanish government committees, juntas are perhaps most often associated with military dictatorships in Central or South America. A "junta" refers to the governing body that comes to power after a military coup d'état, usually formed of the heads of armed forces. However, the word is often used pejoratively today to describe governments, or senior groups within organizations, that are perceived to be dictatorial in some aspects of their policy.

> *Sir Richard was desperate to get something in writing about the extension of the hunting ban, but he knew he'd have a hard time getting it past the pro-hunting junta.*

K

---⟊⟊⟊---

Kaftan

floor-length cotton or silk tunic (Persian)

The "kaftan" was an elaborately embroidered and symbolic item of clothing when it was first worn by the fourteenth-century Sultans of the Ottoman Empire; the colors, designs, and trimmings denoted the status of the wearer in strictly hierarchical Ottoman society. They were also popular in Morocco, where they were traditionally a women's garment and where they were picked up by free spirits on the 1960s "hippie trail." The kaftan has had a fashion resurgence in the past couple of years as an item of summer beachwear.

As she tried on her twenty-sixth bikini of the day, Katrina clenched her buttocks, sucked in her stomach, and said a prayer of thanks for the return of the kaftan.

Kahuna

priest, expert, or wizard (Hawaiian)

In Hawaiian culture any expert in a particular art, such as boat-building, navigation, or healing, was described as a "kahuna." Many of these ancient practices began to die out after the arrival of Christian missionaries in the 1820s, but since the 1970s, some practitioners have come forward and reclaimed this ancient title. In English it is used as part of the phrase "the big kahuna"—coined in the 1959 surfing film *Gidget* and used in the 1999 film *The Big Kahuna* starring Kevin Spacey—which means "most important person" or "top dog."

Okay, who's the big kahuna here? I've got a proposition to make.

Kamikaze

divine wind (Japanese)

The word "kamikaze" refers to the legendary typhoon in 1281 that saved Japan from a Mongol navy assault by destroying the invader's fleet of ships. More than 660 years later the same name was given to the fearless Second World War Japanese fighter pilots who loaded their planes with explosives and deliberately crashed into enemy targets. In 1941 kamikaze pilots destroyed four U.S.

Navy battleships during the invasion of Pearl Harbor. Today the term is frequently used both seriously and more lightheartedly to describe behavior or actions so reckless as to be suicidal.

High on drugs, with police in hot pursuit, the carjacker was on a kamikaze mission through the busy streets.

Kaput

broken (German)

The German word "*kaputt*" means "lost," "ruined," or "broken," but it comes from the comparatively undramatic French phrase "*être capot*," which means to score zero at a round of cards. The Germans picked it up as a term for being defeated or ruined. In English, where it began to be used in the late-nineteenth century, it usually refers to objects that are broken. The explosion of the Vanguard TV3 rocket shortly after launch in 1957 led the press to dub it "Kaputnik."

There was no way Owen could salvage his turbo hair dryer now. It went completely kaput when he tried to blow-dry his dog.

———— ❦ ————

Karaoke

empty orchestra (Japanese)

"*Kara*" in Japanese means "empty" and "*okesutora*" means "orchestra." Japanese drummer Daisuke Inoue was often asked by guests in the coffee shops where he played to provide an instrumental recording of his performance so that they could sing along in their own homes. Inoue saw a gap in the market and manufactured a machine that would play his backing tracks for a hundred yen per song. He then leased his karaoke machines out to restaurants and hotels, and the craze for amateur performances of popular songs took off, soon finding a much-loved place in bars and pubs.

Somehow Joseph's karaoke performances improved as the night wore on, and by midnight he could sing both Elton John's and George Michael's parts in "Don't Let the Sun Go Down on Me."

———— ❦ ————

Karma

act, action, performance (Sanskrit)

Karma is the idea that one's actions actively influence one's future in a cycle of cause and effect. Originating in ancient India, the concept is a key feature of many philosophies and generally asserts that an individual's own actions influence his or her future happiness. Today the idea is framed more by notions of an action bringing good or bad luck than by spiritual goodness.

Okay, five more minutes of complaining, and then we stop—it's bad karma.

Kayak

hunter's boat (Inuit)

The Inuits used small one-person paddle boats for hunting in the icy sub-Arctic waters, and it is thought that the word was imported into European languages by Dutch or Danish whalers and then made its way into English by the early eighteenth century. Though no longer made from animal skins, the modern version of the boat is very like the original in shape and is popular with white-water adrenaline-seekers who like to bob about in the rapids in just a thin plastic shell.

"I'm just not ready for a relationship at the moment," Tina told Ralph at the end of the night. It seemed kinder than telling him she'd rather paddle a kayak over Niagara Falls than endure his halitosis for a moment longer.

Kebab

marinated meat cooked on a skewer (Arabic)

The Arabic word *"kabab"* is possibly derived through ancient Semitic languages from *"kababu,"* meaning "to burn or char." *"Döner kebab,"* in Turkish, literally means "rotating meat." *"Shish"* means "skewer," hence *"shish kebab."* One modern version was invented by Mahmut Aygün (1921–2009), known as the kebab king, who opened a Turkish restaurant in Berlin that served traditional sliced lamb in warm pita bread instead of on a plate. However, he failed to patent his invention. . . . The ancient institution of the British pub and the ancient traditions of delicious

Middle Eastern cuisine combine so well that they're now an indispensable part of our culture.

When the bartender called for last orders and Paul suggested a kebab, Julie realized they would be together always.

Ketchup

fish brine (Malay, from "*kichap*")

Yes, Heinz's most popular condiment began life as a spicy pickled fish sauce in seventeenth-century China. The word is a westernized version of the Malay word "*kichap*," which came from the Min Chinese "*koechiap*," meaning "fish brine." The sweet red version we're familiar with began to take shape when American seamen added tomatoes—excellent for preventing scurvy. In 1876 John Heinz launched his tomato ketchup, and it's been a staple of British and American diets ever since.

Thanks so much for agreeing to look after him, Sarah. Here's his toothbrush and his pajamas, oh, and his bottle of ketchup— he won't eat anything without it.

———⁓⊙⁓———

Khaki

dusty (Hindi)

Until the early nineteenth century the uniform of the British Army featured bright scarlet tunics—a useful means of identifying who was on your side in the confusion of battle. However, it also made soldiers highly visible targets for ambushes and enemy snipers, and heavy casualties in colonial wars led to the introduction of the dun-colored uniforms still worn by soldiers today. The word comes from the Hindi for "dust" or "earth," with which the troops blended well in their new attire, and can be used to describe the fabric of the uniforms as well as the color.

Neville smoothed down his hair and turned to look in the mirror. He'd always fancied himself as a young Alec Guinness, and in his new khaki shirt, he felt sure he looked just like him.

———⁓⊙⁓———

Kiosk

pavilion, palace (Turkish)

The telephone kiosk sounds like a quintessentially British invention, but the word itself has far more exotic origins. In seventeenth-century Turkey kiosks were porticoed palaces grand enough to attract the attention of Lady Wortley Montagu, wife of the English ambassador to Istanbul, who wrote a letter home about them. In modern English, however, kiosks tend to refer to somewhat less genteel freestanding carts, where hot drinks or cheap goods are sold on the street or in shopping malls.

I can't possibly drink this coffee, Muriel. You may as well confess now—you got it from that kiosk on the corner, didn't you?

Kitsch

tat, gaudy merchandise (German)

Language experts believe that this word is derived from the German verb "*kitschen*," which means "to scrape mud from the street." It is believed to have become associated with garish, shoddily produced artwork in late-nineteenth-century Munich, where cheap, gaudy paintings that appealed to the uncultivated tastes of the newly wealthy Munich middle classes were hot produce. The word signified socially aspirational poor taste, though in the past decade "kitsch" has become fashionable (in a postmodern, ironic sort of way, of course).

How much for that red-and-gold version of the Mona Lisa? It's so kitsch I just have to have it.

Klutz

blockhead (Yiddish)

This comes from the Yiddish word "*klots*," which translates literally as "wooden beam," and perhaps also from the German word "*klotz*," meaning "block" or "lump." "*Klotz*" is related to the

English words "clot" and "clod," both of which mean "lump" (of earth in the latter case) and also "stupid person."

The president blushed as he walked head-on into the glass swinging door. He liked his reputation as a man of the people, but he didn't want anyone thinking he was a klutz.

Kohl

black powder (Arabic)

Kohl is the name for the dark gray or black powdered mineral that has been used in the Middle East since the Bronze Age, when it amplified the beauty of Egyptian queens and was also used as a protection from eye infections due to its antibacterial properties. It is still used in its original form in South Asia, where it is often put around the eyes of infants to protect them from the evil eye. We now use the word to describe heavily applied chemical-based eyeliner.

Kirsty staggered to the bathroom and braved the mirror—her hair stood on end as if she'd been electrocuted, and last night's sexy, kohl-ringed eyes now made her look like a despondent panda.

Kosher

suitable and pure (Yiddish)

Food that has been prepared according to Jewish dietary rituals and laws is deemed "kosher," or "fit to eat." It came from the Hebrew word "*kasher*," meaning "fit and lawful," around 1851, but since the end of the nineteenth century, the word has been used more generically outside the Jewish community to mean "legitimate." It is still commonly used with this meaning, especially in the East

End of London, where cockneys use it to indicate that something is all aboveboard.

Do you want to come in with me on this horse, then, Stan? It's kosher, I promise you.

Kowtow

knock the head (Chinese)

The most deeply respectful act of submission in Han Chinese culture was the "kowtow." The word describes a kneeling bow so deep that the forehead touches the ground. By the 1820s the word had come to mean an obsequious manner of acting, and it is in this sense that the word has been adopted into English. In the less strictly hierarchical West the term is usually used in a negative sense, to describe the actions of someone who is groveling or "sucking up" to his superiors.

Mark Stainton dressed with care on the morning of his interview. He had no intention of kowtowing to the new manager, but he hoped that a clean shirt and tie would create the right impression.

Kudos

glory, renown (Greek)

"Kudos" is a singular noun in Greek, and it entered British English in this form at the end of the eighteenth century, but in the United States the final "s" is mistakenly thought to mean that the word is plural, so the word "kudo" has been adopted as a singular. "Kudos" is found in American English, but only when someone has received more than one accolade. Both spellings are used to denote public respect or acclaim.

By the final leg of the squadron's assault course, Melanie could barely breathe, let alone run. But she wouldn't give up; she wanted the kudos of being the first female officer to finish before the sergeant.

Sudoku champion of Athens ten years ago, and he never lets you forget it.

L

Lacrosse

game of hooked sticks (French Canadian)

Lacrosse was originally a Native American team game played using curved sticks to scoop and throw the ball and was adopted by French Canadians in the early eighteenth century. They named the game "*jeu de la crosse*," literally meaning "game of the hooked stick," and an abbreviated version of the phrase—lacrosse—found its way into North American English. It is now particularly popular in girls' schools where the hooked end of the sticks inflicts serious damage to bony shins.

Okay, girls, today we're going to have a mini lacrosse tournament, but let's keep it clean, shall we? We don't want a repeat of "Bloody Thursday."

Lager

storehouse (German)

The term is short for "*Lagerbier*"—a "*Lager*" being the storehouse or cellar in which beer ferments. A vast range of flavors and degrees of dryness exist in Germany, less so elsewhere. In certain regions, like Bavaria, lager is central to traditional culture. Lager is the drink of choice for many youngsters in the UK, including a rowdy subset called "lager-louts." Older people tend to prefer bitter, less fizzy native beers at cellar temperature. (The American notion of warm English beer is a misconception.) Lager is best enjoyed cold, and in the United States it may be served in a frosted mug.

Roy's philosophy was mellower, and Melissa prettier, after six pints of lager.

Laissez-faire

let do, leave alone (French)

"Laissez-faire" typically describes an economic or political philosophy that promotes a reduction of government intervention in aspects of society, particularly business and industry. The phrase's first recorded use was by French minister René de Voyer in his famous outburst, "*Laissez faire, morbleu! Laissez faire!*" ("Leave them be, damn it! Leave them be!") Today the term is used to describe noninterventionist approaches in other settings, such as schools with liberal discipline policies. More generally it is used to describe an individual with a laid-back, or even lazy, attitude.

This is the last straw, Mr. Streathers. The students are running riot, one of them is hot-wiring a teacher's car as we speak. The time for a laissez-faire approach is well and truly over.

Lebensraum

living space (German)

This comes from the German words "*Leben*," meaning "life" and "*Raum*" meaning "space," but its meaning is more complex than it seems. "*Lebensraum*" was the living space that Hitler decided the German people needed to become a truly great race, and it was to acquire this extra space that he invaded his neighboring countries to the east. The term was first used in this sense in 1897 by geographer and ethnographer Friedrich Ratzel, who studied the English and French colonies and thought Germany should have its own. It is usually used today to describe territory that is being fought over.

Sidney looked around his dingy room in despair. In his dreams of the city, he'd been living in luxury, not competing for Lebensraum with a swarm of cockroaches.

Leitmotif

leading theme (German)

This is a musical theme that recurs whenever the composer wants the idea of a certain character, place, or concept to come across. The word stems from "*leiten*," "to lead," and "*Motif*," meaning "theme." The first use of the term dates back to the late 1800s when it was used exclusively in reference to music and became associated with Wagner's epic operas. It is still used in reference to classical music as well as for modern compositions and film scores. It has also expanded to include recurrent themes in other creative works, such as poetry, dance, painting, and fiction.

The sea was wonderfully warm, but Kerry could only paddle. As soon as the water reached her knees, the shark's leitmotif from Jaws boomed inside her head and made her run for dry land.

Lingua franca

Frankish language (Italian)

In the medieval Middle East, Europeans were collectively known by Arabic speakers as Franks, and the Frankish language was primarily Italian with a mixture of Persian, French, Greek, and Arabic words. It was a language cobbled together to allow people of different native tongues to communicate. We now use the term to refer to any common language used by speakers of different languages, especially where that language is not the native tongue of either. English, for instance, has become the lingua franca of the international business world.

Have you ever tried taking minutes of a meeting where half the delegates are Chinese and the other half Icelandic? I'm just praying English is the lingua franca.

Loot

plunder (Anglo-Indian, from the Hindi "*lut*")

"Loot" or "*lut*" originally described the items stolen following a war or riot and was brought into the English language by British soldiers who served in India in the late-eighteenth century. Over time it has also become a verb, and "looting" is often reported in war-torn towns. We also use the word more casually as slang for money or a particularly pleasing haul of presents.

Hermione loved birthdays. Before bed she arranged her gifts in rows on her bedroom floor and surveyed her loot with glee.

That is looting – this is connoisseurship.

Louche

decadent, shady (French)

This comes from the Old French word "*lousche*," which means "squint-eyed." A squint was clearly a suspicious affliction in those days because the term gave rise to the more modern "louche," meaning "devious" and "of questionable repute." The word was first used in English in the early nineteenth century and can be used in reference to a person of dubious moral values or her debauched behavior. It is also often used to describe a decadent or possibly slightly seedy place.

It's very tricky to know what sort of place you're going into in that part of town. Some of the bars look terribly louche.

M

Macho

virile, domineering (Spanish)

In Spanish culture (and in Hollywood), the macho man is celebrated as a strong, patriarchal, responsible example of the alpha male. The word comes from "machismo," which has also been adopted by English speakers and means "masculinity." It has been used in English since the 1920s, but in the UK and the United States (apart from in the movies), it is most often used negatively to denote aggression, chauvinism, or the kind of male physical posturing that starts fights after last call.

Don't you dare go all macho on me, Darren; you're no Sylvester Stallone, and anyway, you know I prefer a man who's in touch with his feminine side.

Maestro

master, teacher (Italian)

This, like so many musical words, is Italian and usually refers to composers, conductors, and some musicians of classical music and opera. It has its origins in the Latin "*magister,*" meaning "master," and in modern usage it has expanded to include masters in other artistic fields, particularly fine art, and some sports, such as fencing, where it means "instructor," though its principal use is still in the musical world.

With a final frantic wave of his baton and a wild flick of his hair, the maestro brought the opera to its magnificent conclusion.

Magnum opus

great work (Latin)

This grand term refers to the largest or most substantial piece of work by an established composer, author, or artist. These days we tend to use the phrase as a synonym for "masterpiece," and in many cases both terms apply, but a magnum opus is not always an artist's best work. It might refer to a piece of work that is remarkable more for its scale or the time it took to produce— than its success.

Lucille scanned the desk in front of her: seven lined notepads, fifteen pens and a box of twenty-four Krispy Kreme doughnuts. Yes, she had everything she needed to begin her magnum opus.

Mañana

tomorrow (Spanish)

This comes from the Latin "*maneana*," which translates as "early tomorrow," but to the Spanish and to most English-speaking users of the phrase, it means "at an unspecified time the next day." Though it is used straightforwardly in Spain, in English it has taken on an additional sense of vagueness or reluctance to commit to a deadline. We sometimes say that someone has a *mañana* attitude, which means he is so laid-back that he never gets anything done.

All you ever tell me is, mañana, mañana! Well, I'm sick of hearing it—we both know mañana never comes.

Mandarin

official (Malay)

The name given to sixteenth-century Chinese officials is derived from the Malay word "*mantri*," meaning "minister of state." English speakers have adopted the term to describe government officials of our own, and also for the small, sweet citrus fruit, so named because its color is the same shade as the Chinese mandarins' robes. In their honor, the word is also put to use as a name for society's elite, such as influential figures in the art world.

Personally, I don't think that a banana placed on top of a toilet tank constitutes art. Whether the mandarins in charge of the Turner Prize will agree remains to be seen.

Mantra

instrument of thought (Sanskrit)

This comes from the Sanskrit root "*man*," meaning "to think," and the suffix "*tra*," meaning "tool." It refers to a chant or sound, made either out loud or in the mind, that advances spiritual development. Mantras have found their way into English through the teachings of Buddhism and Hinduism, though we now use the word in a more secular sense. Any saying or statement that helps us to focus on achieving something can be labeled a mantra.

I've borrowed my New Year's resolution from a sportswear company: Just Do It! I'm going to make that my mantra.

Maven

expert (Yiddish)

"Maven" comes from the Yiddish word "*meyvn*," which stems from the Hebrew word "*binah*," meaning understanding. It traditionally referred to someone who gathers information and passes his knowledge on to others. It arrived in English in the 1950s and was popularized in England in the 1960s, thanks to a popular ad campaign featuring "The Beloved Herring Maven." Sociologist Malcolm Gladwell uses it in his best-selling book *The Tipping Point* to describe intense information gatherers who are quick to pick up new trends. We also use it to describe someone who is an authority on a subject.

Douglas had a job he loved—selling fishing bait. In fact, he was so skilled at breeding worms for the wire that the angling community nicknamed him the "Maggot Maven."

Mazel tov

good fortune (Yiddish)

With its origins in the Mishnaic Hebrew word "*mazzal*," meaning "destiny," this word is used to celebrate good fortune having come someone's way. It is traditionally used on significant occasions such as weddings and bar mitzvahs, though it is also now widely used even outside the Jewish community as an alternative to congratulations for anything from buying a new house to passing your exams.

Hi, Louise, guess what? I was lucky this time and passed my driving test on the third try.

That's awesome! Okay—stay where you are, I'm coming over to say mazel tov.

Mea culpa

my fault (Latin)

This phrase comes from a Roman Catholic prayer for Mass called "*Confiteor,*" meaning "I confess," which includes the cheery line: "I have sinned exceedingly in thought, word, and deed: through my fault, through my own fault." This English translation appeared beside the Latin in prayer books, and the phrase was absorbed into general use. Now a "mea culpa" is an admission of guilt for a mistake, often rendered as "mea maxima culpa" by people into serious breast-beating.

Someone among us has left his underwear in the microwave, where I can only assume he was attempting to dry it. I suggest that he perform a swift mea culpa if he wants the chance to salvage the offending item.

Memento mori

be mindful of death (Latin)

Something ... something... where is thy sting?

In ancient Rome, where life could, though disease or war, be brutally short, this phrase was used as a reminder of mortality. It is said to have been delivered by an appointed slave to victorious generals after a celebration of victory to help them guard against complacency. Under the influence of Christianity, the phrase came to refer to works of art—paintings, elegies, and engravings on tombs were common versions.

> *Don't be too hard on the boy about those plastic skulls he likes to dangle off his ears, Pete. Try to think of them as religious ornamentation—they're the perfect memento mori.*

————∾⊙⊙∾————

Ménage à trois

household of three (French)

In the affair-fueled society of late-nineteenth-century England, this French term for a domestic arrangement in which three people live together and have a sexual relationship came in rather handy for the British aristocracy. Any household in which a married couple lives with the lover of one partner can be described with this word. It is sometimes used in modern times to refer to the act of sex between three people, more colloquially known as a "threesome."

I wouldn't mind a ménage à trois if I'm honest. It'd get him off my case every night, and it'd be nice to share the housework.

————∾⊙⊙∾————

Mi casa es su casa

my house is your house (Spanish)

This welcoming Spanish phrase is used widely in Spanish and Mexican households to make guests feel at home. It passed into American English through the Latin American and Spanish communities and subsequently reached British shores. While it can be used quite formally by Spanish speakers, it is more of a lighthearted phrase in English, where people tend to say it with arms thrown theatrically wide.

Friends, come on in. No, no need to take off your shoes, James, mi casa es su casa. Let me get you a drink.

Mise en scène

staging, direction (French)

This term is central to the critical analysis of film and theater and refers to everything that can be seen in the picture or onstage: the set, costumes, and lighting, and the use of movement and expression by the actors. It was first used by critics in the French film journal *Les Cahiers du cinéma* in the 1950s and is still central to the vocabulary of film and drama critics today.

Walter Jackman wasn't happy. He sat in the director's chair, but the damned actors seemed to be running the show. And what did any of them know about the mise en scène?

Modus operandi

mode of operation (Latin)

This started as a term used by the police to describe the favored methods of criminals. In cases where a series of crimes had been committed, the investigating team would try to establish the criminal's characteristic techniques and patterns of movement to plan their capture. It is still used in this way today (often shortened to MO), though it is most often applied generally to a person's method of working that has proved successful.

Good lord, Gwynneth, seven children to ferry to ballet class, football club, Mandarin for beginners, and orienteering practice, and you still have to squeeze in the shopping for dinner. Tell me how you manage it—what's your modus operandi?

---✎🙂✎---

Moratorium

delay (Latin)

In law a "moratorium" is an officially authorized period of delay in complying with a legal demand, such as payment of a debt, or a legally enforced suspension of an activity while discussions take place concerning its future. Since its introduction into English around 1875, there have been moratoria on activities as diverse as hunting, mining, nuclear testing, and the death penalty. In more general modern use it means a pause or break from something.

Can we please have a moratorium on these awful round-robin joke e-mails? They're blocking up my inbox, and they're not even funny.

N

---✎🙂✎---

Nabob

wealthy man/dignitary (Hindi)

During the Mogul Empire, a governor in India was known as a "*nawab*," or "nabob," which comes from the Arabic "*na'ib*," meaning "deputy." The riches they took home after their time in the East marked them as wealthy men, and the term "nabob" was coined to describe a man with immense riches, especially one who had made his fortune in the Orient. It is now used as an alternative to "bigwig" to denote someone in a position of influence who has power and wealth.

Janet smoothed the wrinkles out of her jacket and stepped closer to the VIP bar; she wasn't used to mingling with nabobs and felt in need of a smooth martini.

NB (Nota Bene)

note well (Latin)

This useful Latin phrase is usually abbreviated to NB and means "note well" in the sense of "pay attention." Though used in conversation in Roman times, the phrase is reserved for text in modern English, where it is used to draw attention to a particularly important fact that is linked in some way to the primary reading material. It is most commonly used by teachers who wish to highlight information that their students need to take into account.

Sophie's note taking had never been sophisticated. Usually she got down the gist of what the teacher said and then put NBs in the margins whenever she realized she'd missed something important.

Nil desperandum

nothing to be despaired at (Latin)

Like so many of our best maxims, this comes from Roman lyric poet Horace, who wrote it in *Odes I*, published in 23 BC. "Nil" comes from "*nihil*," meaning "nothing," and "*desperandum*," meaning "to be despaired at." It was probably adopted into English as a salve to the soul in difficult times, and we still use the phrase when we need to cheer someone up as an alternative to "it's not the end of the world."

Nil desperandum, Bill; there's no shame in playing on the B team.

———∽⟨⟩∾———

Noblesse oblige

nobility obligates (French)

This term sums up the idea that those of high birth have an obligation toward the rest of society. Originally it implied that noblemen owed it to themselves and to others to become strong leaders of common men, though over time it has become less explicit. Nowadays it is used to suggest that those with wealth and status should do something to help those less fortunate than themselves.

I do like Prince Charles, you know. I don't know if it's noblesse oblige, but he really does seem to do a lot of good with his charity work.

———∽⟨⟩∾———

Nom de plume

pen name (French)

Though the phrase is French, it is rarely used in France, where "*nom de guerre*," meaning "war name," has served as an alternative to "pseudonym" since the establishment of the French Resistance. The phrase "nom de plume" was in fact made up by the English, who wanted a literary-sounding phrase for writers wishing to disguise their identity. They were especially useful to female writers in the male-dominated world of publishing. Mary Ann Evans famously wrote under the name George Eliot to ensure that her work was taken seriously.

What do you think of Crumpet Delamore as my nom de plume? I think it has the perfect ring of romance for an author of a romance novel.

---◦◦◦◦---

Non sequitur

does not follow (Latin)

This term refers to a statement or response that seems utterly meaningless in the context of whatever preceded it. It came into English around 1540, and when a non sequitur is used deliberately, it is usually the preserve of comedians who aim to make a comment so ludicrously absurd and irrelevant that it becomes funny. It may also be used in an argument when someone wants to outwit his opponent by confusing him with nonsense.

I think I'll have cake, but should it be apple or pound?
Don't try and evade me with your non sequiturs. Did you clean up the kitchen or not?

---◦◦◦◦---

Nosh

snack food (Yiddish)

This beautifully onomatopoeic word comes from another Yiddish word "*nashn,*" which means "to eat sweets" or "to nibble on." It was adopted into English by the working-class communities in the

East End of London, where there was a large Jewish population in the early 1900s. It has become a slang word for food and for snacking.

That tukey is still not done. Do you want something to nosh on while waiting?

———◦◦◦———

Nous

mind, intellect (Greek)

To Homer it meant "mental activity," to Plato it denoted the conscious part of the soul, while for Aristotle it represented the intellect. However, in spite of these varying interpretations, "nous" was generally accepted as a philosophical term for the mind. It continued to be used in this way by later philosophers, but in modern English it has far less cerebral connotations and is used simply to mean "common sense."

That hairdresser could make a fortune out of all the secrets she knows about the rich and famous, but she just doesn't have the nous—that's why they all like her.

———◦◦◦———

Nouveau riche

new rich (French)

Trade and economic growth have led to shifting fortunes between the social classes since the earliest civilizations, but during the Industrial Revolution the British borrowed the French term for those with newly acquired wealth who were breaking into aristocratic social circles for the first time. It was used as it is today, as a derogatory term, laden with the suggestion that as the beneficiaries of new money rather than old, the "nouveau riche" would lack the taste and breeding to know how to use their wealth wisely and discreetly.

I'm sorry, darling, but we really can't go for dinner with the new neighbors; those big china bulldogs in their driveway are so painfully nouveau riche.

O

Oeuvre

work (French)

The French use this word to mean work in the sense of an artist's work, rather than the daily grind, and "*oeuvre*" usually refers to the complete body of work by a writer, artist, or composer. It entered English in 1875 and is used primarily in artistic criticism or by academics who are looking at the life's work of an individual to assess it in its widest possible context. It is generally viewed as a rather pretentious word, though it has seen resurgence through use by modern music reviewers.

Henry had studied the entire Bee Gees oeuvre, but he still could not fathom how Barry hit those high notes.

Ombudsman

commission man (Swedish)

This word can be traced back to the Danish law of Jutland in 1241. It was then written as "*umbozman*" and meant "royal civil servant." By 1809 the term was established with its modern meaning of "official" with the creation of the Swedish Parliamentary Ombudsman to protect the rights of its citizens. In the United States the word describes someone who acts as a trusted intermediary to investigate a complaint.

How dare they give me a speeding fine when I was doing twenty-six miles per hour in a twenty-five-mile-per-hour zone! I'm telling you, Penelope, there should be an ombudsman to deal with this kind of injustice.

Outré

exaggerated, eccentric (French)

Used in English since around 1720, this French word is derived from "*outre*," meaning "beyond," and originally described any behavior, design, or action that broke the boundaries of eighteenth-century convention. It is now regularly used in reference to extravagant fashions, where it might be taken as a compliment by an innovative designer, or to outlandish interior decoration, where it would probably be taken as an insult.

I don't think I'd go back there again, would you, Gordon? The food was delicious, but the faux tiger-skin rugs and zebra-hide chairs seemed rather outré for a family restaurant.

P

Panache
plume (French)

There's always someone who has to go over the top.

The literal translation refers to the feather worn in the helmet of King Henri IV of France, whose bravery and flamboyance gave the word its idiomatic meaning. It describes an almost reckless heroism best exemplified by French dramatist Edmond Rostand's most famous character, Cyrano de Bergerac (created in 1897), who admired King Henri's courage and was partly responsible for establishing "panache" as a desirable quality in a person. We now also use it in reference to anything that exudes flair, from a musical performance to an outstandingly cooked meal.

There are some who say The Boulder's wrestling days are over, but he delivered that pumphandle slam with real panache.

—◦◦◦◦◦◦—

Paparazzi

mosquitos (Italian)

This word is now used across the world for freelance photographers who pursue celebrities to take candid shots of them, but it didn't acquire this meaning until the 1966 release of Federico Fellini's *La Dolce Vita*. Fellini had based one of the film's characters on a street photographer called Tazio Secchiaroli, who made his name with surreptitiously taken images of famous people having angry outbursts or arguments. He supposedly named the character Signore Paparazzo, after a school friend whose buzzing energy had earned him the nickname "The Mosquito."

Tamara never used the front entrance to department stores; the paparazzi made window-shopping impossible.

—◦◦◦◦◦◦—

Par excellence

preeminent (French)

The very best thing of its kind or the most skilled person in his or her field is referred to with this phrase. Its literal and original meaning—"to a degree of excellence"—has been largely superseded by a still more effusive one: "the most excellent of all." Exactly when and why it was adopted into English is unclear, especially since our own word "preeminent" does the job equally well, but the French flourish adds a certain distinguished flair.

Fred Hurlington spent most of his days reminiscing about his time in the armed forces; in his day he'd been hailed as a military tactician par excellence, but he was now reduced to waging war on the moles in his back garden.

Pariah

untouchable, social outcast (Anglo-Indian)

The original pariahs, or "Pariars," are a Tamil tribe of drummers named after the Pari drum. After the introduction of the Indian caste system around 1500 BC, they were segregated from the Hindu majority and are discriminated against as "untouchables" who are outside the caste system—literally "outcasts." British colonialists witnessed the exclusion and social rejection of the Pariahs and from 1819 used their name to describe all those who are spurned by society.

> *Attorney Waterford was beginning to regret his decision to support plans for a new giant supermarket in the area. He had become a pariah in his town.*

Passé

past (French)

It is fitting that a country where being in fashion is a matter of national pride should have provided us with a neat little word to indicate when something is looking a bit jaded. We use this word as the French do, in the sense of "past it," to indicate something that is no longer, ahem, à la mode. It can be applied to artistic, culinary, and musical styles as well as to clothing and is most frequently used by those who believe their own tastes to be unimpeachable.

No, Martha, there's nothing that will work for me here; cream makes me look washed out, and chiffon is so passé.

———⌘———

Passim

throughout, everywhere (Latin)

This is a rather bookish word that has been passed on to us by ancient Roman scholars. It is used in footnotes, indexes, or other explanatory material to show that an idea or particular word is referred to repeatedly at various points in the work being cited. It comes from the Latin word "*passus*," which is the past participle of "*pandere*," meaning "to spread," and allows references to be made to a text as a whole rather than pinpointing precise passages.

New evidence suggested that evolution was dependent on a process of natural selection (Darwin, On the Origin of Species, *1859, passim).*

———⌘———

Peccadillo

small sin (Spanish)

This word came to us in the late-sixteenth century from the Spanish, who got their word from the Latin "*peccare*," meaning "to sin." But it refers only to the mildest of transgressions; an individual's bad habits are often described as their "peccadillos," as long as they are mildly annoying rather than seriously antisocial, and a one-off trivial misdeed might also be described as such.

At the start of their relationship, Jean had been charmed by Alfred's little peccadillos, but as she swept his toenail trimmings off the edge of the bathtub for the hundredth time, she knew she had to say good-bye.

———⟨♥⟩———

Per se

by, of itself (Latin)

Another Latin term useful in argument, "per se" means by virtue of itself; "per" is Latin for "by" or "through," and "se" means "itself." It is used in law as part of the phrase "illegal per se," which is used to refer to something that is against the law in its own right and also in general argument in place of the word "necessarily."

Melanie wasn't averse to fancy dress per se, but in her opinion attempting to look like a Playboy bunny after the age of forty was taking things too far.

———⟨♥⟩———

Persona non grata

unwelcome person (Latin)

This phrase has endured in the English language primarily through its usefulness in diplomatic circles. It refers to a member of diplomatic staff who is deemed to be no longer welcome in a country, either because he is suspected of being a spy or there has been a breakdown of trust between the two nations. The phrase has taken on a broader meaning in general use and is applied to people who have been cut off or ostracized from a group.

Eddie had stopped attending the Poetry Society's live perform-ance nights; he felt he'd been made persona non grata when he admitted to not having read Beowulf in the original Old English.

Pied-à-terre

foot on the ground (French)

A small city apartment that serves as a temporary home during the working week is known as a "pied-à-terre." The literal trans-lation of the phrase gives a sense of its purpose as a foothold in a metropolis. It is usually a second home, with the owner's primary property being larger and in a more rural setting, and so the phrase has a certain sense of luxury.

Oh, Bob, I'm sick of this long journey home every time we go out in the city. Can't we get ourselves a sweet little pied-à-terre like Bruce and Susan's?

Placebo

I shall please (Latin)

In the seventeenth century a "placebo" was a treatment given by a doctor purely to please a patient. Later, with the advent of clin-ical trials, the word was adopted to describe the mock medication given to some patients in the control experiment, in order to ensure that the changes being observed in the main experiment are the result of the drug being tested, rather than the patient's belief in the medication. We now also use the term "placebo effect" to describe any positive outcome that is caused by a belief in something's effectiveness.

Those pills definitely did something for me, Doctor. I don't know if it was just the placebo effect, but the minute I got home from the drugstore, I've been like clockwork.

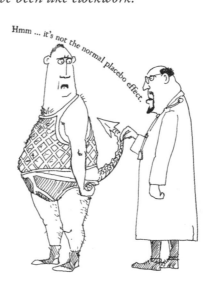

⤳⟡⤳

Poltergeist

noisy ghost (German)

Distinct from apparitions that materialize, poltergeists remain unseen but make noises and perpetrate acts of mischief, such as throwing objects around. In German "*poltern*" means "to make noise," and "*Geist*" means "ghost." Sceptics say poltergeist activity that can't be dismissed as fraud has physical explanations, such as static electricity, electromagnetic fields, or infrasound. However, some well-documented cases with reliable witnesses are hard to explain. Traditionally, poltergeist activity may occur around disturbed or hysterical individuals.

Stephan went to sleep each night that week hoping he'd wake up with the Norovirus: Poltergeist was his favorite horror film of all time, and he wanted to experience projectile vomiting for himself.

Postmortem

after death (Latin)

A "postmortem" is the examination of a body after death. They have been carried out for more than two thousand years; one of the earliest was performed on Julius Caesar in 44 BC, and by the early twentieth century they had become standard practice for any death where the cause was uncertain. We still use the term to describe this procedure, though it is also commonly used to describe any review or analysis that takes place after the completion of an event.

Okay, guys, I think we all know we could have played better, but there's no need for a big postmortem—let's just focus on the games we've still got ahead of us.

Prêt-à-porter

ready-to-wear (French)

High-end fashion designers used to make all their clothes on a personal basis for their individual, high-paying clients, but by the mid-1950s there was a widespread desire for designer clothes at more accessible prices. Prêt-à-porter, or ready-to-wear, collections were the answer to this, allowing greater access to skillfully designed but mass-produced clothes. Many designers still make made-to-measure outfits for their most loyal clients, but the vast majority now focus on their prêt-à-porter range.

It is gorgeous, Felipe, but you know I can't go in prêt-à-porter—I'd never live it down if someone else was wearing the same thing as me.

Prima donna

first lady (Italian)

This term was coined in Italian opera houses to describe the leading female singer in the company, usually a soprano, who, according to opera mythology, was self-important, demanding, and egotistical. The phrase is now more commonly used to describe self-obsessed female stars with a reputation for a bad temper and an outrageously long list of dressing room requirements, such as freshly painted white walls, rare Guatemalan orchids, and full kitchen facilities for their personal chef.

I'm telling you, Yvonne, I've done hair and makeup for some of the biggest stars out there, but that little one-hit wonder is the biggest prima donna I've ever come across.

———◦◦◦◦◦———

Pro bono

for good (Latin)

This is a shortened version of the phrase *"pro bono publico,"* which means "for public good." It refers to the work that lawyers do without payment for clients who are unable to pay their fees or for charities or non-profit-making organizations. In recent years it has also been used to describe the ethos of public service organizations, like the National Health Service and the BBC, which are run to provide a service rather than to make a profit.

I'm leaving the law firm. I have so much pro bono work, I'm going to set up a charity instead.

———◦◦◦◦◦———

Protégé

protected person, apprentice (French)

A person being mentored or guided in their profession by someone more experienced is known as a "protégé." The word, which entered English in 1778, comes from the French *"proteger,"* meaning "to protect," and was originally used in relation to someone apprenticed to an established tradesman in order to learn his skills. These days it is often used in a looser sense to refer to someone who is favored, though not necessarily trained, by an expert in his field.

Brad, I believe that you have great potential. The world of bathroom and kitchen tile grouting needs someone like you—I'm going to make you my protégé!'

Pukka

cooked, ripe (Hindi, from "*pakka*")

The word "*pakka*," which means "cooked" or "ripe," is used in India to denote something that is first-class or completely authentic. The term entered the English language during the days of the Raj and is now generally used as slang for "top quality." It has been popularized in recent years by celebrity chef Jamie Oliver, who coined the phrase "pukka tukka" to describe an expertly cooked dish.

Come on, ladies and gents, salt and pepper shakers, a dollar a pair. That's a pukka pot of pepper if ever I saw one.

Pundit

learned man (Sanskrit)

Red Sammy, to win, in the 3.30 at Epsom.

When Britain began trading with India in the 1600s "pundits," sometimes known as "*pandita*," were wise men who had studied Sanskrit history and traditions. They were revered as teachers and were important to the English traders in helping them to understand Indian customs. Over time, the word has come to be used for any expert or commentator who can explain events or developments in their area of expertise.

For viewers unfamiliar with the rules of llama racing, our pundits at the racetrack will talk you through the basics.

Purdah

curtain, veil (Hindi)

Originating in Persia in around 1000 BC, "purdah" is a system of rules governing the movements and dress of women in some Hindu and Muslim societies. It requires women to cover themselves with a veil or burqa and to be separated from male non-family members by a curtain. In England the word is also used to mean any period of isolation, and in politics it refers to the inactive period after the announcement of a general election or budget.

Come on, Hannah—put this sparkly wig on and come for a drink. There's no point going into purdah just because you're having a bad hair day.

Pajamas

trousers (Persian, from "*paijama*")

The original "*paijama*" are loose, lightweight trousers with drawstring waistbands worn in Asia by both sexes—literally "*pai,*" meaning "leg," and "*jama,*" meaning garment. In the UK, the United States, and Canada, pajamas are loose-fitting, two-piece garments worn for sleeping but sometimes also for lounging. For U.S. children, pet abbreviations are popular and differ between families. These include "jamas," "pj's," and "jammies." Whatever word you're brought up with is correct, and the other terms are weird.

If Molly could only get out of her pajamas before noon, it would be a big step toward getting a career.

Q

QED (Quod Erat Demonstrandum)

that which was to be demonstrated (Latin)

Ancient Greek mathematicians, including Archimedes and Euclid, used a similar phrase at the conclusion of a proven mathematical truth to indicate that they had worked out their solution ("that which" they had intended to show) using logical deductions. Mathematical books were written in Latin during the European Renaissance, when the phrase was adopted by philosophers to add weight to their arguments. We now use it at the end of any statement we deem to be irrefutable.

A diet low in red meat and high in fruit and vegetables is good for controlling obesity. You never see a fat vegetarian. QED.

Quasi

as if (Latin)

In Latin this phrase was employed in exactly the same way that we would use the words "as if," but over time it has come to be used as a prefix to words such as "scientific," "historical," "official," and "religious," to indicate that something is almost, or has some resemblance to the word it precedes. It provides us with a useful linguistic tool for describing things that can nearly, but not quite, be placed into a category we are familiar with.

I want a new TV, not a science lesson, so skip the quasi-technological sales pitch and tell me how much it costs.

———⌒☙⌒———

Que sera sera

whatever will be, will be (Portuguese/Spanish/French)

It's not actually clear which language this happy-go-lucky phrase comes from. It was the title of a 1956 song by Jay Livingston and Ray Evans, which became a hit after Doris Day sang it for the Alfred Hitchcock film *The Man Who Knew Too Much*. Livingston said he'd adapted it from "*che sera sera*," a motto from the 1954 film *The Barefoot Contessa*, which may in turn have been taken from Christopher Marlowe's sixteenth-century play *Dr. Faustus*.

Kay's attempt at seeming nonchalant about the promotion was rather spoiled by the volume at which she belted out "Que Sera Sera" on her way to the interview.

———⌒☙⌒———

Quid pro quo

something for something (Latin)

In law this Latin term is used to describe an equal exchange, either to ensure good behavior by requiring that services or goods are exchanged for something of equal value or to prevent bad behavior by ensuring, for example, that donors to political parties don't expect favors in return. We now also use it more generally to describe a situation that is mutually beneficial. The British slang word "quid" for "pound sterling" is also derived from this phrase and its association with currency and exchange.

An excellent meal, Neil, and it's my treat. No, really, I insist; quid pro quo—you've been a marvelous host all week.

R

Raconteur

skilled storyteller (French)

This French word comes from the verb "*raconter*," meaning to "relate" or "recount," and is used to describe people with a sort of refined version of the "gift of the gab"; in other words, someone known for her wit and skill at telling stories. It was first used in English in the nineteenth century, just in time for one of the world's most celebrated raconteurs, Oscar Wilde, to be labeled with the term.

Billy felt a bead of perspiration trickle down his neck as the first of his witty anecdotes was met with silence. He'd never been much of a raconteur, and suddenly he understood that he just wasn't cut out to be best man.

—⁓⁓⁓—

Raison d'être

reason for being (French)

Originally used straightforwardly to rationally justify the existence of a thing, person, or organization, the phrase has been used in English since 1864 to describe an individual's primary motivation in life or dearest passion. If there is a cause that someone dedicates all his time to fighting for, or a project or hobby that he feels more passionate about than anything else, that might be described as his raison d'être.

Quentin came to life as he heard those rumba rhythms; dancing had been his raison d'être since the day he first realized his hips knew how to wiggle.

—⁓⁓⁓—

Rapport

harmonious relationship (French)

When this word was first used in English in the mid-1800s, it was in the context of the psychologist–patient relationship. The earliest written record is Edgar Allan Poe's 1844 short story "A Tale of the Rugged Mountains," in which Poe uses it to describe the magnetic bond between a practitioner of mesmerism (early hypnosis) and his subject. The word is still used in psychology, though we now also use the term to refer to any feeling of connection or emotional affinity between two people.

Lucy stood at the edge of the red carpet and quivered; Brad had only glanced at her for a second while he signed his autograph on her fake plaster cast, but she was sure he, too, had felt the rapport between them.

———∘⟨⟩∘———

Reductio ad absurdum

reduction to the absurd (Latin)

Another Latin term useful in both mathematics and philosophy, "reductio ad absurdum" is a process of logical reasoning in which a mathematician or debater might prove his or her own theorem to be correct by starting out with the opposite claim and showing that it leads to a ridiculous outcome. When their careful calculations demonstrate that it is wrong, they have succeeded in proving that their own claim is right.

> *Birds are most certainly vertebrate animals that fly.*
> *Are they? You don't think that the flightless emu and the ostrich furnish the reductio ad absurdam for your proposition?*

———∘⟨⟩∘———

Renaissance

rebirth (French)

This is the name given to the period of radical cultural change that took place across Europe in the fifteenth and sixteenth centuries. The movement began in Italy, where scholars called it the "*rinascita*"—the rebirth—in recognition of the fact that they had escaped the barbarism of the Middle Ages and were rediscovering the cultural values of ancient Rome and Greece. The French translated the word, and as England entered its own modern era, it borrowed the French term. We now use it to describe any kind of revival.

> *Sandra carried her old clothes down from the attic with reverence. She was a shoulder-pad girl at heart and was thrilled that 1980s fashions were having a renaissance.*

Rickshaw

man-powered carriage (Japanese)

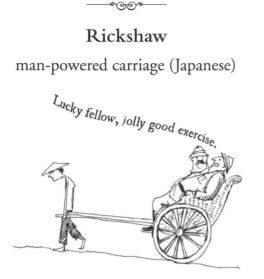

These two-wheeled carriages were originally pulled along by a runner and were first used in Japan in around 1868. The word is a shortened version of "*jinrikisha*"—a blend of three Japanese words: "*jin*," meaning "man," "*riki*," meaning "power," and "*sha*," meaning "carriage." It was popularized in English by Rudyard Kipling's 1888 ghost story "The Phantom Rickshaw" and is now used to describe the bicycle-drawn carriages that clog the streets of Central London and downtown New York.

Jack had always agreed with Samuel Johnson that when a man is tired of London, he is tired of life, but the day he was run over by a rickshaw, he realized that Johnson's London was sadly not comparable with his own.

———⸪———

Rigor mortis

stiffness of death (Latin)

Ancient Roman physicians carrying out the earliest autopsies used this term to describe the rigidity of the body after death. Within three to six hours of death, chemical changes in the muscles, combined with a buildup of lactic acid, cause the body to stiffen unless it is carefully cooled ready for embalming. The development of rigor mortis can be useful in determining the time of death in police investigations.

> *I'm afraid Snowy's grave is going to have to run the full length of the garden; it didn't occur to me that rabbits got rigor mortis.*

———⸪———

Robot

drudgery (Czech)

The Czech word "*robota*" means "drudgery," hence "robot" for devices that can do tedious work for humans. The Czech writer Karel Capek first introduced the concept, and name, of "robot" in his play *R.U.R. (Rossum's Universal Robots)*, whose first scene takes place in a factory that manufactures artificial people to work for humans. There are many different definitions of what constitutes a modern robot, but broadly speaking, they are programmable electromechanical systems that can sense and interact with their environment. In popular imagination robots are machines with human qualities and capabilities, but whether they could ever possess true intelligence continues to intrigue philosophers, scientists, writers and filmmakers alike.

Professor Zoton deliberately didn't give his robot, Epsilon-TransnegativeElectrostabilizer, a name in case he became too attached to him. Nevertheless it would have been easier to call him "Pete."

<hr>

Roué

debauched or lecherous man (French)

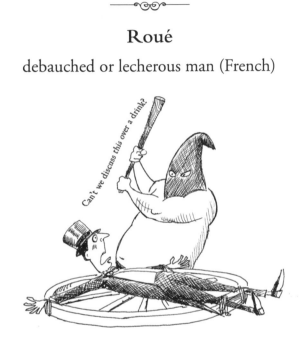

This is a rare example of a term that is derived from the kind of punishment that ought to befall the person given it. The word is the past participle of "*rouer*," which means to "break on a wheel" or "beat harshly," which the French felt was a fitting treatment for such a dissipated creature. These days, society is less critical of lechery, and the word is often used for sex-hungry men who are regarded as "players."

I'd steer clear of that Les Fisher if I were you, Jeanette. Apparently he's become a bit of a roué since he discovered hair color for men.

Rucksack

back bag (German)

What is often thought of as a peculiarly British word is actually borrowed from the Germans. It may have come into use during the era of Romanticism, which thrived in Germany and saw many an awe-inspired poet seeking the sublime on the kind of mountain walks that it would have been foolhardy to attempt without a rucksack of provisions. In Germany itself, the rucksack is often called a "body bag," which doesn't sound quite so wholesome.

For goodness' sake, Doreen, how do you expect me to find the compass when you insist on filling every crevice of the backpack with peanut butter and jelly sandwiches?

S

Safari

journey (Swahili)

In Swahili a "safari" is any journey, even just popping out to the local market and back, but in English it is reserved for tours of the savannah made especially to see and photograph the wildlife. It is thought to have been brought into the English language by explorer Sir Richard Francis Burton in the nineteenth century, when the phrase "point and shoot" had rather different connotations. Hunting safaris are now rare, and the term has extended to include wildlife-watching trips to rain forests, frozen tundra, and remote parts of the ocean.

We thought about going on a safari this year, didn't we, Jeff?
But then we thought, well, we get a lot of quite sizable cats in
the backyard at home, so we stuck with the Jersey Shore.

———◦◦◦———

Sangfroid

cold blood (French)

Though the literal translation makes the term sound vaguely
reptilian, "sangfroid" is—in both French and English—a desirable
quality in a person. It arrived in English during the Enlightenment
in the eighteenth century and means "cool-headedness" and
"composure." An important attribute in all reasoning individuals,
sangfroid implies an ability to keep a clear mind and an even
temper in the most testing of circumstances.

Did you see her face as the nominations were read out? It was
completely expressionless; I don't know whether to admire her
sangfroid or blacklist whoever does her Botox.

———◦◦◦———

Sarong

covering (Malay)

The "sarong" is the Malay national garment and the word was first
recorded in 1834. It is made from a long sheet of fabric, often
batik dyed, or woven with checks for men, which is tied at the
waist. It is still worn by both men and women in Southeast Asia,
but in the West they are worn exclusively by women and David
Beckham.

Toby waited for a good ten minutes after Sophie had left the
house and then crept over to her closet. He'd once been told he
looked like David Beckham, and he wanted to see if he could
carry off a sarong.

Savoir faire
know how to do (French)

In both French and English this phrase refers to the kind of innate social knowledge possessed by tactful people who know instinctively how to behave, though the French version has more practical overtones and can refer to depth of knowledge in a particular field. The phrase was first recorded in English by Sir Walter Scott in his 1815 novel *Guy Mannering*, in which a character called Gilbert Glossin is described as having "great confidence in his own savoir faire" when it came to his polished behavior in society. Today we also use the informal shortened "savvy" for "know-how."

This isn't a job for Daniel—I know he tries hard, but he has as much savoir faire as a baby chihuahua.

Schadenfreude
pleasure taken from another's suffering (German)

This comes from two German words, "*Schaden*," meaning "damage" or "harm," and "*Freude*," meaning "joy." Though it sounds like a mean and disturbed emotion to feel, *Schadenfreude* actually forms the basis of much of our comedy. From the slapstick antics of Charlie Chaplin to the self-deprecatory humor of modern stand-up comedians, as long as suffering isn't permanently damaging, it can be enjoyable to witness. The modern obsession with following the downfall of troubled celebrities is proof of the word's continuing usefulness.

Mary couldn't bear circus clowns, the Schadenfreude the rest of the audience experienced from watching them fall over just left her with a nervous headache.

Schlep

drag (Yiddish)

Damn it, Curuthers, I didn't mean that sort of drag.

This comes from the Yiddish word "*shlepn*," meaning to "drag" or "pull," and it has retained this meaning in one of its modern uses, in which it is synonymous with the English word "lug." It is more frequently used, though, to describe an arduous or difficult journey and, most recently, to describe any journey, however short or simple, that you simply can't be bothered to make.

Oh, darling, please can we just get in a taxi. It's such a schlep to get to the West End, and my Manolos don't deserve this kind of pounding.

―✦⟳✦―

Schmaltz

rendered fat (Yiddish)

In brutally literal terms "schmaltz" is rendered chicken or goose fat that is clarified and eaten spread on bread, in the way that lard used to be before we knew about the dietary causes of heart disease. It arrived in English in the 1930s courtesy of Yiddish-speaking Jews who used it in this culinary sense, but it has been adapted by English speakers, along with the newly coined "schmaltzy" to describe something excessively maudlin or "dripping" with sentimentality.

I know Broadway musicals are meant to be sentimental, but the schmaltz levels in this one are just suffocating.

―✦⟳✦―

Schmooze

converse casually (Yiddish)

This is one of those brilliant words that perfectly distils into a single syllable a fairly complex social interaction. It is believed to originate from the Hebrew word "*schmu'ot,*" which translates as "reports" or "gossip," and is used in Yiddish, and now English, to describe the act of exchanging small talk with someone in order to establish a mutually beneficial relationship with them. It's the "chatting-up" of the business world.

Tara downed her glass of pinot grigio, applied a fresh coat of lipstick, and spritzed on some perfume—she was ready to schmooze.

---❧ঔ❧---

Schmuck/schmo

penis (Yiddish)

"Schmuck" and its slightly less offensive derivative "schmo," have meanings synonymous with "idiot," "sad case," and the somewhat less refined "dickhead." Like the latter of these derogatory appellations, both come from the Yiddish word for penis and are used in English, primarily in the United States, as insults. The Yiddish "schmuck" is linked to the same word in German, where it means "jewels," which may or may not be the source of the popular euphemism "the family jewels."

> *Gregory, you've got to help me; some schmuck's just let his dog do its business on the wheel of my vintage Aston Martin.*

---❧ঔ❧---

Shaman

priest (Russian/Evenki)

A religious practitioner serving the small nomadic communities in Siberia, Mongolia, and northern China is known by the local Evenki-speaking people as a "shaman." Shamanism works on the principle that the lives of those on earth are shaped and influenced by spirits, over whom a shaman has power. The word is now used in many different cultures to describe a priest or sorcerers and in the West, the New Age community uses the term for its spiritual leaders.

> *Get those bits of half-chewed chicken bone off me, Steve! Thinking you saw a ghost on a short cut through the cemetery does not make you a shaman.*

———⋱⟨∘⟩⋰———

Sic

thus, in such a way (Latin)

Used in publishing to indicate a misspelling or unconventional use of a word, "*sic*," written in brackets, is the editor's way of indicating that she is aware of the error but is simply quoting material in exactly the form in which it first appeared. It is especially useful for publications whose readership is proud of its pedantry and takes pleasure in writing in to point out syntactical oversights.

> *In a heartfelt letter to the president, five-year-old Scarlet Jones wrote, "I'm getting to like you more now, but I do miss George Brush [sic]."*

———⋱⟨∘⟩⋰———

Sine qua non

without which not (Latin)

This phrase, in its Greek form, was originally used by Aristotle to describe a legal condition that was absolutely essential and could not be done without. It has been used in English since around 1600, and the term is still used in this way in the British legal system but has also been adopted more widely to mean any crucial ingredient or prerequisite without which the normal order of things could not proceed.

> *Let me just call Gustav to ask for a recommendation. Really, how could you think of cooking for yourself; these days a personal macrobiotic chef is the sine qua non of the Hollywood elite.*

Skol

cheers (Danish/Norwegian/Swedish)

Like all groups of marauding invaders, the Vikings liked a little tipple at the end of the working day. The word they used to accompany a toast was "*skol*," which has often been mistranslated as "skull" because of the Vikings' mythical practice of drinking out of the skulls of their victims. In fact, the word comes from the old Norse word "*skál*," meaning "shell" or "bowl."

Martin woke up dressed in a tutu and tied to a lamppost. He tried to piece together the events that had led him there, but all he could remember was shouting "skol" before everything went dark.

Smorgasbord

sandwich table (Swedish)

In Sweden a "*smörgåsbord*" is a type of varied meal in which numerous dishes are arrayed on a table for guests to choose whichever items they like. It consists of both hot and cold dishes and traditionally includes smoked fish and meatballs. English speakers borrowed the word as an alternative to "buffet," but its idiomatic meaning has since broadened and it is used to describe any situation in which a range of choices are presented.

You are all in for a treat tonight, ladies and gentlemen; we've got a veritable smorgasbord of acts to tempt and bedazzle you.

<hr>

Spiel

a play or game (German)

Exactly what playing has to do with long-winded speeches isn't clear, but the German word "*spiel*" has been absorbed into English to describe an extravagant address or argument that is generally delivered in order to convince the listener to believe in something or buy it. It comes from the Middle High German "*spilon*," meaning "to revel," so perhaps giving a spiel was more fun in the Middle Ages than it is today.

An hour and twenty minutes I was trapped at the front door this morning trying to fend off that salesman! I thought I knew about cleaning, but after his spiel, I was an expert in all twenty-seven different kinds of dust.

<hr>

Spiritus mundi

soul, spirit of the world (Latin)

The concept of "*spiritus mundi*" has its roots in the philosophy of Plato, but the phrase itself was coined by fifteenth-century German astrologer and occult philosopher Agrippa von Nettesheim. He used it as a label for the spirit element that he believed permeated the whole world and was the force behind alchemy and occult occurrences. The psychologist Carl Jung elaborated on these ideas when he discussed the idea of a collective subconscious, and the term is still used by astrologers and spiritualists today.

Runa closed her eyes and jangled her bangle-laden wrists; she was about to channel images from the spiritus mundi and liked there to be an appropriately grandiose buildup.

⁓❦⁓

Status quo

state in which (Latin)

Shortened from the longer Latin phrase "*status quo ante bellum,*" meaning "the state in which things were before the war," this was used in Roman diplomacy to negotiate a return to the previous order of things before a conflict. The phrase is still used to describe an existing political situation—Ronald Reagan famously said, "Status quo, you know, is Latin for 'the mess we're in.'" And we now use it for any abiding set of circumstances that are either under threat of change or need changing.

Norman liked the fact that he'd worked in the same office for thirty years. For him, maintaining the status quo was one of life's true pleasures.

⁓❦⁓

Subpoena

under penalty (Latin)

A subpoena is an official written instruction to an individual to testify in, or bring evidence to, court or face punishment. However, in their bid to be more accessible to those unfamiliar with Latin legal terms, civil courts in England and Wales have recently replaced the word with the phrase "witness summons," which does explain rather neatly what the Latin word means.

Oh, no, I can't believe it—I've got a subpoena.
I'm so sorry, Frank—that's terrible. Is it contagious?

T

Temet nosce

know thyself (Latin)

"*Temet nosce*," the Latin translation of the Greek phrase "*gnothi seauton*," which was engraved in the forecourt of the Temple of Apollo at Delphi, dates back to the fourth century. It translates as "know yourself" and carries with it the idea that you must first understand yourself before you can understand others around you. Exactly which of the great Greek scholars came up with this profound aphorism is not clear; it may have been Socrates, or possibly Pythagoras, or one of four other sages. It has long been used in English by those of a philosophical bent and has been widely quoted since it was used by the character of the Oracle in the 1999 dystopian sci-fi film *The Matrix*.

Higgins was a terrible drunk—his school motto had been " Temet nosce," and he'd taken it so much to heart that he regularly bored his companions to tears with his obsessive self-analysis.

⎯⎯⎯ ⟿⟾ ⎯⎯⎯

Terra firma

solid ground (Latin)

This phrase was used in the labeling of maps in the seventeenth century in order to distinguish areas of dry land from the parts covered by seas or oceans. We also use "terra" as the scientific name for our planet, and "terra firma" more colloquially to describe being on solid ground, rather than aboard a ship or in a plane.

Well, Stephanie, I've loved every minute of our cruise, but after last night's rough waters, I have to admit I'm glad to be back on terra firma.

Tête-à-tête

head-to-head (French)

Come on, lads, don't argue.

This phrase can be used in French and English to describe any intimate meeting between two people where the arrival of a third party would be considered an intrusion. It flourished in eighteenth-century tearooms, where gossip was rife and whispered exchanges of confidences over a muffin were the best form of entertainment available. Sadly in modern usage it has been appropriated by pushy middle managers who are prone to suggesting "a quick tête-à-tête" as if they wanted a cozy chat, when they actually mean "an intimidating personal assessment."

Michael, have you got a moment? Let's have a little tête-à-tête over coffee in the chill-out zone.

Thug

thief (Hindi/Marathi)

In Hindi and Marathi (the fourth most spoken Indian language) "*thag*" was the name given to a member of an Indian network of gangs who murdered and robbed travelers and often strangled their victims. They operated well into the nineteenth century, when they were driven out by the British, and by 1839 the term had come to mean "ruffian" or "cutthroat." These days we use "thug" to describe someone hired by criminal groups to do their dirty work as well as any brutishly violent male.

Beverley walked like a thug, swore like a thug, swung a baseball bat like a thug, and terrorized all the local businesses. And yet nothing could quite play down the fact that he had a woman's name.

Tour de force

feat of strength (French)

Not to be confused with the Tour de France, an annual long-distance bicycle race, this epic-sounding French expression denotes an achievement that has required great skill or endeavor to complete. In recent years it has been somewhat devalued in literary circles through overuse by critics who employ it too often to describe a well-crafted novel, but it's still a valid term of praise for an outstanding sporting or artistic achievement.

Well, Jim, we were expecting to see some good bowling from you, but that was a tour de force!

Tout de suite

at once (French)

This phrase became common in English during the Great War, when many British soldiers spent time fighting in France. Like many French phrases adopted by the English, it was often misspelled and sometimes deliberately mispronounced. In 1917 an edition of satirical magazine *Punch* ran a cartoon featuring a soldier saying to inquisitive French children, "Nah, then, alley [go] toot sweet, an' the tooter the sweeter."

Mrs. Kendle watched in horror as the head of the marzipan bride-groom wobbled off the wedding cake. She could hear the guests outside and knew she must reverse the decapitation tout de suite.

Trek

a long journey (Afrikaans)

"Trek" entered English in the nineteenth century from South Africa, where the word was used by the Boers for a journey by ox wagon. The Groot Trek (1835 onward) refers to the journey made by ten thousand Boers, who journeyed north and north-east from the Cape Colony to escape British colonial rule. The word is universally familiar thanks to *Star Trek*, the hugely popular long-running sci-fi series created by Gene Roddenberry, whose ashes made perhaps the longest trek possible when they were sent into space aboard space shuttle *Columbia* in 1992.

It was quite a trek up the hillside and along the ridge, but Sally was determined to boldly go where no girl in kitten heels had gone before.

Tzar

emperor (Russian)

In Russia, Bulgaria, and Serbia, "tzar" has been the term for the sovereign since the fourteenth century. The word is a Russian adaptation of the Latin *"caesar"* (also the root of the German

"*Kaiser*") and was used to describe all Russian emperors until 1917. English speakers have in turn adopted the word to describe any politically powerful figure with jurisdiction over a certain problem area, such as a drug tzar or a terrorism tzar.

Okay, staff, I'd like to announce a new appointment this term; Mr. Jacobson is going to take on the role of punctuality tzar, so arrive by eight thirty at the latest, or you'll have him to answer to.

Tsunami

harbor wave (Japanese)

The literal meaning of this Japanese word comes from "*tsu*," "harbor," and "*nami*," "waves." However, the waves that the word describes are not confined to harbors, nor do they have anything to do with tides, but rather deep sea earthquakes. They were observed as early as 426 BC, when the Greek historian Thucydides correctly suggested that they might be caused by tremors under the ocean. Nearly two hundred Japanese tsunamis have been officially recorded, and the high incidence of the phenomenon in the oceans around Japan has resulted in the adoption of their word across many languages, including English. The Japan tsunami of 2011 was one of history's worst natural disasters, with hundreds of thousands of casualties.

I've never really liked the sea. All the seaweed and sharks and tsunamis—no, a bath once a week has always been more than enough splashing about for me.

Tycoon

great lord (Japanese)

Shoguns or generals in the Japanese army were given the title "*taikun*," meaning "great lord or prince," and when Matthew Perry, commodore of the U.S. Navy, compelled Japan to open trading with the West in 1854, he took the word back home with him. Abraham Lincoln's cabinet members used it as a nickname for the president, and it has since come to describe powerful and wealthy businessmen who have made their fortune from a particular industry, such as oil or shipping.

Mr. Chakrabarti's ever-expanding chain of menswear stores had led some gossips to dub him "the shirt tycoon."

U

Übermensch

superman (German)

This word was coined by Friedrich Nietzsche in his 1883 work *Thus Spoke Zarathustra*, in which he described a more evolved version of humankind—a superhuman in comparison with which mankind as we know it would seem as underdeveloped as apes. The word is used in English primarily in a philosophical context, though "*über*" is often turned into a prefix as an alternative to "extremely" in phrases like "*über* cool."

> *It would take ten people working flat out on that project to get it done inside a week, and there are only three of us—what does he think we are—team Übermensch?*

Ukulele
jumping flea (Hawaiian)

The ukulele was a Portuguese instrument originally called a "*braghuina*," but when Portuguese immigrants arrived in Hawaii in the nineteenth century and played it in front of the locals, the Hawaiians adopted it as their own. They rechristened it the "jumping flea" in reference to the way in which the musician's fingers jump up and down the fret board. The "uke" reached mainland America in 1915 at the Panama Pacific International Exposition and has been a part of American music ever since.

> *The hot favorite at the Alabama Ukulele Play-Offs stepped onto the stage with a swagger—they didn't call him "Fourteen-fingered Frankie" for nothing.*

Utopia
no place (Greek)

In 1516 Sir Thomas More wrote a book about a fictional island on which the community functioned in perfect harmony. He called the eponymous island "Utopia" from the Greek words "*ou*," "not" (which sounds nearly the same as "*eu*," "good") and "*topos*," "place," and the word has been used ever since to describe a flawless society. Over the centuries many people have chased the ideal of a utopia, sometimes with disastrous results. The word's antonym is "dystopia" ("*dus*" being Greek for "bad") and is a nightmarish imagined world, such as the one created by George Orwell in *1984*.

Sunshine, sangria, friendly neighbors, and endless golf courses— the map might have told him it was southern Spain, but Mick felt as if he had found utopia.

V

Vade mecum
go with me (Latin)

In the Middle Ages physicians, astrologers, parsons, and tradesmen often carried with them small manuals filled with useful references and calculation aids appropriate to their field of expertise. These were called "vade mecums" or "go-with-mes" because they were taken everywhere, often suspended on a string or ribbon from the belt. We still use the term for any handy object or booklet that is carried on the person and more widely for specialist handbooks.

Alan patted his top pocket anxiously and felt his heart rate calm as his fingers touched on the hard cover of his angler's vade mecum, knowing he had never had a successful fishing trip without it.

Vampire

a nocturnal reanimated corpse
(Hungarian/Bulgarian/Ukrainian)

In folktales vampires were said to revisit loved ones and cause mischief or deaths where they had once lived. The etymology of the word is unclear, but it possibly stems from a Kazan Tatar word for "witch." The ancient vampire was bloated and dark-countenanced, unlike the nineteenth-century reinvention, which is gaunt and pale. The term entered English in the eighteenth century, when vampire superstitions arrived from the Balkans and Eastern Europe. Our best-known fictional vampire is the eponymous villain of Bram Stoker's *Dracula* (1897), which was inspired by the legends surrounding fifteenth-century Wallachian Prince Vlad the Impaler. It wasn't until 2005 that vampires once again earned such widespread fame, with the debut of Stephanie Meyer's *Twilight*, the first novel in a series of modern-day vampire love stories. When *Twilight* was made into a movie in 2008, the series quickly became a worldwide phenomenon.

Poised over the alabaster neck of his beautiful victim, the vampire sniffed the air. Had she been eating garlic?

—◦◦◦◦◦◦—

Vendetta

blood feud (Italian)

Originating from the Latin word *"vindicta,"* meaning "revenge," the Italian term "vendetta" is most associated with Corsica. There it was the name for a social code whereby if a serious wrong was committed against a member of a family, it could only be righted by the murder of the wrongdoer. The word has now come to be used to describe any kind of long-standing grudge.

Hello, I'd like to book an appointment for a fake tan, please, with anyone but Jacqueline. She's had a vendetta against me since I asked if she'd been tangoed, and I don't want her deliberately giving me streaks.

—◦◦◦◦◦◦—

Verbatim

word for word (Latin)

This term made its transition into English through the printed word. The full phrase *"verbatim et literatim,"* meaning "word for word and letter for letter" was used to indicate that a piece of text had been copied precisely, with no alterations to the spelling, grammar, or meaning. It is now most commonly used in spoken English to explain that something someone has said has been repeated exactly.

You know John Lennon didn't really write "Imagine," don't you? In actual fact, I did. I read it at a poetry recital in 1969; he must have been there and copied it down verbatim.

Verboten

forbidden (German)

This word had been an unremarkable feature of the German language from the end of the Middle Ages until the autocratic policies of Wilhelm II and later the Nazis imbued it with sinister undertones. It became familiar to English speakers during World War II, when signs reading "*Juden verboten*" appeared everywhere, from shop doors to park benches. We now use it in place of "forbidden," usually when we want to imply an element of authoritarianism.

> *Have you heard the latest from the new management? No talking between breaks—they'll have "Laughter is verboten" flashing on our screensavers before we know it.*

Verbum satis sapienti

a word is enough for the wise (Latin)

This saying is attributed to the ancient Roman playwright Plautus. It means that just a few words of explanation are adequate to explain a situation or concept to someone who is wise. It is used in English as an alternative to the phrase "enough said."

Okay, Marge, it's not brain surgery. Verbum satis sapienti. I'll feed Felix half a tin of cat food in the morning and half a tin at night.

Via

by way of (Latin)

This is such a commonly used word in English that it seems strange to think of it as foreign, but we owe its usefulness to the ancient Romans, who said in three letters what the English language needs three words for. It is almost synonymous with our word "through," but it implies more strongly that a solution or destination has been arrived at by dint of a little detour.

The package was sent via overnight mail because it simply had to get there for the next morning's meeting.

Vice versa

a switched change (Latin)

The term is used to mean that the reverse of the previous statement, with the main items transposed, is also true. It is usually used to imply the complement of a statement without expressing as much in words. For example, "Fish can't live where we are most comfortable, and vice versa." It is usually pronounced as spelled, but in fact, the Latin pronunciation is "wee-ce wer-sah." The first English usage is found in print as early as 1601.

Wives may bring their husbands to the celebration and vice versa (husbands may bring their wives).

——◦⌒◦——

Vis-à-vis

face-to-face (French)

This French expression was first used in English in the 1750s with a trio of different meanings. The name given to a carriage in which the passengers sat facing one another with their knees almost touching; a term used to describe a person or object opposite you; and an alternative to "in relation to." The last of these is how we most commonly use the term today, with the idea that it's a more stylish substitute for "regarding."

Hi, Katie! I wondered if I could talk to you vis-à-vis what happened the other night. It's just that I'd had a few drinks, and I didn't know if you, you know. So, anyway, give me a call. If you want to. Obviously.

——◦⌒◦——

Voilà

see there (French)

This exuberant exclamation comes from the French word "*voir*," meaning "to see," combined with "*là*," meaning "there." It's used in France and in English-speaking countries when some sort of action has been demonstrated successfully, and it is particularly popular with television chefs, who often deliver it with a smack of the lips as they take a perfect pie out of the oven. The closest equivalent in English is "there you have it," which doesn't have quite the same triumphant ring to it.

Simply throw the chicken into a pan with the turmeric and bean sprouts, pop it in the oven for 30 minutes, and voilà!

——⁘——

Vox populi

voice of the people (Latin)

This phrase is a reduced version of "*Vox populi, vox dei*," meaning "the voice of the people is the voice of God," a phrase believed to date back to the eighth century that referred to a belief that the views of the masses should rule the day. Shortened to "vox populi," it has come to mean "the view of the majority," or a belief shared by most people. It is often shortened further to "vox pop," which is now used in broadcasting to describe interviews with members of the public giving their views on a subject.

I know we're all in agreement, sir, but according to the vox populi, it's cruel to hunt deer, so we'll have to stick to shooting clay pigeons, I'm afraid.

W

Wanderlust

desire to travel (German)

This is a blend of German words "*wandern*," meaning "to hike," and "*Lust*," meaning "desire." The word was first used in English in the late-nineteenth century, possibly as a result of our association of German Romanticism with carefree wandering. We still use it to refer to a yearning for the open road.

Pete had always planned to settle down by the time he was thirty, but wanderlust kept gripping him by the throat and dragging him back to mosquito-ridden swamps in far-flung places.

Wunderkind

wonder child (German)

In nineteenth-century Germany this phrase often referred to musical child prodigies such as Mozart and Beethoven, but the phrase has since expanded to include anyone at an early age with a specific skill, art, or talent. A ten-year-old with expert skills in, say, mathematics, chess, or art deserves the title. In English the term has come to include those with remarkable talent or ability who achieve great success or acclaim early in their adult lives. The computer industry has plenty of modern examples.

Troy may be the new wunderkind of alternative theater, but his mother still does his laundry.

Y

Yin and yang

balance of opposites (Chinese)

In Chinese "*yin*" denotes negative, dark, calm and feminine qualities, "*yang*" positive, bright, fiery, masculine ones. In Chinese philosophy the concept of yin and yang describes how seemingly opposing forces are interconnected and interdependent in the natural world, giving rise to each other in turn. This idea lies at the heart of classical Chinese science and philosophy and is a fundamental principle in traditional Chinese medicine. Many natural dualities—for example, dark and light, female and male, low and high—are cast in Chinese thought in this way and are represented by the symbol ☯.

"Yin and yang is a dynamic equilibrium," said Huaqing sagely. "Because they arise together, they are always equal; if one disappears, the other must disappear as well, leaving emptiness."

Z

Zeitgeist

spirit of the time (German)

The word describes the atmosphere of an era but can also refer to a trend. Literally translated: "*Zeit*" is time; "*Geist*" spirit. In German the word has more layers of meaning than in English, including the fact that zeitgeist can only be observed for past events. The English usage is looser, and the word carries a compelling literary ring, for anything that seems to perfectly capture a mood or a trend.

Lots of students in the sixties got caught up in street protests; the zeitgeist of the age compelled it. At least that was Bartholomew's excuse when he became a judge.

A brief list of sources

A New Dictionary of Eponyms, by Morton S. Freeman, Oxford University Press, 1998.

Chambers Dictionary of Etymology, edited by Robert K. Barnhart, Chambers Harrap, 1999.

Faux Pas? by Philip Gooden, A&C Black, 2007.

Oxford Dictionary of English Etymology, edited by C. T. Onions, Oxford University Press, 1966.

http://french.about.com

http://germanenglishwords.com

http://hinduism.about.com

http://latin-phrases.co.uk

www.absoluteastronomy.com

www.answers.com

www.bhashaindia.com

www.encyclopedia.com

www.muslimheritage.com

www.phrases.org.uk

www.thefreedictionary.com

www.uklegal.com

www.urbandictionary.com

www.websters-online-dictionary.org

www.word-detective.com

www.yourdictionary.com

"They have been at a great feast of languages, and stolen the scraps."

—William Shakespeare, *Love's Labour's Lost, V.i.*